International Finance

FOR DUMMIES®

A Wiley Brand

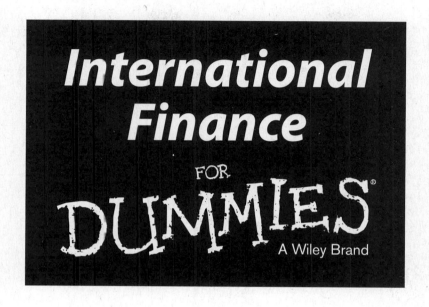

International Finance

FOR DUMMIES®

A Wiley Brand

by Ayse Y. Evrensel, PhD

International Finance For Dummies®

Published by
John Wiley & Sons, Inc.
111 River St.
Hoboken, NJ 07030-5774
www.wiley.com

About the Author

Ayse Y. Evrensel holds a PhD from the University of Zurich (Switzerland) in Economic and Social Geography (1984) and a PhD in Economics from Clemson University (1999). As a geographer, she worked at University of Zurich and Clemson University (SC). In geography, her areas of teaching and research focused on international migration, economic development, multilateral organizations, and the European Union.

As an economist, she worked at Ball State University, Portland State University, and University of California San Diego. In Economics, she has taught a wide range of courses such as Macroeconomics, Microeconomics, Econometrics, International Finance, International Trade, and Financial Markets. She has published on the effects of IMF programs, banking regulations, banking crises, preferential trade arrangements, corruption, and the relationship between institutional quality and culture.

Ayse is currently an associate professor of Economics at Southern Illinois University Edwardsville. She lives in Edwardsville, Illinois.

Dedication

I dedicate this book to Myles Wallace, my teacher and dear friend.

Author's Acknowledgments

I have been teaching International Finance for many years. Over the years, my students have become my teachers, especially when it comes to how to teach the subject. I am deeply grateful for their genuine involvement and contribution to the course.

I could not have had the courage to get involved in this project without David Lutton and Erin Calligan Mooney holding my hand and showing me the ropes at the very beginning of the writing process. I am very appreciative of their support, encouragement, and trust.

I wish I could give everything I write to Linda Brandon for editing because she is such an amazing editor. I hope to have learned one or two things from her about writing. I am grateful to Linda for her patience and professionalism. I also thank Krista Hansing for her involvement in the project.

I am very grateful to technical editors Jerry Dwyer and Allen Brunner for their valuable comments and suggestions.

Publisher's Acknowledgments

We're proud of this book; please send us your comments at http://dummies.custhelp.com. For other comments, please contact our Customer Care Department within the U.S. at 877-762-2974, outside the U.S. at 317-572-3993, or fax 317-572-4002.

Some of the people who helped bring this book to market include the following:

Acquisitions, Editorial, and Vertical Websites

Project Editor: Linda Brandon

Acquisitions Editor: Erin Calligan Mooney

Copy Editor: Krista Hansing

Assistant Editor: David Lutton

Editorial Program Coordinator: Joe Niesen

Technical Editors: Allan Brunner; Jerry Dwyer

Senior Editorial Manager: Jennifer Ehrlich

Editorial Manager: Carmen Krikorian

Editorial Assistant: Rachelle S. Amick

Art Coordinator: Alicia B. South

Cover Photos: © klenger / iStockphoto.com

Composition Services

Project Coordinator: Katie Crocker

Layout and Graphics: Carl Byers, Melanee Habig, Joyce Haughey

Proofreaders: John Greenough Eveylun Wellborn

Indexer: BIM Indexing & Proofreading Services

Publishing and Editorial for Consumer Dummies

> **Kathleen Nebenhaus,** Vice President and Executive Publisher

> **David Palmer:** Associate Publisher

> **Kristin Ferguson-Wagstaffe,** Product Development Director

Publishing for Technology Dummies

> **Andy Cummings,** Vice President and Publisher

Composition Services

> **Debbie Stailey,** Director of Composition Services

Contents at a Glance

Table of Contents

Introduction

· ·

1 understand when people are perplexed about international finance. Been there, done that. But being perplexed about something can be good motivation to understand it. As a noneconomist (and a much younger person), I had the privilege of experiencing life in different countries such as Turkey, Brazil, and Switzerland, which greatly affected my career choice later.

Throughout the 1970s, the 1980s, and partly the 1990s, Turkey and Brazil experienced political struggles and economic problems. You could feel it in the streets, and bad news was everywhere in the media. Hyperinflation — annual inflation rates reaching 100 percent in Turkey during the early 1980s and several hundred percent in Brazil until the mid-1990s — was simply stunning. At the same time, these countries' currencies were depreciating. I sort of understood that part because I experienced it in my everyday life. I needed more of these countries' currencies to buy one unit of a hard currency such as the dollar, the German mark, or the Swiss franc.

By the way, although I didn't understand what was going on at that time, both official and unofficial (black market) places existed for buying or selling hard currency. Now I would call it *foreign exchange restrictions,* but then, it was just reality. Needless to say, when you sell your hard currency unofficially, you receive a lot more domestic currency than the official place gives you. Also, the International Monetary Fund (IMF) was part of these countries' daily life then. I understood that, for some reason, the central banks of these countries were losing hard currency. Sometimes they had problems paying imports. The IMF representatives visited these countries and worked out an austerity program in exchange for a large amount of hard currency. Then all newspapers published articles against the IMF and how awful the proposed austerity program was. People held demonstrations in the streets, shouting, "IMF, go home!"

Switzerland was a whole other experience. My experience in this country didn't include any of the previous stories about Turkey and Brazil. I could tell that Switzerland was a very expensive but low-inflation country. Its currency was holding its own against other currencies. I didn't experience any difficulty with exchanging currency there. In Switzerland, no restrictions governed exchanging foreign currency, so no black market in foreign currency existed. I didn't hear anything about a large deficit of any kind. Certainly, the IMF wasn't a part of everyday life there.

I had to learn international finance in a systematic way to understand my experiences when I was younger. This book reflects the same systematic way, which hopefully will help you understand international finance.

About This Book

A variety of people are the primary readers of this book. A student of economics can use it to supplement lectures and the textbook. A practicing economist may want to brush up on existing knowledge of international finance. Maybe learning more about exchange rates has been on your mind for awhile, and now that you have more time, you want to give it a shot. This book provides the fundamental knowledge necessary for people of all backgrounds to understand international finance. It contains the nuts and bolts of the subject, without going into great detail.

No matter who you are, your goal should be to *understand* the subjects of international finance. I've been a teacher for almost three decades. Sure, I can pose problems such as, "Suppose the demand–supply model of exchange rate determination, and graph the market for euros; show the effects of a higher inflation rate in the U.S. on the exchange rate." But I value the comments of my students on a news article much more as an assessment tool than their answers to exam questions. A news article has a lot of information, and sifting through information and using the relevant information to predict the change in the exchange rate is an accomplishment. Similarly, you may be part of conversations about China revaluing its currency or the gold standard being a much better system than the current one. When people talk, they say a lot of things, some that are relevant and some that aren't. Distinguishing between them and giving a straightforward and correct answer isn't easy at first. But practice makes perfect. Therefore, I recommend that you put your knowledge to the test by reading exchange rates–related news and getting into conversations with others.

Another challenge in economic analysis is that this discipline offers alternative theories that explain the same subject. Therefore, this book offers two alternative theories of exchange rate determination, to help you compare the predictions of different models.

The best way to deal with model- and calculation-related challenges is to work with paper and pencil. Reproducing the models and calculations helps you make them your own.

Conventions Used in This Book

Italics emphasize an important point. In the previous section, I put *understanding* in italics because I wanted to emphasize gaining a fundamental knowledge, not just acquiring short-term knowledge that you lose the next day.

Bold is used when new terminology is presented.

✔ Bullet points such as this one indicate several points related to a certain subject. This convention makes it easy to visually separate different aspects of the same conversation.

What You Are Not to Read

I'm not sure whether I should say *unfortunately*, but you can't skip many parts of this book. I've included only a few "technical stuff" items and sidebars — you can skip those parts, if you want. Even though I've kept the details to a minimum, the nuts and bolts of the subject require quite a bit of analysis.

Foolish Assumptions

On the first day of all my courses, I distribute a couple subject-related questions among my students. I assure them that this isn't an exam and tell them to give me their honest opinion. At the second class meeting, I summarize their responses and post them on our class Blackboard site. Going over their answers sparks interesting conversations.

Based on the answers in my upper-level undergraduate international finance course, I can say that some students can do currency conversions and, looking at a time-series graph (say, with years on the x-axis and the dollar–euro exchange rate on the y-axis), can also tell when the dollar depreciated or appreciated against the euro. However, most of them cannot explain why the dollar depreciates or whether the world should return to the gold standard. The average reader of this book may be in the same situation as my students on the first day of the class. But most of my students eventually get a grasp of the subject, and it is my hope that you, the reader, will become equally (if not more) knowledgeable about international finance.

International finance is an area of economics — more precisely, macroeconomics. You may be aware of economics' approach to analyzing the subject based on models. Curves are shifting for whatever reason, and then you predict the changes in the variables on the x- and y-axis of the model. I hope that you don't think of it as boring. Remember my life experiences that I talked about at the beginning of this Introduction. These models were instrumental in making sense of my life experiences. If you don't already see this, I hope that you come to appreciate their power in explaining the world.

How This Book Is Organized

The parts of this book (Parts I through V) are its backbone. They are well defined in terms of their content. The sequence of these parts also is helpful for learning the material. Parts start with definition- and calculation-related subjects and progress over exchange rate determination and then later to the historical and current structure of the international monetary system. In terms of the content and sequence of chapters in each part, chapters correspond to the title of the part and are cohesive within each part.

In the following, you find information regarding the content of each of the five parts in this book, which helps you determine where you want to start in this book.

Part I: Getting Started with International Finance

Part I is about understanding the basics of exchange rates, such as definitions, conversion calculations, and the use of correct terminology when exchange rates change (see Chapter 2). In Chapter 3, I discuss the relevance of exchange rates for all sorts of international business. Even though this part doesn't give you the reasons for the changes in the exchange rates, it makes a visual start. Therefore, in Chapter 4, I show a couple graphs to illustrate how the relevant macroeconomic variables affect the changes in the exchange rate.

Part II: Determining the Exchange Rate

The chapters in Part II answer the question of why exchange rates change. This question is important to answer because Part I shows that all sorts of international business and speculators are interested in predicting which way exchange rates will change. Part II introduces two models of exchange rate determination. First, the demand–supply model represents a basic approach to exchange rate determination (see Chapter 5). Second, it introduces the Monetary Approach to Balance of Payments (MBOP). Because the MBOP is a more extensive model, two chapters are devoted to it. Chapter 6 examines how to develop this model. Chapter 7 shows how you can use it to predict the change in the exchange rate.

Part III: Understanding Long-Term Concepts and Short-Term Risks

The first two chapters in Part III are related to the MBOP, which Part II examines. Among them are the concepts of interest rate parity (see Chapter 8) and purchasing power parity (see Chapter 9). These concepts relate the changes in the exchange rates to the interest rate and inflation rate differential, respectively. The last chapter in this section, Chapter 10, discusses foreign exchange derivatives such as forward, futures, and options contracts. Multinational firms use these financial instruments to hedge against exchange rate risk and investors use them to speculate.

Part IV: Conducting a Background Check: Currency Changes through the Years

Part IV is about exchange rate regimes and alternative international monetary systems. This subject requires discussing underlying macroeconomic subjects such as the connection between the type of money and the exchange rate regimes. Additionally, the chronological order in previous international monetary systems starts with the gold standard era of pre-1944 years (see Chapter 11). Chapter 12 examines the exchange rate regime and the associated problems during the Bretton Woods era (1944–1971), starting with the Bretton Woods Conference. Chapter 13 discusses diverse exchange rate regimes of the post-Bretton woods era, including floating and unilaterally pegged exchange rates, as well as currency crises. Finally, Part IV also examines the unique subject of the optimum currency area (OCA) and the challenges and opportunities associated with its materialization in the example of the euro (see Chapter 14).

Part V: The Part of Tens

As in every subject, there are some things you should and should not be thinking about international finance. Chapter 15 summarizes some helpful points to consider. Chapter 16 points out some misleading considerations.

Appendix

To round out the book, famous puzzles in international macroeconomics and international finance put into perspective the exchange rate determination discussed throughout the book.

Icons Used in This Book

 To aid you in your reading, this book uses the following icons:

This icon is used for all kinds of examples, both numerical and conceptual, to help you better visualize the subject in question.

 Whenever you need to remember something that was discussed earlier to understand the current subject, you see this icon.

 Sometimes the subject matter of international finance gets a bit academic — it can't help itself. This icon helps you weed through these more technical concepts — read them if you want a deeper understanding of subjects; otherwise, just pass them by.

 Sometimes thinking about a subject in a certain way is helpful in learning. This icon is used whenever a suggestion is made.

 Some subjects or expressions are open to misunderstandings. When you see this icon, you can expect an explanation of why it's a mistake to think about the subject in a certain way.

Where to Go from Here

Starting with Part I and moving forward with successive parts gives you nice insight into international finance. Follow this approach if you want to gain control over the subject in a reasonable amount of time.

But if you want, you can focus on one part at a time. For example, if you're more interested in the fixed vs. flexible debate or how the euro works, start reading the chapters in Part IV. If you want to know what depreciates or appreciates a currency against other currencies, start reading the chapters in Part II. However you choose to tackle this subject, *International Finance For Dummies* helps you grasp the concepts and enjoy the journey.

Part I

Getting Started with International Finance

getting started with

International Finance

In this part . . .

✔ I start you off with a look at how international finance touches so many aspects of daily lives around the world.

✔ I give you an introduction to the most important subject in international finance: the exchange rate. I share some very handy basic information on exchange rate lingo and calculations.

✔ You get to meet the users of the foreign exchange market and understand what risks they face.

✔ I introduce a visual approach to changes in exchange rates.

Chapter 1

Money Makes the World Go 'Round

In This Chapter

▶ Understanding the terminology associated with exchange rates

▶ Identifying the factors that change the exchange rate

▶ Realizing excessive short-run volatility in the exchange rate and hedging against it

▶ Examining alternative exchange rate regimes

Internutional finance is a vast and, at times, complex subject. My goal is to break it down for you into easy-to-manage parts. Although on the surface international finance may seem a daunting subject to learn, it really is fascinating and can help you understand the world of exchange rates. Time to get started!

This chapter aims to inform you about what's to come throughout this book. Each section in this chapter corresponds to each of the five parts of the book and gives you a glimpse of what each part covers.

Checking Out Definitions and Calculations

When learning about any new subject, gaining a basic understanding of the important terminology and, whenever applicable, calculations is important. This fact is also true for international finance. The main subject in international finance is exchange rates. Therefore, Part I includes chapters that cover the basic knowledge of exchange rates, which involves their definition, calculations, and the use of correct terminology when exchange rates change. Among the calculations-related subjects, you'll read about how to calculate the percent change in exchange rates as well as how to convert an amount of money denominated in a currency into a different one. It turns out that all sorts of international business pros, as well as investors (or speculators), care about the changes in exchange rates.

What's an exchange rate?

An *exchange rate* (also known as the *nominal exchange rate*) represents the relative price of two currencies. For example, the dollar–euro exchange rate implies the relative price of the euro in terms of dollars. If the dollar–euro exchange rate is $0.95, it means that you need $0.95 to buy €1. Therefore, the exchange rate simply states how many units of one currency you need to buy one unit of another currency.

Throughout the book, you see the term *consumption basket.* Basically, think about the content of your shopping cart when you go grocery shopping, such as milk, bread, eggs, and so on. The consumption basket of a country includes goods and services that are bought or consumed by the average person in this country.

Other types of exchange rates also exist, including the real and effective exchange rates. The *real exchange rate,* for example, uses the nominal exchange rate and the ratio of the prices of two countries' consumption baskets in respective currencies. In this case, the real exchange rate compares the price of two consumption baskets in a common currency. Therefore, unlike the nominal exchange rate, which only implies the exchange of currencies, the real exchange rate compares the price of two countries' consumption baskets. The effective real exchange rate considers the comparison of the price of the home consumption basket to that of the weighted-average price of the most important trade partners of the home country.

What do you say when the exchange rate changes?

Using the proper terminology is important when referring to a change in the exchange rate. It's true that this terminology relates to the exchange rate regime in question. I discuss alternative exchange rate regimes much later, in Part IV. For now, you can think of a **floating** (or **flexible**) regime and a **pegged** regime. In a floating exchange rate regime, mostly market forces determine exchange rates — in other words, the sale and purchase of the relevant currencies affect exchange rates. I ignore the nuances among the pegged exchange rate regimes for now and state that, for the most part, governments set the exchange rate in pegged exchange rate regimes.

An exchange rate regime implies whether or how a country decides to manage its currency with respect to other currencies. In a flexible exchange rate regime, the country leaves the determination of its currency's price mostly to international foreign exchange markets. Alternatively, a country may decide to exercise varying degrees of control over the exchange rates involving its currency. Chapters in Part IV discuss the factors that affect countries' decisions regarding the exchange rate regime.

Appreciation and revaluation have the same meaning: The value of one currency increases against the other. But these terms are used for the floating and pegged exchange rate regimes, respectively. For example, both the dollar and the euro are floating currencies. If the dollar–euro exchange rate decreases from $0.95 to $0.85, it implies appreciation of the dollar. If China decreases the yuan–dollar exchange rate from CNY6.23 to CNY6.02, it's revaluation because China pegs its currency. In both cases, you need less of the domestic currency to buy one unit of the foreign currency.

Depreciation and devaluation also have the same meaning: The value of one currency decreases against the other. Again, these terms are used for the floating and pegged exchange rate regimes, respectively. If the dollar–euro exchange rate increases from $0.95 to $1.05, it implies depreciation of the dollar. If China increases the yuan–dollar exchange rate from CNY6.23 to CNY6.35, it's devaluation. In both cases, you need more of the domestic currency to buy one unit of the foreign currency.

Who cares about exchange rates?

First, various multinational firms care about the changes in exchange rates. Some domestic firms export to or import from other countries. Some firms have licensing and franchising agreements with foreign firms. Some have production facilities in foreign countries, with or without local partners. The important point about international business is that these firms have account payables or receivables in foreign currencies. A change in the exchange rate makes their payables or receivables in domestic currency smaller or larger in terms of their home currency.

Multinational companies cannot ignore the changes in exchange rates, but as an investor, you can, if you want to. You may not follow the changes in exchange rates if your portfolio consists of domestic equity and debt securities. But if you have foreign assets in your portfolio or you're a speculator trying to make a profit by buying currency low and selling high, you'll be very interested in which direction and how much exchange rates change.

Finding Out What Determines (Or Changes) Exchange Rates

You may know today's dollar–euro exchange rate. But it will be something else next year. How do you predict what the exchange rate will be? Which factors are helpful in predicting the change in exchange rates? Part II of this book focuses on these important questions.

Which model to use?

In this book, I show you two alternative ways of looking at exchange rate determination. First, you can apply a microeconomic approach to exchange rate determination and assume that currencies are exchanged just like oranges. The question as to how many oranges do you need to buy one apple is fundamentally similar to the one as to how many dollars do you need to buy one euro. In the demand–supply model, the demand and supply curves shift for various reasons, some that relate to international trade and others that relate to international investment.

Second, you can focus only on international investment. In this case, you can think of yourself as an investor deciding between dollar- and euro-denominated securities (of similar maturity and risk). How do you decide between these securities? The answer involves two factors: real interest rates associated with these securities and the expected change in the exchange rate. Keep in mind that monetary policies of two countries affect the real returns in this model, as well as your expectations regarding the future exchange rate. Therefore, you need to keep a close eye on monetary policies of both countries, form your expectations regarding the real returns and the future exchange rate, sell one of the currencies, buy the other currency, and buy securities denominated in the latter currency. The currency you're buying appreciates in the current (spot) foreign exchange market.

Are there any prediction rules to live by?

Yes, certain generally accepted factors lead to predictable changes in the exchange rates. Two main factors are nominal interest rates and inflation rates. Higher inflation rates generally lead to higher nominal interest rates. If you ask why inflation rates increase, the major culprit, in this case, is an expansionary monetary policy, implied by higher growth in nominal money supply accompanied by declines in central banks' key interest rates. Therefore, all three factors (monetary policy, inflation rates, and nominal interest rates) are related and have a predictable effect on exchange rates. Most empirical evidence implies that expansionary monetary policies resulting in higher inflation rates and higher nominal interest rates lead to the depreciation of a currency.

In terms of real variables (variables that are adjusted for inflation), higher real interest rates and growth rates of real GDP (gross domestic product, or output of a country) lead to the appreciation of a currency.

Getting to the Long and Short of It

The chapters in Part III focus on two main subjects. First, they expand upon the subject of exchange rate determination and discuss long-run relationships. Second, the chapters put your knowledge in perspective by pointing out the high short-term volatility of exchange rates.

What's the percent change in the exchange rate?

You can both predict the direction of change in the exchange rate and also calculate your best guess regarding the percent change by examining two important concepts: interest rate parity (IRP) and purchasing power parity (PPP). The IRP relates the percent change in the exchange rate to the nominal interest rate differential between two countries. The PPP, on the other hand, explains the percent change in the exchange rate based on the inflation differential between two countries. Actual changes in exchange rates may not reflect the IRP- or PPP-suggested changes every time you observe them, but both concepts give you a best guess regarding the direction and size of the change in the exchange rate.

The empirical evidence confirms that both the IRP and the PPP are helpful long-run concepts with which you can predict exchange rates.

Can anything be done about the risk due to short-term volatility in exchange rates?

Because predicting the exchange rates is difficult in the short run, market participants such as multinational firms are exposed to exchange rate risk. Foreign exchange derivatives help multinational firms hedge against this risk. Additionally, speculators use these derivatives to make profits. Part III discusses three types of foreign exchange derivatives: forward contracts, futures contracts, and options. They have important differences, such as whether they imply an obligation to buy or sell currency, which, in turn, affects their attractiveness to different market participants.

Answering Questions about the System: Fixed, Flexible, or Pegged?

In Part IV, I talk about the international monetary system, which refers to implicit or explicit arrangements governing exchange rates. Because the type of money affects the type of exchange rate regime, I first discuss the different types of money throughout history and the associated exchange rate regimes. Then the focus shifts to the international monetary systems since the late 19th century. These systems, the associated exchange rate regimes, and their challenges are discussed in chronological order, starting in the 19th century and ending with the euro.

Does the type of money matter for the exchange rate?

A close relationship exists between the type of money and the exchange rate regime. A monetary system based on a metallic standard such as the gold standard leads to a fixed exchange rate regime. For a good part in human history, some kind of a metallic standard governed. However, don't assume that the reign of the metallic standard was continuous throughout history. Mostly because a metallic standard such as the gold standard doesn't allow monetary policy, countries left the metallic standard whenever they had to endure a war or a military conflict so that they could print money and finance the war effort.

Money that's not backed by a precious metal has no intrinsic value. It's called fiat money. Therefore, the type of money used during the gold- (and/or silver-) standard periods interrupted by wars or revolutions was fiat money. This type of money has been used from 1971 through today (see Chapter 12 for information on the post-Bretton Woods era, when this type of currency was introduced).

Previously in this section, you read that a metallic standard, such as the gold standard, leads to fixed exchange rates. What kind of exchange rates would we have when currencies are fiat? The answer is that fiat money doesn't imply a certain kind of exchange rate regime. It's up to countries to decide what kind of an exchange rate regime they want to have. In fact, following the end of the metallic era in 1973, developed and developing countries decided differently about this matter. While all developed countries adopted a floating exchange rate regime, most developing countries adopted some kind of pegged exchange rate regime.

In a pegged exchange rate regime, governments announce the exchange rates between the domestic currency and other major currencies. Pegging is done for a variety of reasons. First, pegging can support the country's development strategy. For example, if a country wants to industrialize and needs to import a variety of intermediate goods, it can make its imports cheaper by overvaluing its currency. On the other hand, if a country wants to promote its export sector as the engine of growth, undervaluation of the currency can accomplish this goal. In addition, a pegged currency can function as a nominal anchor to signal economic stability. In particular, developing countries used the pegged regime to attract foreign investors. In this case, the investment in question is portfolio investment and implies investing other countries' equity and debt securities.

Unilaterally pegged exchange rates in developing countries, especially in emerging markets with a potential to grow, sounded like an ingenious plan. These countries needed hard currency in large amounts, and international investors wanted to have higher nominal returns with virtually no exchange rate risk. But this kind of hot money comes in fast and leaves fast. When investors became anxious that these countries couldn't continue with the peg, they cashed in their portfolio in return for hard currency, leaving the countries in a currency crisis.

When talking about exchange rate regimes and currency crises, the International Monetary Fund (IMF) has to be included in the discussion. The IMF was introduced during the Bretton Woods conference in 1944 as the coordinator of the post–World War II international monetary system. The post–World War II system was a variation of the metallic standard and was called the reserve currency system. The dollar was pegged to gold, and all other currencies were pegged to the dollar. As in the case of any metallic standard, an agency such as the IMF needed to keep an eye on current account imbalances and redistribute funds from countries with a current account surplus to countries with a current account deficit. As early as the late 1940s, it became clear that the IMF didn't have enough funds to fulfill its objective.

Following the end of the Bretton Woods era in 1973, the IMF remained in business even though there was no metallic standard and therefore fixed exchange rates. However, as developed countries adopted floating exchange rates, most developing countries believed that if they adopted a floating exchange rate regime, their countries' fiscal and monetary problems would depreciate their currency too much. Therefore, after 1973, most developing countries unilaterally pegged their currency to the currencies of major developed countries. But pegged currencies experience crisis, meaning that countries lose their international reserves when fiscal and monetary policies aren't consistent with the peg. Therefore, the IMF remained in business, this time to provide balance of payments support to developing countries. Over the decades, the IMF has been criticized for providing financial support to countries that implement macroeconomic policies inconsistent with their currency peg.

Which international monetary system is better?

Economics is all about tradeoffs, and there's no such thing as a flawless international monetary system. All systems have their benefits and costs.

Any variety of a metallic standard, such as the gold standard of pre–World War II years and the reserve currency standard of the Bretton Woods era (1944–1971), avoids volatility in exchange rates. But the stability in exchange rates comes at a high cost. Evidence suggests that, when trying to keep the fixed exchange rate, achieving internal balance (growth and full employment) and external balance (no large current account surplus or deficit), and allowing free flow of funds between countries, the internal and external balance was sacrificed for the fixed exchange rate. This situation led to persistent current account deficits, lower growth, and higher unemployment in many countries. Especially during the early 1930s, retaliatory trade restrictions were introduced as a desperate attempt to promote growth and employment, which only worsened the overall economic outlook.

The floating exchange rate regime that developed countries have adopted since the early 1970s has the benefit of requiring no internal or external balance. It's virtually maintenance free. But because currency trading in foreign exchange markets determines the exchange rates, countries' monetary and fiscal policies or expectations regarding these policies have an effect on exchange rates. The problem is that short-run fluctuations in floating exchange rates don't reflect the changes in macroeconomic fundamentals. In fact, the short-run volatility seems to be excessive compared to the changes in macroeconomic fundamentals.

Many developing countries have adopted pegged exchange rates, and they have their benefits and costs as well. A pegged currency can signal stability and encourage much-needed hard currency flowing to the country. If the country has a well-developed financial system that can distribute these funds efficiently among borrowers, hot money can stimulate growth. If the financial system of the country is weak or the government's policies aren't consistent with the peg, investors will expect that the peg will be broken. If they wait until the peg is actually broken, they suffer losses because, when the peg is broken, the currency substantially depreciates. Therefore, investors convert their investment into hard currency right away. Clearly, a large amount of hard currency leaves the country in this case. The peg is broken, the currency is let to float (and depreciate), and the country has lost most of its international reserves.

Is the Euro-zone an optimum currency area?

One of the most interesting developments in international finance took place with the introduction of the euro in 1999. At the time of its introduction, 11 European countries (among them, Germany, France, and Italy) gave up their national currencies to take part in a common currency area, known as the euro-zone. As of 2011, there were 17 European countries in the euro-zone. Of course, the European common currency didn't happen overnight. Starting in the 1950s, European countries went through various stages of economic and monetary integration.

The euro raises issues addressed by a theory known as the optimum currency area (OCA) theory. Consider a number of countries, and call them a region. If these countries experience similar macroeconomic shocks, and if there's labor mobility between these countries, this region may be an OCA. After adopting the common currency, countries of the region are expected to trade with each other more because of lower transaction costs and, consequently, enjoy price converge. However, as problems in some of the Euro-zone countries, such as Greece, Ireland, and Spain, revealed in the late 2000s, a common currency can also be problematic. A common currency requires coordination in both monetary and fiscal policy. The European Central Bank (ECB) has worked to achieve monetary policy coordination, but it seems that there is no supranational authority in the European Union (EU) similar to the ECB to coordinate fiscal policies.

The lack of fiscal policy coordination has led to some of the euro-zone countries having high levels of debt. If financial markets view these countries' debt as excessive, they may expect that highly-indebted Euro-zone countries may not be able to make payments on their debt, which means that these countries may default on their debt. Therefore, higher levels of debt in some of the euro-zone countries may threaten the Euro's credibility.

Gaining Insight into the Do's and Don'ts of International Finance

Some absolutes and some falsehoods arise in the subject of international finance. In Part V, you find a summary of some main ideas to take from this book. These ideas are presented in terms of what to think and what not to think about the most important concepts in international finance.

You definitely need to know that macroeconomic fundamentals such as inflation rates, exchange rates, and growth rates affect the long-run changes in exchange rates. But you also must realize that short-term changes in the exchange rate don't reflect the changes in fundamentals, although they may well reflect expectations of changes in those fundamentals. This fact certainly motivates the use of foreign exchange derivatives to hedge against the foreign exchange risk in short-term transactions. In terms of the international monetary system, no perfect system exists. Alternative international monetary systems have their costs and benefits. Although a common currency area such as the Euro-zone sounds like a great efficiency-enhancing idea, it requires a great deal of policy coordination.

In terms of warnings, the fact that macroeconomic fundamentals cannot explain short-term changes in the exchange rate doesn't mean that the theory of exchange rate determination is useless. The theory is helpful in determining the long-run changes in exchange rates. Additionally, because most developed countries' exchange rates are determined in foreign exchange markets, you don't want to ignore policymakers. Monetary but also fiscal authority significantly affects exchange rates. Finally, in terms of the international monetary system, exchange rates that don't change or that change infrequently, as in the case of fixed or pegged exchange rates, don't necessarily imply stability.

Looking at Finance Globally

Exchange rates imply the relative price of one currency in terms of another currency. In a way, countries are related to each other through exchange rates. Remember that what one country does affects another. Macroeconomic decisions made in your home country affect people that live thousands of miles away. Our world isn't so big, after all. International finance shows how economies are intertwined and how currencies change the way businesses run. Read on!

Chapter 2

Mastering the Basics of International Finance

....

....

*E*xchange rates are the cornerstone of international finance. An exchange rate tells you the relative price of one currency in terms of another. In this chapter, you get familiar with the different types of exchange rates, such as nominal, real, and effective exchange rates. Additionally, although this chapter doesn't discuss why exchange rates change (turn to Chapters 5, 6, and 7 for that information), it talks about the proper terminology to use when exchange rates change. The chapter also includes a little math, showing both how to convert an amount of money from one currency into another one and how to calculate the percent change in exchange rates, cross rates, and bid–ask spreads.

Making the Exchange: Exchange Rates

An exchange rate is nothing but a relative price — for example, how many apples you need to buy one orange. In fact, how many Mexican pesos you need to buy one U.S. dollar indicates the Mexican peso–dollar exchange rate. It implies the relative price of the dollar in terms of Mexican pesos.

Understanding exchange rates as the price of currencies

You pay $5 for a sandwich or $1 for a soda. It's not surprising that we pay for goods and services with money. Everything has a price. Currencies are also exchanged, so they have a price as well. An exchange rate indicates the price of a currency in terms of another currency. If the dollar–euro exchange rate is $1.31, then you need $1.31 to buy one euro. In other words, the price of a euro in dollars is $1.31.

You can also look at an exchange rate as the *relative price* of a currency in terms of another currency. Consider a barter economy, where people exchange goods for other goods. In this situation, the price of a good is expressed in terms of the units of another good, which implies the relative price. Suppose you have only two goods, apples and oranges. The price of apples is expressed in terms of oranges — that is, the number of oranges you give up to buy one apple. If the answer is 2, then the price of an apple is two oranges. Conceptually, there's no difference between the price of an apple (two oranges) and the price of a euro ($1.31).

Applying relative price to exchange rates

An exchange rate is a relative price because it represents the price of one currency in terms of another currency.

Assume that the dollar is the domestic currency and the euro is the foreign currency. The exchange rate between these two currencies implies how many dollars, the domestic currency, are necessary to buy one euro. However, because an exchange rate is a relative price, you can also define it as the number of euros necessary to buy one unit of the domestic currency (the dollar).

If you define the exchange rate as the amount of domestic currency necessary to buy one euro, this definition implies the price of the euro in dollars. If you define the exchange rate as the number of euros necessary to buy one dollar, this definition indicates the price of the dollar in euros.

Section C4 of the *Wall Street Journal* (*WSJ*) of September 10, 2012, listed the euro–dollar exchange rate as €0.7048. This rate means that you need €0.7048 to buy one dollar. This particular exchange rate implies the price of dollars in euros.

Although the *WSJ* doesn't list the dollar–euro exchange rate or the price of euros in dollars, you can easily calculate it. Inverting the current exchange rate yields the dollar–euro exchange rate. If

$$\frac{€}{\$} = 0.7048$$

then

$$\frac{1}{\frac{€}{\$}} = \frac{1}{0.7048} = \$1.42$$

Therefore, the dollar–euro exchange rate implies that you need \$1.42 to buy one euro, which indicates the price of a euro in dollars.

Taking on Different Exchange Rates

This section explains the three main types of exchange rates and the information each type conveys. Nominal exchange rates are the ones the financial media quotes most commonly, but real and effective exchange rates are mentioned as well.

Nominal exchange rates

All reported exchange rates in financial media are nominal exchange rates, unless indicated otherwise. The nominal exchange rate reflects the relative price of two currencies.

Consider the previous euro–dollar exchange rate that was taken directly from the *WSJ* of September 10, 2012: €0.7048. This is an example of a nominal exchange rate. The only information the nominal exchange rate provides is the amount of one currency necessary to buy one unit of the other currency. Therefore, this exchange rate means that you need €0.7048 to buy one dollar.

Real exchange rates

You may be interested in getting more information than the relative price of two currencies, or the nominal exchange rate. For example, you may want to know what one dollar can buy in the Euro-zone countries or what one euro can buy in the United States. In this case, you're interested in the real exchange rate (RER). The RER compares the relative price of two countries' consumption baskets. Therefore, to calculate the RER, you need to know two things: the nominal exchange rate and the price of the two countries' consumption baskets.

A country's consumption basket tells you what the average consumer buys, and its price indicates how much consumers pay for it. For example, in the U.S., the Consumer Price Index (CPI) is calculated based on a consumption basket consisting of about 80,000 goods and services. Each country's consumption basket is expressed in its domestic currency. If you know the nominal exchange rate and the prices of two countries' consumption baskets, you can express the price of one country's consumption basket in the other country's currency. This information enables you to calculate the RER. In other words, you can compare the prices of two countries' consumption baskets in the same currency.

Suppose you know the dollar–euro nominal exchange rate, the euro price of the European consumption basket, and the dollar price of the U.S. consumption basket. You may think, "Hey, I know! I can divide the two!" Nope! You can't divide the price of the European consumption basket by that of the U.S. consumption basket because the prices of these consumption baskets are denominated in different currencies. Therefore, follow this concept:

RER = (Nominal exchange rate × Price of the foreign basket) / (Price of the domestic basket)

The next equation reflects this concept:

$$RER = \left[\left(\frac{\$}{€} \right) \times P_E \right] \div P_{US}$$

Here, RER, P_E, and P_{US} indicate the real exchange rate, the price of the Euro-zone's consumption basket, and the price of the U.S. consumption basket, respectively.

Consider a numerical example for the RER. Assume that the dollar–euro exchange rate is $1.42 per euro, P_E (the price of the Euro-zone's consumption basket) is €100, and P_{US} (the price of the U.S. consumption basket) is $142. In this case, the real exchange rate is 1:

$$RER = \frac{\$1.42 \times €100}{\$142} = 1$$

In the previous equation, first note that, in the numerator, you multiply the dollar–euro exchange rate with a euro amount. Doing so changes the European basket so that it's expressed in dollars. Second, note that you have the dollar price of the American basket in the denominator. Because now the price of both consumption baskets is expressed in dollars, you can compare them.

Suppose that the dollar–euro exchange rate increases to $1.52, but the prices of the Euro-zone and U.S. consumption baskets remain the same. In this case, the real exchange rate increases to 1.07:

$$RER = \frac{\$1.52 \times €100}{\$142} = 1.07$$

This increase in the real exchange rate implies that the dollar price of the Euro-zone's consumption basket increases, or the dollar's purchasing power over the Euro-zone's consumption basket falls. Alternatively, you can increase the price of the Euro-zone's consumption basket or decrease the price of the U.S. basket to achieve an increase in the real exchange rate.

Suppose that the nominal exchange rate decreases to $1.35, with the prices of the Euro-zone and U.S. consumption baskets remaining the same. In this example, the real exchange rate decreases to 0.95:

$$RER = \frac{\$1.35 \times €100}{\$142} = 0.95$$

A decline in the real exchange rate indicates that the dollar price of the Euro-zone's consumption basket decreases, or the dollar's purchasing power over the Euro-zone's consumption basket increases. Again, you can also decrease the price of the Euro-zone's consumption basket or increase the price of the U.S. basket to achieve a decline in the real exchange rate.

Effective exchange rates

Effective exchange rates compare a country's currency to a basket of other countries' currencies. The most common way to identify the basket of currencies is to consider a country's major trade partners. In this case, the effective exchange rate is called the *trade-weighted index* because the weights attached to other countries' currencies reflect the relevance of the home country's trade with these countries.

The effective exchange rate measures the value of the domestic currency against the weighted value of a basket of foreign currencies, where the weights reflect the foreign countries' share in the domestic country's trade. Therefore, you use the effective exchange rate if you're interested in the domestic currency's performance compared to the country's most important trade partners.

The effective exchange rate is usually expressed as an index number out of 100. An increase in the effective exchange rate indicates a strengthening of the home currency with respect to other currencies considered in its calculation. Conversely, a decline in the effective exchange rate means a weakening of the home currency.

Figure 2-1 shows that, during the early 1980s and the late 1990s, the trade-weighted index for the dollar increased, indicating a strengthening of the dollar against its major trade partners. But the overall trend since 1973 shows a weakening of the dollar.

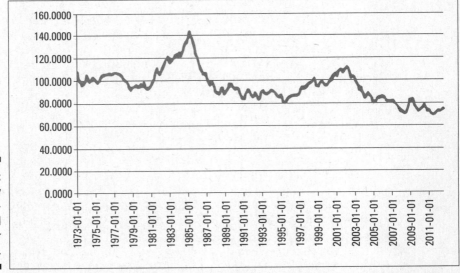

Figure 2-1:
Monthly trade-weighted U.S. dollar index.

Notes: FRED, St. Louis Federal Reserve Bank. The data are available at http://research.stlouisfed.org/fred2/series/TWEXMMTH?cid=95. The index includes the Euro-zone, Canada, Japan, the United Kingdom, Switzerland, Australia, and Sweden. March 1973 =100.

Tackling Terminology: Changes in Exchange Rates

This section is all about calculating the changes in the exchange rate and using the correct terminology to express these changes. For now, don't worry about why they change: Chapters 5, 6, and 7 discuss exchange rate determination and explain the reasons for the changes in exchange rates.

Also keep in mind that the change in exchange rates involves whether the currencies in question are freely exchanged in international foreign exchange markets, with minimum restrictions and interventions by governments or central banks. Chapter 14 examines government restrictions and central bank interventions.

Calculating the percent change

The percent change formula is a basic but useful tool. You can apply it to any variable that's observed at various points in time. For all variables for which you want to measure the percent change, use the following formula:

$$\%\Delta X_t = \frac{X_t - X_{t-i}}{X_{t-i}} \times 100$$

Because the subject here is the exchange rate, suppose that X denotes the exchange rate. Also:

- ✔ $\%\Delta$ is the percent change.
- ✔ X_t is the exchange rate in the current period (t).
- ✔ X_{t-i} is the exchange rate in the previous period ($t - i$), where i can be yesterday, last month, last year, or ten years ago.

To find the percent change in the exchange rate, start with the current exchange rate minus the previous exchange rate, divide that answer by the previous exchange rate, and then multiply by 100 to express the change as a percent.

Table 2-1 shows the monthly dollar–euro exchange rates as of the first of every month between January and August 2012.

Table 2-1	The Dollar–Euro Monthly Exchange Rate (2012)		
Date	**Exchange Rate**	**Percent Change**	**Terminology (Refers to the Dollar)**
January	1.2910		
February	1.3238	+2.54	Depreciation
March	1.3208	−0.23	Appreciation
April	1.3160	−0.36	Appreciation
May	1.2806	−2.69	Appreciation
June	1.2541	−2.07	Appreciation
July	1.2278	−2.10	Appreciation
August	1.2406	+1.04	Depreciation

Notes: FRED, St. Louis Federal Reserve Bank. Available at http://research.stlouisfed.org/fred2/series/EXUSEU/downloaddata?cid=95.
All monthly rates imply the exchange rate on the first of the month.

Even though the table title doesn't explicitly indicate it, the exchange rates in Table 2-1 are *nominal* exchange rates. Remember that all exchange rates provided are the nominal exchange rates unless otherwise noted.

Table 2-1 lists the percent change in the exchange rate in the third column and the associated terminology in the fourth column. Focus on the percent change column for now. You don't see any entry for January (the first observation) because you lose the first observation in percent change calculations. Take the percent change for February 1, 2012, which is +2.54 percent. Apply the percent change formula to the exchange rates (E) in January and February:

$$\%\Delta E_{Feb-2012} = \frac{E_{Feb-2012} - E_{Jan-2012}}{E_{Jan-2012}} \times 100 = \frac{1.3238 - 1.2910}{1.2910} \times 100 = +2.54\%$$

Another example is the percent change in the exchange rate in July 2012, which is a 2.1 percent decline:

$$\%\Delta E_{July-2012} = \frac{E_{July-2012} - E_{June-2012}}{E_{June-2012}} \times 100 = \frac{1.2278 - 1.2541}{1.2541} \times 100 = -2.10\%$$

All other percent changes in the third column are calculated similarly.

Defining appreciation and depreciation

The fourth column of Table 2-1 states the terminology associated with each change in the exchange rate. When you use the term *appreciation* or *depreciation*, make sure you're referring to currencies that are traded in foreign exchange markets with no government interventions. As Chapter 14 explains, a country may unilaterally peg its currency for various reasons. In the absence of such government interventions, the exchange rate or the relative price of two currencies is determined mainly in foreign exchange markets through the buying and selling of currencies by market participants. Because the example exchange rate in Table 2-1 is the dollar–euro exchange rate, and both currencies are traded in international foreign exchange markets, you can use appreciation or depreciation to describe the changes in the exchange rate.

Table 2-1 shows that the dollar–euro exchange rate increased in February and August 2012 . Compared to the previous period, the changes in both months imply that more dollars were needed to buy one euro. Therefore, the fourth column refers to these months as depreciation in the dollar. In February and August 2012, there was a 2.54 and 1.04 percent depreciation in the dollar from their respective previous periods.

Because the example exchange rate is the dollar–euro rate, depreciation in the dollar means appreciation in the euro. You can invert the exchange dollar–euro rates in Table 2-1 and express them as euro–dollar rates. You can see that, in February and August 2012, the euro appreciated.

The following equations show that, from January to February 2012, fewer euros were needed to buy a dollar, which indicates the appreciation of the euro:

$$\left(\frac{€}{\$}\right)_{Jan-2012} = \frac{1}{1.2910} = 0.7746$$

$$\left(\frac{€}{\$}\right)_{Feb-2012} = \frac{1}{1.3238} = 0.7554$$

All other observation points in Table 2-1 (March, April, May, June, and July) indicate a negative percent change in the exchange rate, meaning that fewer dollars were needed to buy one euro. Therefore, Table 2-1 refers to these changes as appreciation of the dollar against the euro.

Check out the graph in Figure 2-2 and apply the terminology for changes in the exchange rates. Figure 2-2 shows changes in the monthly dollar–euro exchange rate since the introduction of the euro in 1999. Note that the dollar appreciates following the euro's introduction until 2001, and then the dollar depreciates until early 2008.

Figure 2-2: The dollar–euro monthly exchange rate.

Notes: FRED, St. Louis Federal Reserve Bank. The data are available at http://research.stlouisfed.org/fred2/series/EXUSEU?cid=95.

Note that Figure 2-2 illustrates the change in the nominal dollar–euro exchange rate, which indicates only the number of dollars necessary to buy one euro. Figure 2-3, on the other hand, shows the nominal effective exchange rates (NEER) for the euro and the dollar, which compare currencies with those of their respective trade partners.

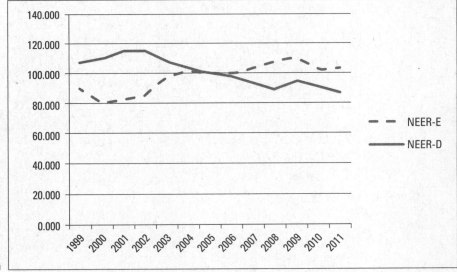

Figure 2-3:
Nominal effective exchange rate (NEER) index for the euro and the dollar (2005 = 100).

Notes: The data are available at www.imf.org. NEER-E and NEER-D denote the nominal effective exchange rates for the euro and the dollar, respectively.

Figure 2-3 shows an increase in the NEER for the dollar until 2001. This movement indicates an appreciation of the dollar compared to the currencies of major trade partners of the U.S. Then the NEER declines until 2008, indicating a depreciation of the dollar. After a slight appreciation until late 2009, the NEER for the dollar indicates depreciation again.

Figure 2-3 also shows the NEER for the euro. Compared to the currencies of the Euro-zone's major trade partners, the euro depreciates following the introduction of the new currency in 1999. But between 2001 and 2009, the euro appreciates compared to the currencies of the Euro-zone's major trade partners.

Finding revaluation and devaluation

When you read any financial newspaper, you note that a weakening in the dollar is reported as depreciation of the dollar. But if the same happens to the Chinese yuan, it's phrased as the yuan being devalued. Professional people use a certain language, and it's important to understand and use this language.

The terms *revaluation* and *devaluation* are used instead of *appreciation* and *depreciation,* respectively. However, to use the terms *revaluation* or *devaluation,* you need substantial government interventions in the exchange rate. The Chinese yuan is a good example for a currency whose value with respect to other currencies is determined by the Chinese government. This section doesn't explain why China intervenes in the value of its currency in terms of other currencies; Chapter 14 examines these issues in detail. For now, the goal is to identify devaluation and revaluation, for example, on a graph.

Figure 2-4 shows the yuan–dollar annual exchange rate for the period 1981–2011. The yuan–dollar exchange rate was CNY1.71 per dollar in 1981 and then steadily increased until 1994, when it reached CNY8.6397. Between 1994 and 2005, the yuan–dollar exchange rate remained above CNY8 per dollar. Beginning in 2005, the exchange rate declined, from CNY8.1936 in 2005 to CNY6.4630 in 2011. In the graph, you can use this information to calculate the percent change in the Chinese yuan and apply your knowledge of the terminology associated with the change in the exchange rate.

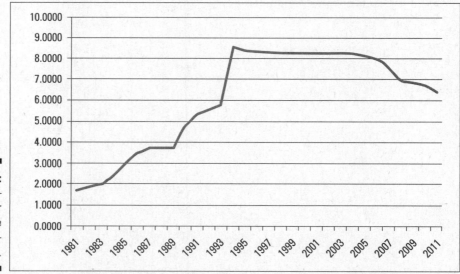

Figure 2-4:
The yuan–dollar exchange rate (1981–2011).

Notes: FRED, St. Louis Federal Reserve Bank. The data are available at http://research.stlouisfed.org/fred2/series/AEXCHUS?cid=32219.

Consider the period of 1981–1994:

$$\%\Delta E_{1981-1994} = \frac{E_{1994} - E_{1981}}{E_{1981}} \times 100 = \frac{8.6397 - 1.71}{1.71} \times 100 = +405.25\%$$

Here, E stands for the yuan–dollar exchange rate. A 405 percent increase in the yuan–dollar exchange rate is shown over a period of 14 years, which translates into an average annual devaluation of the yuan of almost 29 percent (405 ÷ 14).

Now apply the percent change formula to the 2005–2011 period:

$$\%\Delta E_{2011-2005} = \frac{E_{2011} - E_{2005}}{E_{2005}} \times 100 = \frac{6.4630 - 8.1936}{8.1936} \times 100 = -21.12\%$$

This result indicates an average annual decline in the number of yuan necessary to buy one dollar of about 3.02 percent in the past seven years (21.12 ÷ 7), which is called a revaluation.

Grasping Exchange Rate Conversions

One of the most frequently used functions of exchange rates is to convert an amount of money denominated in one currency into another currency.

Exchange rate as the price of foreign currency

The dollar–euro exchange rate implies the price of the euro in dollars. You can use this exchange rate to convert a dollar amount into euros, or vice versa.

Suppose you're an American exporter of backpacks. The importing firm in Germany wires a payment of €135,000 to your bank for the August 2012 shipment of backpacks. The bank deposits the money in your account as dollars, at an exchange rate of $1.24. What's the total number of dollars deposited into your account?

The exchange rate is defined as \$/€, and the amount of money is denominated in euros. You cancel the euros to find the amount in dollars by multiplying the euro payment by the dollar–euro exchange rate:

$$€ \times \frac{\$}{€} = \$$$

or

$$€135,000 \times \$1.24 = \$167,400$$

In this case, your bank deposits $167,400 into your account.

Suppose you're an American importer of French cheese. You receive a new shipment for which you have to pay the French firm $185,000. If the French firm's bank applies the dollar–euro exchange rate of $1.24, how many euros does the French firm receive?

Again, the exchange rate is defined as $/€, and the amount is denominated in dollars. You cancel the dollars to find the amount in euros by dividing the dollar payment by the dollar–euro exchange rate:

$$\frac{\$}{\frac{\$}{€}} = \$ \times \frac{€}{\$} = €$$

or

$$\$185,000 \div 1.24 = 149,194$$

The German firm receives €149,194 from this transaction.

Exchange rate as the price of domestic currency

In this case, you work with the euro–dollar exchange rate, which implies the price of the dollar in euros. You can use this exchange rate to convert a dollar amount into euros, or vice versa.

Using the same example of the American exporter of backpacks who expects €135,000 as a payment for its latest shipment, this time you have the euro–dollar exchange rate of €0.80645 (the inverse of $1.24, or 1 ÷ 1.24; try to keep more than two decimals so that the amounts are the same as in the previous example). The exchange rate is defined as €/$, and the amount is denominated in euros. You cancel the euros to get the amount in dollars by dividing the euro total by the euro–dollar exchange rate:

$$\frac{€}{\frac{€}{\$}} = € \times \frac{\$}{€} = \$$$

or

$$€135,000 \div €0.80645 = \$167,400$$

Therefore, the American exporter receives $167,400, as in the previous example.

In the example of the American importer of French cheese, the French exporter is paid $185,000. The French firm's bank applies the euro–dollar exchange rate of €0.80645 and deposits the dollar amount as euros.

This time the exchange rate is defined as €/$, and the amount is denominated in dollars. You cancel the dollars to get the amount in euros by multiplying the dollar amount by the euro–dollar exchange rate:

$$\frac{€}{\$} \times \$ = €$$

or

$$\$185,000 \times 0.80645 = €149,193$$

The French firm receives €149,193 from this transaction. (Note that the small discrepancy between this total and the previous result is due to rounding.)

Calculating Cross Rates

Financial media provide information only about the most frequently used exchange rates. Therefore, you may not have all the exchange rate information you need. No worries — the concept of cross rates helps you here. You can deduce information about other exchange rates based on the given exchange rates. The idea of cross rates implies two exchange rates with a common currency, which enables you to calculate the exchange rate between the remaining two currencies.

For example, you can easily find, say, the euro–dollar or the yen–dollar exchange rates in financial media. However, the euro–yen exchange rate may not be listed. Because the dollar is the common currency in this example, you can calculate the euro–yen (and also the yen–euro) exchange rate.

Section C4 of the *WSJ* of Monday, September 10, 2012, listed the yen–dollar and euro–dollar rates as ¥78.56 and €0.7802, respectively. Suppose you want to know the euro–yen exchange rate. In this case,

$$\frac{¥}{\$} = 78.56$$

and

$$\frac{€}{\$} = 0.7801$$

and you want to know what the following is:

$$\frac{€}{¥}$$

Because the dollar is the common currency here, cancel it. Think in terms of the currencies involved: When you divide the euro–dollar exchange rate by the yen–dollar exchange rate, the dollars cancel and you get the euro–yen exchange rate:

$$\frac{€}{\$} \div \frac{¥}{\$} = \frac{€}{\$} \times \frac{\$}{¥} = \frac{€}{¥}$$

Therefore, if you divide the euro–dollar exchange rate by the yen–dollar exchange rate,

$$\frac{€}{¥} = \frac{0.7801}{78.56} = 0.0099$$

the euro–yen exchange rate turns out to be €0.0099.

Figuring the Bid–Ask Spread

The bid–ask spread is important for two reasons. First, it gives you another opportunity to have more numerical exercises with exchange rates. Second, and most important, if you're an international traveler, it helps when you exchange currencies. Otherwise, you'll be surprised to find that the exchange rate at which you buy euros is different than the rate at which you sell euros on the same day and at the same bank.

Everybody has to make a living! This section describes the banks' attempts to make a living by buying foreign currency at a lower price and selling it at a higher price, which is essentially what the bid–ask spread is all about. The bid and ask quotes or rates are essentially exchange rates at which the bank buys foreign currency from you and sells foreign currency to you.

Gaining insight at an international airport

You may have seen banks or exchange offices at airports. Usually, they have displays at their windows indicating their bid–ask rates for various currencies. Next time you see their displays, look closely: Their bid and ask rates differ.

Say you're at Lambert International Airport in St. Louis and you observe the bid–ask rates indicated in Table 2-2. On this table, the ask rate refers to the rate you receive when you sell currency. The bid rate refers to the rate you pay when you buy currency. If the exchange office or the bank at the airport is to make money on this transaction, you pay more when you buy currency than when you sell the same amount of currency.

Table 2-2	Buying and Selling Rates for Selected Currencies per Dollar		
	Ask Rate	**Bid Rate**	**Bid–Ask Spread**
Euro	0.9021	0.6948	22.98%
British pound	0.7187	0.5408	24.75%
Mexican peso	15.3914	11.2714	26.77%
Turkish lira	2.0663	1.5376	25.59%

Notes: The bid–ask rates reflect the rates at the Lambert International Airport in St. Louis on September 25, 2012.

In Table 2-2, you buy euros at €0.6948 per dollar. If you want to buy €100, you pay $143.93 (€100 ÷ €0.6948). But if you want to sell €100, you sell them at €0.9021 per dollar and receive only $110.85 (€100 ÷ 0.9021).

In terms of the Turkish lira (TRY), if you buy TRY100, the rate of TRY1.5376 is applied so that you pay $65.04 (TRY100 ÷ TRY1.5376). If you sell TRY100, the rate of TRY2.0663 is applied and you receive $48.40 (TRY100 ÷ TRY2.0663). If you look at the buying and selling rates associated with the British pound and the Mexican peso, the results are similar: You pay more to buy foreign currency than you receive when selling it.

Finding the spread

The bid–ask spread (S) calculates the difference between the selling (ask) and buying price (bid) of a currency, in terms of percentage based on the following formula:

$$S = \frac{E_{ask} - E_{bid}}{E_{ask}} \times 100$$

Here, E_{ask} and E_{bid} refer to the exchange rate associated with selling and buying a currency, respectively.

Table 2-2 indicates the spreads associated with the currencies on the table. You can use the previous formula to calculate these spreads.

To calculate the spread on the euro–dollar exchange rate:

$$S = \frac{0.9021 - 0.6948}{0.9021} \times 100 = 22.98\%$$

You can use the same formula for other bid and ask rates in Table 2-2 and calculate the spreads. As you can see in Table 2-2, bid–ask spreads vary among exchange rates. Various factors affect bid–ask spreads. First, trade volume associated with a currency is negatively related to spreads, in that currencies with higher trade volumes tend to have smaller spreads. Spreads associated with heavily traded currencies, such as the euro, pound, and yuan, tend to be smaller. Second, spreads increase with the volatility or the riskiness of a currency. If a currency exhibits relatively frequent and larger changes compared to other currencies, the bid–ask spread increases. You can see this in Table 2-2: The bid–ask spreads associated with the euro and the British pound are smaller than the spreads associated with the Turkish lira and the Mexican peso.

Chapter 3

Buy, Sell, Risk! Users of Foreign Exchange Markets

••

In This Chapter

▶ Identifying the participants in foreign exchange markets

▶ Understanding the risk of multinational companies

▶ Understanding the risk of speculators

••

Diverse groups are involved in foreign exchange markets. This chapter identifies these groups, explains the nature of their involvement, and illustrates the risk associated with their involvement. Numerical examples guide you through the concepts and illustrate the risk taken by various participants in foreign exchange markets.

Identifying Major Actors in Foreign Exchange Markets

Multinational firms, speculators, and central banks are the important participants in foreign exchange markets. Multinational companies operate in different countries and, therefore, deal with a variety of currencies in their daily business. Speculators invest in assets denominated in different currencies and, therefore, buy or sell currencies. Central banks may be engaged in foreign exchange markets to increase or decrease the value of their currency with respect to other currencies.

Multinational firms

The term *multinational firm* refers to a wide range of domestic firms that are engaged in business with foreign countries in different ways. One point to remember is that, independent of the type of foreign involvement, all multinational businesses deal with exchange rates. You see in this section that multinational companies have to buy or sell foreign currency as part of their daily business. Therefore, these companies face foreign exchange risk every day. A short definition of foreign exchange risk is the possibility of losing money when you buy or sell currency because of unexpected changes in exchange rates. When you learn about the general characteristics of participants in foreign exchange markets in the next section, you can work on numerical examples regarding foreign exchange risk.

Some multinational companies are export or import firms. These companies are engaged in selling domestic goods abroad or buying foreign goods. Therefore, an American company that exports to Germany is a multinational company. So is an American firm that imports from Germany. Exchange rates affect both types of firms. For example, if the American firm bills the German importer in euros, the former receives its payments in euros. But an American firm can't use euros in its daily business, so it sells euros as soon as it receives them. Conversely, the American firm may bill the German importer in dollars. Then it becomes the German importer's responsibility to buy dollars and pay the American exporter.

Other domestic firms may be involved in the production of goods in foreign countries in a variety of ways.

Licensing means that a firm provides its technology to another firm abroad in exchange for a fee. Depending on the currency in which the fee is denominated, one of the firms faces the foreign exchange risk.

The September 17, 2012 issue of *Pharmaceutical Business Review* reported that the Canadian vaccine developer `Medicago` entered a licensing agreement with the American firm Philip Morris Products (PMP) to allow PMP to use Medicago's proprietary vaccine-manufacturing technologies for developing and manufacturing pandemic and seasonal influenza vaccines in China. Medicago received fees totaling $7.5 million, as well as royalty payments on future sales of pandemic and seasonal influenza vaccines produced by PMP in China.

In this example, you know the amount of the licensing fee, but you don't know the denomination PMP plans to use. If PMP pays the licensing fee from its dollar accounts in the United States, it doesn't face an exchange rate risk. But Medicago, a Canadian firm, is going to receive periodic U.S.

dollar–denominated payments. If Medicago wants to convert these fees into Canadian dollars, it exposes itself to changes in exchange rates. Alternatively, if PMP pays the licensing fee out of its revenues in China by exchanging yuan into dollars (unless the Chinese government has restrictions on payments denominated in yuan), PMP and Medicago are both exposed to exchange rate risk.

Franchising implies that a domestic firm allows its production, sales, marketing, and management strategies to be used in a foreign market in exchange for a periodic payment. You see such chains as Starbucks, McDonald's, and Pizza Hut around the world; to open these businesses in other countries, foreign firms need to have franchising agreements with these American companies.

The September 7, 2012 issue of *Business Day* reports that international franchises are opening new locations in Africa, where the demand for their products is strong, unlike in stagnant developed markets. Hilton Hotels, Kentucky Fried Chicken, and fashion retailer Mango are just a few companies that are expanding their franchising in Africa. The franchising industry employs an estimated 500,000 people in Africa, and nearly 700 brands operate franchises there.

If American firms are franchised in Africa, the American firms collect franchising fees from African owners of these franchises. If American firms want to receive their franchising payments in dollars, the African owners face the exchange rate risk. Because their revenues are in local currencies, they need to convert some of their revenues into dollars to pay the franchising fee.

Domestic firms engage in *joint ventures* with foreign firms. A joint venture is a business arrangement between two businesses to produce a particular good, where these firms share expenditures, revenues, and assets. For example, an American firm may enter a joint venture to test the waters before entering a foreign country on its own. Or an American company may want to use the existing distribution network of a foreign firm to sell its product abroad.

The September 24, 2012 issue of the *Washington Post* reported that breakfast giant Kellogg formed a joint venture to expand the distribution of its cereals and snacks in China in 2013. Kellogg plans to tap the infrastructure and local expertise of Wilmar International, a Singapore-based agribusiness.

In this case, Kellogg is likely to pay Wilmar for the privilege of using the latter's infrastructure and expertise. Suppose Kellogg provides these payments in U.S. dollars. This form of payment shifts the exchange rate risk to Wilmar, which has to convert these U.S. dollars into a combination of Singapore dollars and Chinese yuan to pay for the expenses of including Kellogg in its network in Singapore and China.

Domestic firms may buy existing firms abroad, which involves the *acquisition* of existing foreign firms. An acquisition allows an American firm to enter a foreign market with an existing production facility and a distribution network.

The September 26, 2012 issue of *Businessweek* reported that Canada's Onex Corporation was in talks to buy KraussMaffei AG, a German maker of machinery for processing plastics and rubber. Onex reportedly planned to pay €568 million for KraussMaffei, the company's first European-based acquisition.

In this news article, the payment for the German company is discussed in euros. The Canadian buyer, Onex Corporation, faces exchange rate risk here, especially if acquisition payments are to be made in installments.

Domestic firms establish new subsidiaries in other countries. The term *foreign direct investment* (FDI) refers to establishing a new production facility, distribution network, management, and so forth in a foreign country.

On September 18, 2012, cnbc.com reported on the global appeal of Mexico for FDI. The country attracted more than $19 billion FDI in 2011, and half of this investment went toward manufacturing. Major automakers, such as General Motors, Nissan, Audi, Honda, and Mazda, recently announced plans to open plants in Mexico during the next few years. Many other companies, including aluminum producer Alcoa, General Electric, Honeywell, Hawker Beechcraft, and Swedish appliance maker Electrolux, already have production facilities in Mexico.

These American, Japanese, and European firms are engaged in FDI, which indicates substantial new investment in a foreign country. Therefore, parent companies have to transfer funds denominated in foreign currency to the FDI-receiving country. Also, depending on the FDI-receiving country's restrictions, parent companies may receive income/profits from their foreign operations denominated in foreign currency. All these activities imply exchange rate risk.

Speculators

The generic term *speculator* includes a wide variety of market participants. Foreign exchange traders and brokers make up a relatively small segment among speculators; commercial banks, hedge funds, and other financial companies represent the most important group among speculators. Regardless of type, speculators in foreign exchange markets want to profit from buying currency low and selling it high. In other words, all speculators try to make a profit from fluctuations in exchange rates.

The interbank market, which consists of large commercial banks and financial firms, is a major player in foreign exchange markets. Its activity helps determine the bid (buy) and ask (sell) price of currencies. This market has no trading floor, but banks can trade with each other directly or via electronic brokerage systems that connect market participants.

Multinational companies also engage in speculation because they make or receive payments denominated in various currencies to and from firms around the world. These currencies fluctuate on a daily basis. Therefore, multinational companies are also involved in speculation to hedge against their exchange rate risk.

Central banks

Central banks have a unique place in foreign exchange markets. First, unlike the other groups involved in foreign exchange markets, the central banks' involvement in foreign exchange markets doesn't have a profit motive.

Second, central banks' decisions regarding monetary policy are extremely influential on exchange rate determination. Chapters 5–7 discuss exchange rate determination and how central banks indirectly affect exchange rates through their monetary policy decisions. In every country, central banks are responsible for conducting monetary policy, among their other roles. The main goals of monetary policy are to promote price stability and economic growth. Basically, a central bank addresses the domestic economy's problems by changing the quantity of money and interest rates, which leads to changes in the exchange rate as well.

Third, central banks can directly affect exchange rates through *interventions* into foreign exchange markets. A central bank can use its domestic currency and foreign currency reserves to buy or sell foreign currencies directly in the foreign exchange market. Alternatively, central banks may be involved in foreign exchange markets for reasons that aren't related to their own countries but are related to the common concerns at the international level. For example, several central banks may come together in a joint action in foreign exchange markets to provide liquidity and credit across the world. Chapter 14 shows how central banks directly intervene in foreign exchange markets.

Watching Out for Risk

This section looks at the most important motivation for understanding how exchange rates are determined. When you're involved in foreign exchange markets in any capacity, you face foreign exchange risk. The following examples show the nature of foreign exchange risk, assuming that you're a multinational firm or a speculator.

Note that this section doesn't mention central banks. The reason is that, unlike multinational firms and speculators, central banks don't have a profit motive. Central banks' concerns center on the economic performance of the country. Chapter 14 provides examples for central banks' intervention into foreign exchange markets.

In addition, this section demonstrates only the nature of foreign exchange risk, not how to hedge against it. Chapter 11 examines foreign exchange derivatives that you can use to hedge against exchange rate risk.

FX risk of an exporting firm

Exporting firms may have accounts receivable in foreign currency. The foreign exchange risk of these firms is the possibility of depreciation in foreign currency. In this case, when the exporting firm exchanges foreign currency for the domestic currency, it receives a smaller amount of domestic currency for the same amount of foreign currency.

Suppose you export backpacks to Germany, and your accounts receivable are denominated in euros, totaling €100,000. As an American firm, you don't use euros in your daily operations. Therefore, as soon as you receive the euros from the German importer — say, a week from now — you plan to convert them into dollars. Suppose that the current dollar–euro rate is $1.28, and you observe the dollar appreciating every day until it reaches an exchange rate of $1.25 a week from now, when you convert the euros to dollars.

Note that the exchange rate used here is the dollar–euro rate. A decline in this exchange rate from $1.28 to $1.25 per euro indicates an appreciation of the dollar because fewer dollars are necessary to buy one euro. If the dollar appreciates against the euro, the euro must depreciate against the dollar. As Chapter 2 explains, you can invert this exchange rate and easily see that the euro depreciates. The euro–dollar exchange rate increases from €0.78 (1 ÷ 1.28) to €0.80 (1 ÷ 1.25) per dollar. Clearly, you need more euros to buy one dollar, which means depreciation of the euro.

If the exchange rate of $1.28 had remained constant, the American firm would have received $128,000 (€100,000 × $1.28). However, because the euro depreciated (or the dollar appreciated), the American firm receives only $125,000 (€100,000 × $1.25).

You may argue that most international trade is denominated in dollars. If this case is true, then somebody else is facing foreign exchange risk — namely, the German importer. Suppose that the German importer of backpacks is supposed to pay you $128,000 for the latest shipment. By using the same exchange rates discussed, a week earlier, the company needed €100,000 ($128,000 ÷ 1.28). But when the euro depreciates (or the dollar appreciates) to $1.25 per euro, the company must spend €102,400 ($128,000 ÷ 1.25) to pay for your backpacks.

FX risk of an importing firm

Importing firms may have accounts payable in foreign currency. The exchange rate risk these firms face is the risk of appreciation in foreign currency. Remember, appreciation of a foreign currency means that a dollar buys fewer units of foreign currency. In this case, the amount of a domestic firm's payments in foreign currency gets larger.

Suppose your firm imports cheese from France, and your accounts payable are denominated in euros, totaling €100,000. Again, the current dollar–euro rate as $1.28, but suppose that each day the dollar depreciates. Assume an exchange rate of $1.31 a week from now, when you make your payment.

Note that an increase in the dollar–euro rate indicates depreciation of the dollar. When the exchange rate increases from $1.28 to $1.31 per euro, clearly you need more dollars to buy one euro. If the dollar depreciates against the euro, the euro must appreciate against the dollar. Again, you can invert this exchange rate and easily see that the euro appreciates. The euro–dollar exchange rate decreases from €0.78 (1 ÷ 1.28) to €0.76 (1 ÷ 1.31) per dollar. Clearly, you need fewer euros to buy one dollar, which means an appreciation of the euro.

If the initial exchange rate had remained the same, you would have paid $128,000 (€100,000 × $1.28) for the imported French cheese. However, because the euro appreciated, now you have to pay $131,000 (€100,000 × $1.31) for your imports.

Again, if your accounts payable are denominated in dollars, then the French exporter faces the foreign exchange risk. Suppose you have to pay $128,000 to the French firm for the latest shipment of cheese. By using the same exchange rates, a week earlier, the French firm would have received €100,000 ($128,000 ÷ 1.28) as payment. But when the dollar depreciates to $1.31, it receives €97,710 ($128,000 ÷ 1.31).

FX risk in a domestic company–foreign subsidiary setting

If a domestic firm is involved in foreign operations in any way, such as a joint venture or FDI, funds flow between the domestic and foreign firms. These funds may involve the domestic firm's provision of money to a foreign partner or subsidiary, or the domestic firm may receive income or profits from its foreign subsidiaries.

In terms of the outgoing funds to the subsidiary, the domestic firm may have to provide these funds in foreign currency. In this case, the domestic firm faces the exchange rate risk, which lies in the appreciation of the foreign currency. Suppose an American firm has a subsidiary in Indonesia and plans to wire Rp100,000,000 to the subsidiary for the expansion of the production facility (Rp stands for the Indonesian rupiah). If the current rupiah–dollar exchange rate is Rp9,575 and remains the same for another week until the American firm sends the money, it costs the American firm $10,444 (Rp100,000,000 ÷ 9,575). But if the rupiah appreciates in a week from Rp9,575 to Rp9,250 per dollar, the American firm has to pay $10,811 (Rp100,000,000 ÷ 9,250) for the same amount of rupiah.

Now if the American firm expects some of the profits from its Indonesian operation, the exchange rate risk lies in the depreciation of the rupiah. Suppose the amount of funds coming from the subsidiary in a week is Rp150,000,000. By using the same current exchange rate of Rp9,575, and assuming that the exchange rate doesn't change in a week, the American firm receives $15,666 (Rp150,000,000 ÷ 9,575). However, if the rupiah depreciates to Rp9,950, the firm receives $10,050 (Rp100,000,000 ÷ 9,950).

Speculation: Taking a Risk to Gain Profit

This section provides insight into speculation with exchange rates. Speculation involves profiting from the change in the price of an asset. No matter what kind of asset you consider, the desired change in price is an increase when you sell it. In other words, all speculation involves buying low and selling high.

Currencies can also be bought and sold for a profit. Types of speculation with exchange rates differ, but they all have one thing in common: an expectation regarding the change in the exchange rate in the near future. Other than this expectation, your aim is always to buy low and sell high, as in the case of all speculation. Of course, you can buy and sell currency in *spot* markets or *derivative* markets. In spot markets, assets are traded for immediate delivery. In other words, if you can buy or sell euros now, it means you're trading in a spot foreign exchange market. In derivative markets, although the agreement is done today, the actual transaction (the buying or selling of foreign currency) takes place at a future date (for example, two months from now). Chapter 11 examines various types of derivatives markets and their use in both speculation and hedging. For simplicity, this chapter deals only with spot foreign exchange markets.

The following numerical examples involve a little more than just buying or selling foreign currencies. As before, the change in the exchange rate remains important because you're buying or selling currencies. But when you speculate with foreign currencies, you may want to earn interest on foreign currency while you're holding it. For simplicity, the following examples assume that you want to buy a foreign currency and put it in an interest-earning account. Now this doubles the sources of your profits: You can make money from the changes in the exchange rate and the interest earned on the foreign currency.

The following section includes two numerical examples about speculating with exchange rates. In the first example, the speculator makes a profit. In the second example, the speculator experiences a loss.

When speculation goes right

Suppose USA Bank expects the Swiss franc (SFR) to appreciate from $1.069 to $1.112 a year from now. USA Bank borrows $10,000,000 at an interest rate of 1.5 percent for a year, converts it into Swiss francs at the current rate, and deposits the funds into a Swiss bank account at Helvetica Bank for a year at an annual interest rate of 1.75 percent. A year from now, USA Bank withdraws the Swiss francs, converts them into dollars in the future spot market, and hopes to make a profit.

Now you see the translation of each step into equations. At the end of the calculations, you see how much money the USA Bank makes in this transaction. Here are the steps in calculating the bank's profits:

1. USA Bank converts $10,000,000 into Swiss francs at the exchange rate of $1.069 and receives SFR9,354,537 ($10,000,000 ÷ 1.069).

2. USA Bank deposits SFR9,354,537 into a savings account with Helvetica Bank for a year at an annual interest rate of 1.75 percent. Therefore, you need to calculate how much money USA Bank receives from the Swiss bank a year from now.

At this point, you need a formula that relates an amount of money that you currently hold to its future value, assuming that this money will earn interest for a year. The formula that relates the future value (*FV*) to the present value (*PV*) is:

$$\frac{FV}{PV} = 1 + R$$

The previous formula indicates that the future value is greater than the present value by the interest factor $(1 + R)$. Suppose that you currently have \$100, which is the present value (PV). In a year, you want today's \$100 to become \$110, which is the future value (FV). Plug these numbers into the equation:

$$\$110 \div \$100 = 1 + R = 1.1$$

Note that dollars cancel in the equation. Future value is 10 percent greater than present value, indicating an interest rate (R) of 10 percent.

Now you can manipulate the basic formula, depending upon what is unknown in a situation. In the USA Bank example, you know the present value (PV) and the interest rate (R). Therefore, the unknown variable is the future value (FV). The next formula shows that the future value (FV) equals the present value (PV) multiplied by the interest factor $(1 + R)$:

$$FV = PV \times (1 + R)$$

Now you can plug in the known variables in the previous equation. You know that USA Bank has SFR9,354,537 and that the annual interest rate is 1.75 percent. Therefore, the future value is:

$$FV = SFR9,354,537 \times (1 + 0.0175) = SFR9,518,241$$

So USA Bank will receive SFR9,518,241 a year from now.

3. Suppose USA Bank is correct in its expectation, and the Swiss franc does appreciate to \$1.112 a year from now. Therefore, USA Bank withdraws SFR9,518,241 from Helvetica Bank, converts it into dollars, and receives \$10,584,284 (SFR9,518,241 × \$1.112).

4. But wait! USA Bank still needs to pay off its loan a year from now at the interest rate of 1.5 percent. Here you can also use the future value formula, where the present value is the amount of the loan, \$10,000,000, and the interest rate is 1.5 percent:

$$FV = \$10,000,000 \times [1 + 0.015] = \$10,150,000$$

5. Therefore, after paying off the loan, USA Bank has a profit of $434,284 ($10,584,284 - $10,150,000). To calculate USA Bank's rate of return on this speculation, calculate the percent change between the amount of money the bank received and paid:

$$\frac{\$10,584,284 - \$10,150,000}{\$10,150,000} = 0.0428$$

This result suggests that USA Bank received an annual rate of return (or profit) of 4.28 percent from this speculation. But be careful when you call it a profit. In this example, you're not provided with alternative investment opportunities for USA Bank in the U.S. or elsewhere. As long as the rate of return USA Bank would have received in the U.S. or anywhere in the world is below 4.28 percent (holding the risk constant), this example shows speculation that went right.

The previous speculation example involves a period of one year. But USA Bank may want to consider a shorter time period. What if USA Bank deposited the money with Helvetica Bank for only 60 days and the expected exchange rate of $1.112 refers to the exchange rate expected 60 days from now? In this case, the previous formula for the future value calculation needs to be adjusted. In fact, you want to apply the adjustment to the interest rate because the interest rate is an annual rate, but USA Bank wants to keep its Swiss Francs at Helvetica Bank for only 60 days.

The next future value formula applies the ratio of 60 days to 360 days (60 ÷ 360 = 0.17) to the annual interest rate, essentially lowering the annual interest rate. Also note that using the 360-day year is common practice in international finance.

$$FV = PV \times \left[1 + R\left(\frac{60}{360}\right) \right]$$

Given the data:

$$FV = SFR9,354,537 \times (1 + 0.0175) = SFR9,518,241$$

This time, USA Bank receives SFR9,381,821 at the end of 60 days. Assume that USA Bank is correct in its expectation, and the Swiss franc appreciates to $1.112 in 60 days. Then USA Bank makes SFR9,381,821 at Helvetica Bank, converts it into dollars, and receives $10,432,585 (SFR9,381,821 × 1.112). USA Bank pays off its 60-day loan at the annual interest rate of 1.5 percent:

$$FV = \$10,000,000 \times \left[1 + 0.015\left(\frac{60}{360}\right) \right] = \$10,025,000$$

Therefore, USA Bank's profit from this speculation is $407,585 ($10,432,585 − $10,025,000). In fact USA Bank's rate of return on this speculation is

$$\frac{\$10,432,585 - \$10,025,000}{\$10,025,000} = 0.0407$$

or 4.07 percent.

When speculation goes wrong

Now you see how USA Bank can lose money in speculation. As in the previous example, USA Bank expects an appreciation of the Swiss franc (SFR) from $1.069 to $1.112 in 60 days. USA Bank borrows $10,000,000 at an interest rate of 1.5 percent for 60 days, converts it into Swiss francs at the current rate, and deposits the funds into an account at Helvetica Bank for 60 days at an interest rate of 1.75 percent. At the end of the 60-day period, USA Bank converts its Swiss francs into dollars.

Therefore, most of your calculations associated with the previous example are also correct here, meaning that USA Bank converts $10,000,000 into Swiss francs and receives SFR9,354,537. Then it deposits the money with Helvetica Bank for 60 days at an interest rate of 1.75 percent. At the end of the 60-day period, USA Bank receives SFR9,381,821.

But suppose that USA Bank is wrong this time in terms of its expectations regarding the future spot rate. As USA Bank withdraws SFR9,381,821 from Helvetica Bank, it observes that the Swiss franc has depreciated from $1.069 to $1.059 instead of appreciating to $1.112. In this case, USA Bank receives $9,935,348 (SFR9,381,821 × 1.059), which is less than the payment due on the loan ($10,025,000). In this case, USA Bank suffers a loss of $89,652 ($9,935,348 − $10,025,000).

Chapter 4

It's All about Change: Changes in the Exchange Rate

*I*f you like visualizing concepts, you're in luck! This chapter is all about visualizing changes in exchange rates. Using example exchange rates, we look at how these rates fluctuate over time. Through these examples, you get a good look at the highly volatile nature of exchange rates.

Changes in exchange rates cause you to ask why these changes are happening. You can find the reasons behind why exchange rates change in Chapters 5, 6, and 7. In this chapter, graphs showcase the actual changes in selected exchange rates. In addition to exchange rates, the graphs include macroeconomic fundamentals, including GDP growth, inflation rates, and interest rates. The purpose of this chapter is to introduce a visual approach to the relationship between changes in exchange rates and macroeconomic fundamentals without providing a theory-based discussion.

In this chapter, I use the terminology introduced in Chapter 2, including such terms as *percent change* in the exchange rate, *appreciation,* and *depreciation.* This chapter really serves as a bridge between the definition- and calculation-oriented Chapters 2 and 3 and the upcoming Chapters 5, 6, and 7, which represent the theories of exchange rate determination.

Also in this chapter, you start developing some sensitivity to exchange rate regimes, at least in a visual context. Chapters 11, 12, and 13 focus on the extent of government/central bank interventions in exchange rates, so this chapter prepares you to ask questions regarding exchange rate regimes when you have exchange rate data.

Considering a Visual Approach to Changes in Exchange Rates

Exchange rates behave differently over time. The example exchange rates in this chapter certainly prove this point. I use the Japanese yen–dollar and Indonesian rupiah–dollar exchange rates as example exchange rates for this chapter. The Chinese yuan–dollar exchange rate appears in the section on exchange rate regimes.

This section uses the yen–dollar and the rupiah–dollar exchanges rates as example exchange rates. As Chapter 2 discusses, an increase in these exchange rates implies the depreciation of the yen or the rupiah against the dollar. In addition to using exchange rates in levels, sometimes you see the percent change in exchange rates. If the sign of the percent change is positive, (for example, in the yen–dollar rate), you can express the depreciation in the yen as a percentage. If the sign is negative, it indicates the percent change of appreciation in the yen.

Figure 4-1 shows the quarterly nominal yen–dollar exchange rate for more than 40 years. The general trend is downward sloping, which means a gradual appreciation in the yen against the dollar. The data suggest that the exchange rate in the first quarter of 1970 was ¥360 per dollar and that it declined to ¥77.4 per dollar in the fourth quarter of 2011. Of course, you observe fluctuations around the downward trend. For example, during the mid-1970s and 1980s, the yen depreciated against the dollar.

Figure 4-1:
The yen–dollar quarterly nominal exchange rates (1970:Q1 to 2011:Q4).

Notes: International Financial Statistics of the IMF. Data are available at www.imf.org.

Because the nominal effective and real effective exchange rate data are available for Japan, you can inspect them in Figure 4-2. In terms of the yen–dollar exchange rate, the real effective or trade-weighted exchange rates indicate the cost of the Japanese consumption basket to the weighted average cost of the consumption basket associated with Japan's major trade partners. Figure 4-2 shows effective exchange rates in both nominal (not adjusted for inflation) and real (adjusted for inflation) terms. It also indicates that, between 1980 and the mid-1990s, the purchasing power of the Japanese yen steadily increased. Following a decline in the early and mid-2000s, both the nominal effective and real effective yen–dollar rates increased again until late 2011.

When you compare Figures 4-1 and 4-2, keep in mind that Figure 4-1 shows the nominal yen–dollar exchange rate, whereas Figure 4-2 indicates the nominal effective and real effective rates involving the yen and a basket of currencies that consists of the currencies of Japan's major trade partners. In Figure 4-1, you observe that the yen gradually appreciated against the dollar during the period under consideration (1970:Q1 to 2011:Q4). Based on this figure, you can conclude that, over the years, smaller amounts of yen were required to buy one dollar. Actually, Figure 4-2 expresses something similar, where the comparison isn't between only two currencies, but is between the yen and the currencies of Japan's major trade partners. The rising nominal effective rate means an appreciation of the yen against the basket of currencies. The rising real effective exchange rate shows that, even if you include the cost of the Japanese consumption basket and other countries' consumption baskets in the calculation, the yen appreciated against the currencies of Japan's major trade partners.

Figure 4-2:
The nominal and real effective exchange rate index for Japan, 2005=100 (1980:Q1 to 2011:Q4).

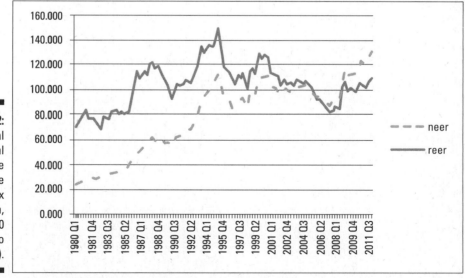

Notes: *International Financial Statistics of the IMF. The consumer price index of Japan and its trade partners are used to calculate the indices. Data are available at* www.imf.org.

Another example exchange rate is the rupiah–dollar rate. Because the nominal effective and real effective exchange rates aren't available for this currency, you observe only the changes in the nominal rupiah–dollar exchange rate in Figure 4-3.

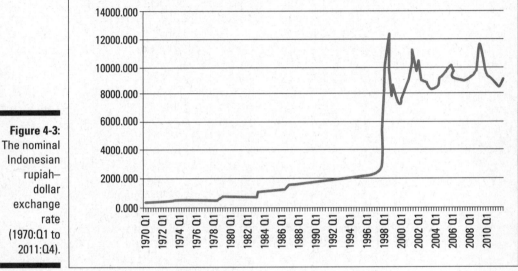

Figure 4-3:
The nominal Indonesian rupiah–dollar exchange rate (1970:Q1 to 2011:Q4).

Notes: International Financial Statistics of the IMF. Data are available at www.imf.org.

The figure starts with Rp326 per dollar in 1970:Q1, and the rate only slightly depreciates until 1971:Q4. At the beginning of the graph, you see a straight line, which reflects the lack of change in the rupiah–dollar exchange rate between 1971:Q4 and 1978:Q3. During this period, the rupiah–dollar exchange rate remained as Rp415 per dollar. Then you observe a steady depreciation of the rupiah approaching Rp1,644 per dollar in 1986:Q4, which continued until 1997:Q3, when the rate reached Rp2,791 per dollar. Next quarter, 1997:Q4, the rupiah–dollar rate increased to Rp4,005, indicating an almost 44 percent depreciation in the rupiah. But worse was yet to come. Next quarter, 1998:Q1, the rupiah increased even further to Rp9,433, which implied a 136 percent depreciation in the rupiah against the dollar. Finally, the exchange rate reached Rp12,252 in 1998:Q3.

These large deprecations of the Indonesian rupiah took place during the Asian crisis of 1997–1998, a currency crises that involved several Asian countries. Chapter 13 examines the Asian crisis and the reasons for currency crises in general.

Looking at How Macroeconomic Variables Affect Exchange Rates

This section provides a visual approach to changes in exchange rates by introducing graphs that capture changes in exchange rates along with changes in the selected macroeconomic fundamentals. The yen–dollar and rupiah–dollar rates continue to be the example exchange rates. Note that upcoming graphs show the change in the exchange rate and the change in Japan's and Indonesia's fundamentals, such as real GDP growth rates, inflation rates, and interest rates.

This section doesn't go into a deep discussion of exchange rate determination. Chapters 5, 6, and 7 cover macroeconomic variables that explain the changes in exchange rates.

Understanding the limitations of this section is important. Clearly, when considering an exchange rate, you must consider two countries' fundamentals (as with the U.S. and Japan or the U.S. and Indonesia, for example). The formal treatment of exchange rate determination in Chapters 7 and 8 examines the change in the exchange rate and the difference between two countries' inflation and interest rates. In this chapter, matters are simpler. Additionally, focusing on the macroeconomic fundamentals of Japan and Indonesia makes sense because of the relatively slower changes in the fundamentals of the U.S. Therefore, you see the change in exchange rates and Japan's and Indonesia's fundamentals, but not fundamentals of the U.S..

Output and exchange rates

Just to clarify the terminology, *output* refers to a country's real gross domestic product (GDP). Because real GDP is adjusted for the changes in inflation (in other words, it has no price effect in it), it can also be referred to as output. The relationship between exchange rates and output, usually the percent change in output (in short, growth rates), is used. Some of the exchange rate determination theories, such as the monetary approach to exchange rates (see Chapter 7), predict that higher growth rates in a country lead to an appreciation of this country's currency.

Figure 4-4 illustrates the relationship between percent change in the yen–dollar exchange rate and growth rates in Japan's real GDP. One striking aspect of Figure 4-4 is that the exchange rate is more volatile than output. You observe that the changes in the exchange rate are much larger than the changes in output. In terms of the expected relationship between changes in the exchange rate and economic growth, some periods, such as the early 1980s, show appreciation of the yen when growth rates are higher and show depreciation of the yen when the growth rates are lower. These associations are consistent with the predictions of the theory that Chapters 6 and 7 cover (the Monetary Approach to Balance of Payments, or the MBOP). However, when you look at the early quarters of 2010, you observe an appreciation of the yen accompanied by slower growth rates.

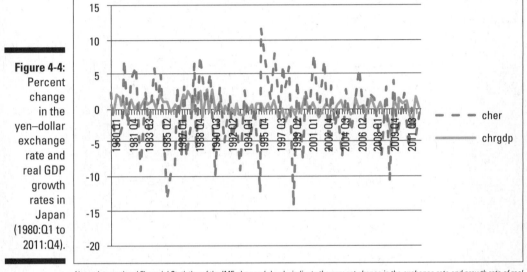

Figure 4-4: Percent change in the yen–dollar exchange rate and real GDP growth rates in Japan (1980:Q1 to 2011:Q4).

Notes: International Financial Statistics of the IMF. cher and chrgdp indicate the percent change in the exchange rate and growth rate of real GDP, respectively. Data are available at www.imf.org.

Another example of the exchange rate output relationship is the rupiah–dollar rate and growth rate of Indonesia's real GDP. Figure 4-5 depicts this relationship. The data availability in the real GDP is the reason the figure starts in 1998:Q1. This figure is interesting because of the spike in the exchange rate, which indicates a 136 percent depreciation in the rupiah after the Asian crisis hit Indonesia (1998:Q1). The corresponding decline in output reached about 18 percent in 1998:Q4. This observation is certainly an outlier. (You call an observation an outlier if it has a much higher or lower value than the surrounding observations.) Still, it confirms the expected relationship between depreciation in the rupiah and slower growth rates in Indonesia.

Although observing such outliers as a 136 percent depreciation in the rupiah is interesting, they make seeing the relationship between the exchange rate and the growth rate difficult for the rest of the available period. Therefore, Figure 4-6 takes out the outlier and starts with the post–Asian crisis period. Now you can better see the changes in the exchange rate and growth rates during the post-crisis period. Again, you observe a higher volatility in the rupiah–dollar exchange rate than that of the GDP growth rate. In terms of the relationship between changes in the exchange rate and GDP growth rate, the first couple quarters in 1999 and 2002, as well as in late 2004 and 2009, indicate the appreciation of the rupiah and higher growth rates. Almost 20 percent depreciation in the rupiah in the fourth quarter of 2008 coincides with declining growth rates, which confirms the theory's expectations.

Figure 4-5:
Percent change in the rupiah–dollar exchange rate and real GDP growth rates in Indonesia (1998:Q1 to 2011:Q4).

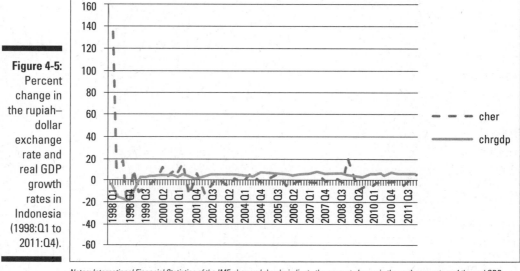

Notes: International Financial Statistics of the IMF. cher and chrgdp indicate the percent change in the exchange rate and the real GDP growth rate, respectively. Data are available at www.imf.org.

Figure 4-6:
Percent change in the rupiah–dollar exchange rate and real GDP growth rates in Indonesia (1998:Q2 to 2011:Q4).

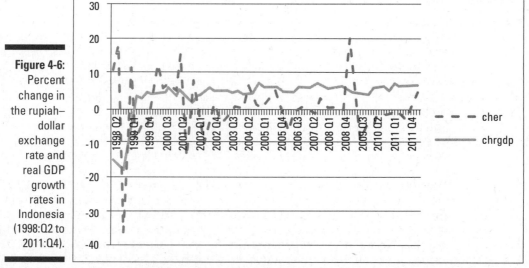

Notes: International Financial Statistics of the IMF. cher and chrgdp indicate the percent change in the exchange rate and the real GDP growth rate, respectively. Data are available at www.imf.org.

Inflation rates and exchange rates

Most theories of exchange rate determination (see Chapters 5, 7, and 9) predict depreciation in the higher-inflation country's currency. *Inflation* refers to an increase in the average price level of a country, which is frequently measured by the consumer price index (CPI). Figure 4-7 shows the change in the yen–dollar exchange rate and the change in the Japanese CPI. Again, you can see higher volatility in the exchange rate compared to changes in the consumer price index.

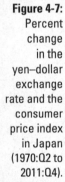

Figure 4-7:
Percent
change
in the
yen–dollar
exchange
rate and the
consumer
price index
in Japan
(1970:Q2 to
2011:Q4).

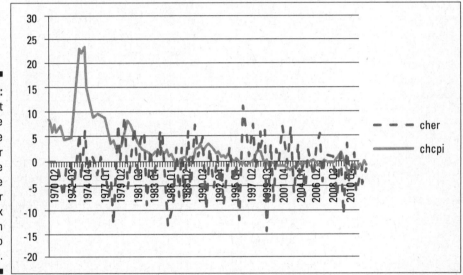

Notes: International Financial Statistics of the IMF. cher and chcpi *indicate the percent change in the exchange rate and the consumer price index, respectively. Data are available at* www.imf.org.

In terms of the relationship between the exchange rate and the inflation rate, certainly the observation in 1974 is consistent with the theory's expectation: As the inflation rate approached 25 percent, you observe a depreciation of the yen about 5 percent. As another example, in 1986, as the inflation rate declined, you observe an appreciation of the yen approaching 15 percent.

Figure 4-8 shows the relationship between the change in the rupiah–dollar exchange rate and the inflation rate in Indonesia. Again, the spike in the exchange rate and the inflation rate indicates the Asian crisis. The 136 percent depreciation in the rupiah in 1998:Q1 was accompanied by higher inflation rates that reached 78 percent in 1998:Q4.

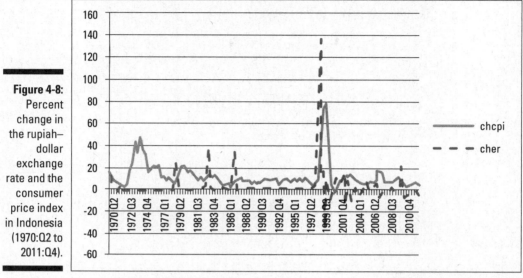

Notes: *International Financial Statistics of the IMF.* cher *and* chcpi *indicate the percent change in the exchange rate and the consumer price index, respectively. Data are available at* www.imf.org.

Because of the outliers associated with the Asian crisis, seeing the relationship between changes in the exchange rates and the inflation rates is difficult. Therefore, Figures 4-9 and 4-10 indicate the pre– and post–Asian crisis periods, respectively. In Figure 4-9, spikes in the change of the exchange rates indicate major depreciations, reaching almost 40 percent in the early 1980s. They're accompanied by higher inflation rates. However, the relationship between changes in the exchange rates and inflation rates is almost nonexistent during the 1970s and the late 1980s and 1990s. The last section of this chapter returns to these periods and provides an explanation.

Figure 4-10 shows the changes in the rupiah–dollar exchange rate and inflation rates in Indonesia during the post–Asian crisis period. Higher inflation rates and depreciation in the rupiah coincide during the later quarters of 2001, the early quarters of 2004, the later quarters of 2005 and 2008, and the early quarters of 2010. Lower inflation rates and appreciation in the rupiah coincide with the early quarters of 2002 and 2003. However, in early 2006, although the inflation rate is above 15 percent, the rupiah appreciates more than 5 percent. This result is inconsistent with the theories in Chapters 5, 6, and 7.

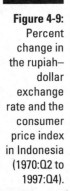

Figure 4-9:
Percent
change in
the rupiah–
dollar
exchange
rate and the
consumer
price index
in Indonesia
(1970:Q2 to
1997:Q4).

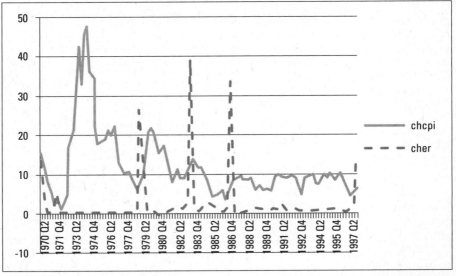

Notes: International Financial Statistics of the IMF. cher *and* chcpi *indicate the percent change in the exchange rate and the consumer price index, respectively. Data are available at* www.imf.org.

Figure 4-10:
Percent
change in
the rupiah–
dollar
exchange
rate and the
consumer
price index
in Indonesia
(1999:Q2 to
2011:Q4).

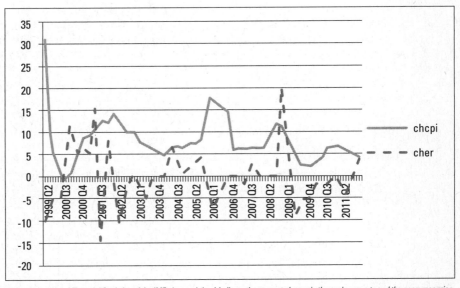

Notes: International Financial Statistics of the IMF. cher *and* chcpi *indicate the percent change in the exchange rate and the consumer price index, respectively. Data are available at* www.imf.org.

Interest rates and exchange rates

All exchange rate determination theories refer to the effect of interest rates on exchange rates. Chapters 5–8 discuss the effects of interest rates on the changes in exchange rates. As these chapters make clear, some theories deal with nominal interest rates, and some deal with real interest rates.

In general, nominal variables include the price effect. Real variables are adjusted for changes in prices.

The relationship between the nominal interest rate and the real interest rate is described thus:

$$r = R - \pi$$

Here r, R, and π denote the real interest rate, the nominal interest rate, and the inflation rate, respectively. This equation implies that the real interest rate is calculated by subtracting the inflation rate from the nominal interest rate. Keep in mind that real interest rates may be negative if inflation rates are higher than nominal interest rates. Upcoming figures have examples of negative real interest rates.

Because nominal interest rates are expected to increase with higher inflation rates, some of the theories in upcoming chapters (for example, see Chapter 8) predict that higher nominal interest rates in a country are consistent with the depreciation of this country's currency. Other theories (see Chapters 5, 6, and 7) work with real interest rates and predict that higher real interest rates in a country are consistent with the appreciation of this country's currency. Therefore, the graphs in this section show both real and nominal interest rates.

The example currencies are still the Japanese yen and the Indonesian rupiah. Because data availability on interest rates varies among countries, the following graphs show the Treasury bill (T-bill) rate in Japan and the discount rate in Indonesia.

In Figure 4-11, you can observe the change in the yen–dollar exchange rate and the nominal T-bill rates. Again, the volatility of the exchange rate is higher than that of the T-bill rates. Especially during the mid- and late 1970s, higher nominal interest rates coincide with the depreciation of the yen. However, this relationship seems to break down starting in the mid-1990s when the interest rates remained very low, but the yen–dollar rate fluctuates substantially.

Figure 4-11:
Percent
change
in the
yen–dollar
exchange
rate and the
Treasury
bill rate
in Japan
(1970:q2 to
2011:q4).

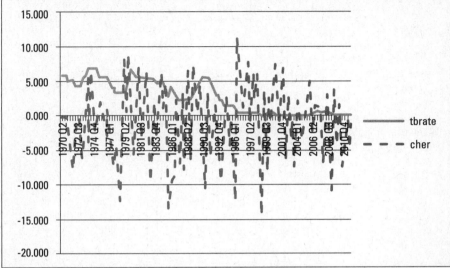

Notes: *International Financial Statistics of the IMF.* cher *and* tbrate *indicate the percent change in the exchange rate and the interest rate on the Japanese Treasury bill rate, respectively. Data are available at* www.imf.org.

Figure 4-12 indicates the relationship between changes in the yen–dollar exchange rate and the real T-bill rate in Japan. In 1974, lower (in fact, negative) real interest rates are consistent with the depreciation of the yen. Although exceptions do exist, during the 1980s and 1990s, higher real interest rates are associated with the appreciation of the yen.

In Indonesia, the graph data starts in 1990:Q1, indicating the data availability in the Indonesian discount rate. Figures 4-13 and 4-14 show the nominal and real discount rates in Indonesia, respectively. In both graphs, the Asian crisis appears as an outlier again. Figure 4-13 shows that higher nominal discount rates are associated with the depreciation of the rupiah. Figure 4-14 indicates that, in late 1998, in the aftermath of the Asian crisis, as the rupiah was depreciating, the real discount rate declined and reached almost –40 percent.

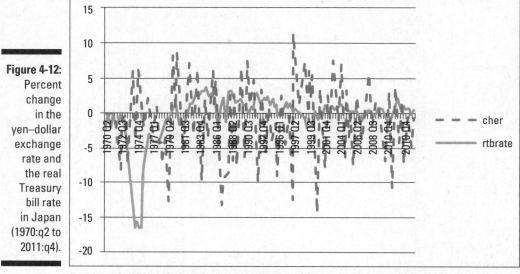

Figure 4-12: Percent change in the yen–dollar exchange rate and the real Treasury bill rate in Japan (1970:q2 to 2011:q4).

Notes: *International Financial Statistics of the IMF.* cher *and* rtbrate *indicate the percent change in the exchange rate and the real interest rate on the Japanese Treasury bill rate, respectively. The inflation rate used in the calculation of the real Treasury bill rate is determined based on the percent change in the consumer price index of Japan. Data are available at* www.imf.org.

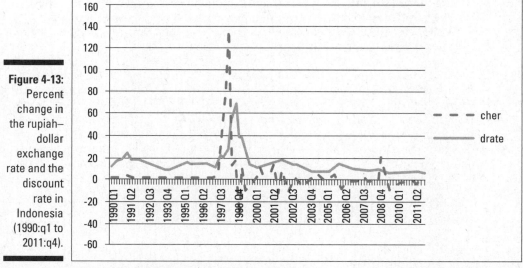

Figure 4-13: Percent change in the rupiah–dollar exchange rate and the discount rate in Indonesia (1990:q1 to 2011:q4).

Notes: *International Financial Statistics of the IMF.* cher *and* drate *indicate the percent change in the exchange rate and the discount rate in Indonesia, respectively. Data are available at* www.imf.org.

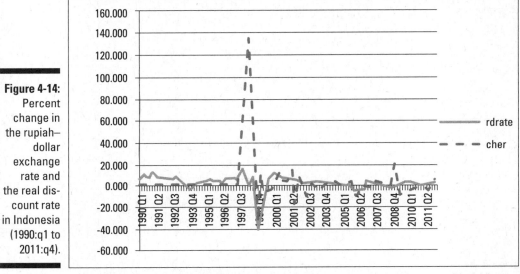

Figure 4-14:
Percent change in the rupiah–dollar exchange rate and the real discount rate in Indonesia (1990:q1 to 2011:q4).

Notes: International Financial Statistics of the IMF. cher *and* rdrate *indicate the percent change in the exchange rate and the real discount rate in Indonesia, respectively. Data are available at* www.imf.org.

Because the outliers associated with the Asian crisis make it difficult to observe the relationship between the interest rate and the exchange rate, Figures 4-15 and 4-16 show the nominal and real discount rates, as well as changes in the rupiah–dollar exchange rate during the pre- and post-crisis periods, respectively.

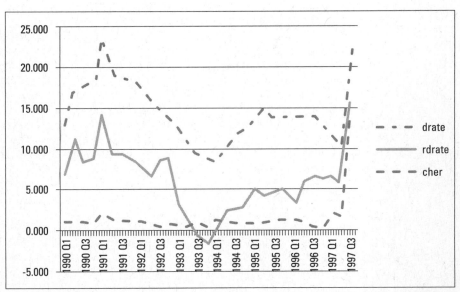

Figure 4-15:
Percent change in the rupiah–dollar exchange rate and the nominal and real discount rates in Indonesia during the pre-crisis period (1990:Q1 to 1997:Q4).

Notes: International Financial Statistics of the IMF. cher, drate, *and* rdrate *indicate the percent change in the exchange rate, the nominal discount rate, and the real discount rate in Indonesia, respectively. Data are available at* www.imf.org.

Figure 4-16:
Percent change in the rupiah–dollar exchange rate and the nominal and real discount rates in Indonesia during the post-crisis period (1999:Q3 to 2011:Q4).

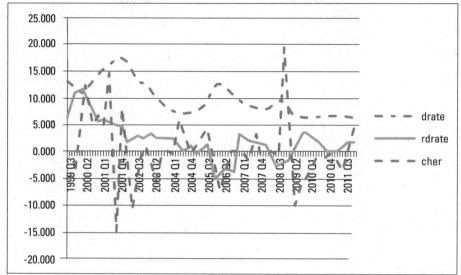

Notes: International Financial Statistics of the IMF. cher, drate, and rdrate indicate the percent change in the exchange rate, the nominal discount rate, and the real discount rate in Indonesia, respectively. Data are available at www.imf.org.

Figure 4-15 covers the pre–Asian crisis period. Still, you can clearly see the start of the Asian crisis, indicated by the large depreciation of the rupiah that starts in the second quarter of 1997. Except for the decline in the nominal and real discount rates in 1993 (in fact, the real discount rate was negative in late 1993), the nominal and real discount rates were positive. The fact that you see only small changes in the exchange rate during the pre–Asian crisis period is related to government interventions in the exchange rate, which the last section of this chapter touches on.

Figure 4-16 shows that the rupiah–dollar exchange rate fluctuated more during the post-crisis period. Nominal interest rates were declining, and real interest rates were fluctuating more in this period. Larger depreciations took place in early 2001 and late 2008, when the real interest rates were declining and negative, respectively. Largest appreciations happened in late 2001, early 2002, mid-2003, mid-2009, and early 2011, all accompanied by higher real interest rates. However, in early 2006, an appreciation of about 7 percent took place when the real discount rate was –5 percent. This scenario isn't consistent with the theories in Chapters 5, 6, and 7.

Uncovering Hidden Information in Graphs: Exchange Rate Regimes

Governments or central banks may intervene in the exchange rate. Chapter 13 discusses such interventions in detail. Still, you can start thinking about this subject now, at least to recognize such interventions on graphs.

Some of the graphs in this chapter show some odd observations. Sometimes an exchange rate is highly volatile, but then in some periods, it seems to be changing only slowly or it remains the same for a number of years. This section refers to some of the previous graphs in this chapter and examines them again to see whether they imply any information about government interventions in exchange rates. In addition to Japan and Indonesia, China is added to this section's discussions on exchange rate regimes.

Defining exchange rate regime

The exchange rate between two currencies may be determined in international foreign exchange markets or in a government office. If an exchange rate — say, the yen–dollar rate — is determined in international foreign exchange markets based on the demand for and supply of the yen, then the markets determine the exchange rate. This situation is similar to the case of any other good, such as oranges, whose price is determined in the market based on the demand for and supply of oranges. If the exchange rate is mainly determined in international foreign exchange markets, it's called a *floating* exchange rate regime.

Exchange rates involving developed countries' currencies, such as the U.S. dollar, the euro, the pound, the yen, and the Swiss franc, are determined in foreign exchange markets — mostly. When referring to these currencies, you may hear the term *dirty float* because of occasional central bank interventions in foreign exchange markets.

If floating or dirty floating currencies are at one extreme of the foreign exchange regime spectrum, *pegged* exchange rate regimes are toward the other end of the spectrum. In a pegged exchange rate regime, governments either don't allow their currency to be traded in international foreign exchange markets or impose restrictions on trade. In fact, governments determine the exchange rate unilaterally and announce it to the world. Although a variety of pegged exchange rate regimes exist, for the purpose of this chapter, you can think about pegged regimes in which the government determines the exchange rate. As Chapter 13 indicates, governments have reasons to keep the exchange rate involving the domestic currency at a certain level.

Don't think of pegging the exchange rate as an easy decision. As any other decision, the decision to peg implies tradeoffs. Governments that decide to peg their currency have to decide whether they want to allow foreign portfolio investment in and out of the country. If governments allow foreign portfolio investment, this approach attracts foreign investors into the country and opens new sources of financing for the country. But it can also spark a currency crisis, as foreign investors cash out their investment in the fear of depreciation, leaving the country in desperate need of foreign currency. Alternatively, a government may decide to peg the exchange rate without allowing foreign portfolio flows. This approach may prevent a currency crisis, but it also makes an additional financing opportunity unavailable.

Visualizing exchange rate regimes

The yen has been a floating currency for almost four decades. Figure 4-1 shows a straight line at the beginning of the data, where the yen–dollar exchange rate seems to remain the same. In fact, the data shows that the yen–dollar exchange rate remained as ¥360 per dollar between 1970:Q1 and 1971:Q2. It's highly unlikely for an exchange rate to remain the same if the currency is almost freely exchanged in international foreign exchange markets. When you look at the exchange rate data earlier than 1970, you see periods of unchanging exchange rates. It seems that Japan did what China is now doing. Before the mid-1970s, Japan pegged its exchange rate with the dollar (and other major currencies of that time) to enhance its export performance.

Assuming away transportation and other costs, a shipment of ¥100,000 costs about $278 to American consumers at the exchange rate of ¥360 per dollar. Suppose the yen appreciates to ¥300. In this case, the same shipment costs $333. With everything else constant, Japan can export more to the U.S. when the peg of the yen implies a lower value of the yen.

A similar situation exists in terms of the rupiah–dollar exchange rate in Figure 4-3. The data starts with Rp326 in 1970:Q1 and only slightly depreciates until 1971:Q4. At the beginning of the graph, you see a straight line, which reflects no change in the rupiah–dollar exchange rate between 1971:Q4 and 1978:Q3. During this period, the rupiah–dollar exchange rate remained as Rp415 per dollar. Then you observe a notable steady depreciation of the rupiah, approaching Rp1,644 per dollar in 1986:Q4. A steady depreciation took place until 1997:Q3, where the rate reached Rp2,791 per dollar.

You can make two observations about Figure 4-3. First, after the Asian crisis, Indonesian governments seem to have stopped pegging the rupiah because the exchange rate fluctuates more during the post-crisis period.

The second observation of Figure 4-3 isn't visible on the graph, but you can discover it by reading about Indonesia's approach to economic development. Until the mid-1980s, the slowly depreciating rupiah reflected a policy similar to the one Japan followed in earlier decades: improving export performance by keeping the rupiah–dollar rate relatively high. In the mid-1980s, the Indonesian government pegged its currency for a different reason. Many developing countries, including Indonesia, recognized the limited financing opportunities associated with exports. They wanted to attract portfolio investment into their countries, which involved foreign investors buying, for example, rupiah-denominated securities (bonds, stocks, and so on). Again, Chapter 13 provides a detailed discussion of these changes in policies and their consequences.

Finally, you can refer to Figure 2-4 in Chapter 2 to see the yuan–dollar exchange rate. As the figure indicates, China has pegged the yuan in accordance with its development policy. Building an industrial base through imports of equipment may have been important to China until the mid-1990s. When China achieved this industrial base, the country's export performance became more important to Chinese policymakers. Then the aim shifted to improving export performance by undervaluing the yuan.

The yuan–dollar exchange rate was as low as CNY1.71 per dollar in 1981, compared to its highest point of CNY8.64 in 1994. The Chinese government tried to keep the yuan overvalued at CNY1.71, to make imports cheaper. Suppose that China wanted to import $100,000 worth of industrial equipment from the U.S., assuming away all transportation and other costs. At the exchange rate of CNY1.71, this shipment costs China CNY171,000 ($100,000 × CNY1.71). However, if the exchange rate is, say CNY8.64, the same shipment costs CNY864,000 ($100,000 × CNY8.64). Undervaluation of the yuan at the level of CNY8.64 is helpful to improve China's export performance because the dollar price of a CNY100,000 shipment is $58,479 at CNY1.71 (CNY100,000 ÷ 1.71) and $11,574 at CNY8.64 (CNY100,000 ÷ 8.64).

Also in Figure 2-4, the slight revaluation since 2006 is indicative of the limited success of developed countries such as the U.S., which have complained about China's extensive use of foreign exchange control to improve its export performance.

Part II
Determining the Exchange Rate

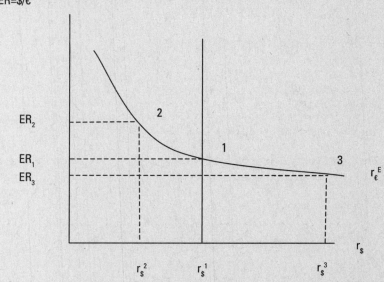

Figuring Out the Exchange Rate Based on the MBOP

In This Part . . .

✔ I supply you with the framework of demand and supply. This easy-to-use model can help you predict the change in the exchange rate.

✔ I break down the Monetary Approach to Balance of Payments (MBOP), another approach to predict the change in the exchange rate.

✔ I show how to use the MBOP to make both short- and long-run predictions regarding the change in the exchange rate.

Chapter 5

It's a Matter of Demand and Supply

• •

In This Chapter

▶ Learning the basics about the demand–supply model

▶ How exchange rates are determined based on the demand–supply model

▶ Which factors change exchange rates

• •

Y ou may know today's dollar–euro exchange rate, but it will be something else tomorrow or the next day. Why do exchange rates change? Reading this chapter is the first step in answering this question.

Economists don't use a crystal ball to predict changes, although some people may think so! But economists have a pretty nice set of tools at their disposal for prediction. This chapter shows that the demand–supply framework enables you to predict the next period's exchange rate. When you understand this framework, you'll be able to predict the direction of the change in the exchange rate — in other words, whether a currency will depreciate or appreciate against another currency.

This chapter introduces a basic microeconomic approach to exchange rate determination. First, the market for oranges illustrates the demand–supply model. Then you can easily change the assumption from the market for oranges to the market for dollars or euros.

Apples per Orange, Euros per Dollar: It's All the Same

Think about a barter economy that uses no money and in which people exchange oranges for apples. Basically, in the orange market, some people do have a demand for oranges. Other people produce oranges and supply them to the market. People who have apples are prepared to exchange them for oranges at a certain price. Producers of oranges are also prepared to exchange oranges for apples at a certain price.

This section develops a demand–supply model that determines the price and quantity of oranges in the market.

Price and quantity of oranges

In this barter economy, we exchange apples for oranges, and vice versa. Therefore, the amount of apples necessary to buy one orange is the price of an orange (in apples). Figure 5-1 shows the orange market.

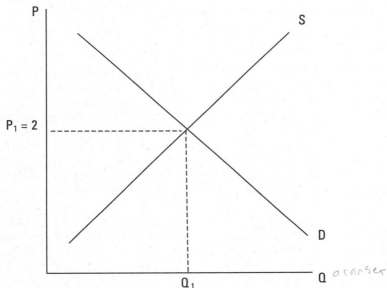

Figure 5-1:
Market for
oranges.

In Figure 5-1, the x-axis indicates the quantity of oranges. Moving to the right on the x-axis, the quantity of oranges in the market increases. Moving to the left on the x-axis, the quantity of oranges in the market decreases. The y-axis measures the price of oranges. As you move up on the y-axis, the price of an orange increases; it means that you give up more apples to buy one orange. As you move down on the y-axis, the price of orange decreases; it means that you give up fewer apples to buy one orange.

Demand and supply in the orange market

In microeconomic analysis, the market for a good, in this case, the market for oranges, is shown by the demand and supply curves. The demand curve represents the consumers' demand for oranges. The negative slope of the demand curve implies that as the price of oranges increases, the quantity demanded of oranges declines, and vice versa. The supply curve shows the behavior of orange producers. The positive slope of the supply curve indicates that as the price of oranges increases, orange producers supply a higher quantity of oranges, and vice versa.

Figure 5-1 illustrates the demand for and supply of oranges. The intersection of the demand and supply curves indicates the *market* price and quantity of oranges. Another term for the market price and quantity of oranges is the *equilibrium* price and quantity of oranges. In this example, the market price of oranges is 2 apples, which means that consumers give up 2 apples to buy an orange, and producers receive 2 apples when they sell an orange.

The equilibrium price and quantity of oranges doesn't stay the same, so you want to predict the changes in the price and quantity of oranges in the market. If any changes occur in the factors that affect either the supply or the demand curve, the equilibrium price and quantity of oranges changes.

In economics jargon, these factors are called *ceteris paribus* conditions (meaning "everything else constant"). The assumption is that the values of these factors are fixed along the demand and supply curves. When they change, the curve shifts in the appropriate direction.

Assume that the latest medical research indicates that oranges cure cancer. The demand for oranges then rises. As Figure 5-2 shows, an increase in the demand for oranges increases the price and quantity of oranges in the market.

Now assume that excessive cold destroyed most of the orange harvest in the U.S. In this case, the supply curve declines. Figure 5-3 shows that a decline in the supply curve increases the price of oranges and decreases the quantity of oranges in the market.

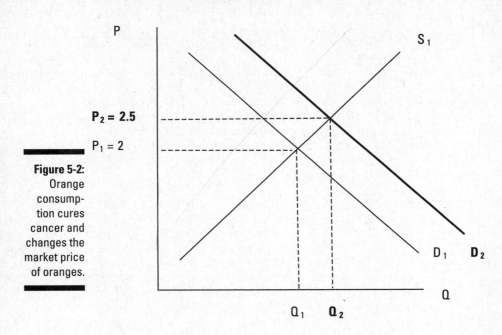

Figure 5-2:
Orange
consump-
tion cures
cancer and
changes the
market price
of oranges.

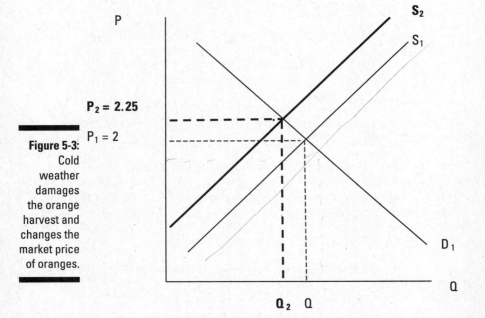

Figure 5-3:
Cold
weather
damages
the orange
harvest and
changes the
market price
of oranges.

These changes can occur simultaneously. As you see in Figure 5-4, if the demand curve increases thanks to the incredible health benefits of oranges and the supply curve decreases because of cold weather, the price of oranges will increase. In Figure 5-4, the price of oranges increases to 2.5 apples per orange. But the effect on quantity is undetermined. Figure 5-4 shows one of the three possible outcomes in terms of quantity and assumes no change in the quantity of oranges because the increase in the demand curve is the same as the decline in the supply curve.

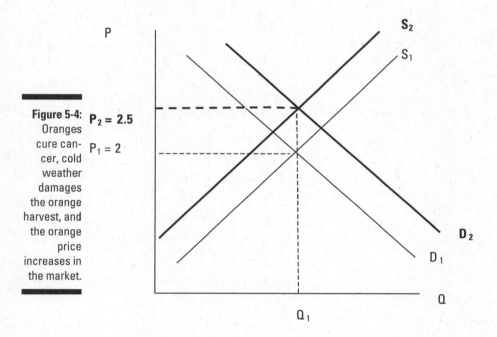

Figure 5-4: Oranges cure cancer, cold weather damages the orange harvest, and the orange price increases in the market.

Of course, you can change your assumptions regarding the nature of the shocks affecting the orange market. This time, assume harmful properties of oranges to health (oranges *cause* cancer) and, at the same time, the introduction of a disease-resistant variety of orange trees. In this case, the demand curve declines and the supply curve increases, lowering the market price of oranges with an undetermined output effect.

In the next section, this demand–supply approach is applied to exchange rate determination.

Determining Exchange Rates through Supply and Demand

Keep the following in mind when applying the demand–supply model to exchange rates:

- ✔ An exchange rate implies the relative price of a currency. For example, the euro–dollar exchange rate tells you how many euros to give up to buy one dollar. Therefore, this exchange rate implies the price of a dollar in euros. If the exchange rate is expressed as the dollar–euro rate, it tells you how many dollars to give up to buy one euro. Therefore, this exchange rate implies the price of a euro in dollars.

- ✔ Certain forces affect the demand for and supply of dollars, or of any other currency, in foreign exchange markets. Because exchange rates are the main subject here, this section identifies which factors affect the demand and supply of currencies.

- ✔ The demand–supply model of exchange rate determination implies that the equilibrium exchange rate changes when the factors that affect the demand and supply conditions change.

This section uses the market for dollars as an example, but you can use any market you want. (The last section of this chapter assumes the market for euros.) Whichever market you use, be careful when labeling the x- and y-axes of your model. When in doubt, remember the setup in the orange market. If you have the quantity of oranges on the x-axis, you have to put the price of oranges on the y-axis. Then the supply and demand curves inside the model refer to oranges.

Also, think about the meaning of the demand for and supply of dollars. Who are these people that want to buy or sell dollars or any other currency? I discuss them in Chapter 3. They are international banks, multinational companies, speculators, and so on. Whenever they want to buy dollars, they'll be along the demand curve. Whenever they want to sell dollars, they'll be along the supply curve.

Let's apply this discussion to the dollar market.

Price and quantity

If you want to graph the dollar market, the quantity on the x-axis must be the quantity of dollars in the market. Therefore, the price indicated by the y-axis must be the price of dollars in another currency (in this example, the euro). In other words, the exchange rate has to be defined as the euro–dollar exchange rate. Consequently, the demand and supply curves indicate the demand for and supply of dollars. Figure 5-5 shows the initial equilibrium exchange rate as €0.89 per dollar.

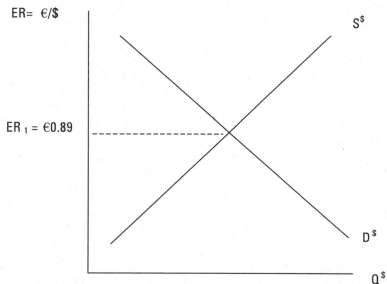

Figure 5-5:
Market for
U.S. dollars.

 Even though this chapter talks about the demand and supply of dollars, don't think about the "domestic" money demand and supply. In terms of exchange rate determination, the domestic money market becomes important in Chapters 6 and 7. For now, think about foreign exchange markets where market participants buy or sell currencies for the reasons explained in the next section.

Also note that Figure 5-5 and the following figures focus on the changes in the exchange rate and don't indicate the changes in the quantity of currency in question.

Factors that affect demand and supply

As in the case of the demand and supply curves in the orange market, *ceteris paribus* conditions are associated with the demand and supply of dollars. These conditions are related to the macroeconomic fundamentals of two countries represented in the exchange rate.

Because the example exchange rate is the euro–dollar rate, the following variables may change in the U.S. or the Euro-zone, which then have an effect on the euro–dollar exchange rate:

- ✔ Inflation rate
- ✔ Growth rate
- ✔ Interest rate
- ✔ Government restrictions

In the demand–supply model, these factors are divided into two areas based on how they affect exchange rates. Inflation rate and growth rate are considered trade-related factors. When you apply the changes in one of these factors to exchange rates, you think about the trade between the U.S. and the Euro-zone.

The interest rate, on the other hand, is a portfolio flow–related factor. It means that when one of the country's interest rate changes, you think about how this change affects the attractiveness of dollar- and euro-denominated securities to American and European investors.

Government restrictions can be related to both trade flows and portfolio flows, depending on the nature of these restrictions.

Note that the changes in inflation, growth, and interest rates, as well as government restrictions, don't have to be actual changes that you are observing right now. If market participants have expectations regarding these changes, they will act on them now, producing the same results as if these changes were actually happening.

Predicting Changes in the Euro–Dollar Exchange Rate

In this section, a change in each of the macroeconomic fundamentals (inflation rate, growth rate, interest rate, and government restrictions) is applied to the dollar market.

Inflation rate

The demand–supply model predicts that the higher-inflation country's currency will depreciate. Continuing with the U.S. and the Euro-zone example, if the U.S. has a higher inflation rate than that of the Euro-zone, the dollar is expected to depreciate against the euro. Following is the explanation for this prediction.

When you work with the demand–supply model of exchange rate determination, first think about whether the relevant factor is related to trade or portfolio flows. Second, think about the people represented by the demand and supply curve and what they would do, given the nature of the change in one of the macroeconomic fundamentals.

Remember that inflation rate is a trade-related variable. If the U.S. inflation rate is higher than that of the Euro-zone, at the given exchange rate, European goods become less expensive to American consumers. Therefore, Americans are inclined to sell their dollars, buy euros, and buy European goods. This increases the supply of dollars in the market.

However, at the given exchange rate, American goods become more expensive to European consumers because of higher inflation rates in the U.S. Therefore, European consumers are now less inclined to buy American goods. Their demand for dollars decreases. Figure 5-6 indicates these shifts.

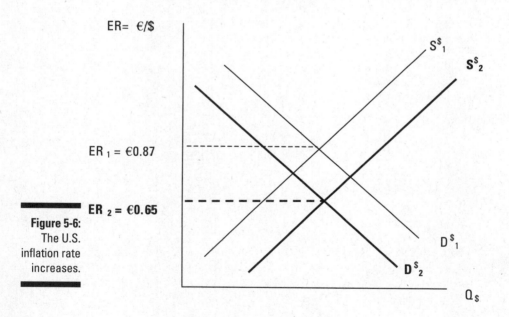

Figure 5-6:
The U.S.
inflation rate
increases.

Figure 5-6 shows that the dollar depreciates (and the euro appreciates) when the U.S. runs a higher inflation rate than the Euro-zone.

Growth rate

Economic growth refers to an increase in a country's output, or real gross domestic product (real GDP). The demand–supply model predicts that the higher growth rate country's currency will depreciate. For example, if the Euro-zone's real GDP growth rate is higher than that of the U.S., this model predicts that the euro will depreciate.

All other predictions of the demand–supply model are consistent with the monetary approach to exchange rates introduced in Chapters 6 and 7. Growth rate of real GDP is the only factor about which different theories provide different predictions. In upcoming chapters, the currency of the country with the higher growth rate will appreciate.

For simplicity, assume that the U.S. growth rate shows no change and the Euro-zone's growth rate increases. Again, remember that growth rate is a trade-related variable. If the Euro-zone's growth rate is higher, then at the given exchange rate, Euro-zone's consumers and businesses are expected to buy more consumption and investment goods from the U.S. Therefore, Europeans are inclined to sell their euros, buy dollars, and buy American goods. As Figure 5-7 shows, this increases the demand for dollars and the price of dollars, which leads to the appreciation of the dollar (or the depreciation of the euro).

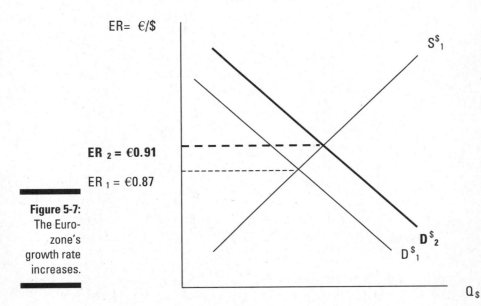

Figure 5-7:
The Euro-zone's growth rate increases.

Interest rate

REMEMBER

Remember, interest rate is a portfolio flow–related factor. Think of yourself as an investor who is deciding between a dollar- and a euro-denominated investment opportunity (with the same risk). Because the main subject is portfolio investment, the interest rate considered here is the real interest rate.

The real interest rate is defined as the difference between the nominal interest rate and the inflation rate (see Chapter 4).

This model predicts that the currency of the country with the higher real interest rate will appreciate. As an investor, and at the given exchange rate, you decide to invest in a security that gives you a higher real return. Suppose that the Euro-zone's real interest rates are higher. Figure 5-8 shows the implications of this change on the euro–dollar exchange rate.

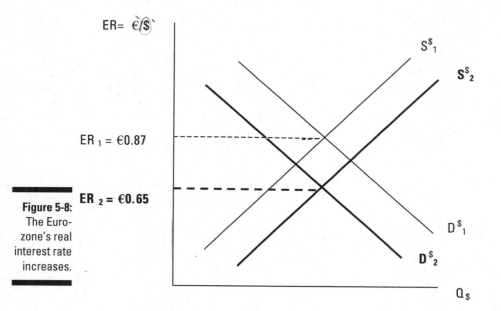

Figure 5-8: The Euro-zone's real interest rate increases.

When you look at the demand and supply curve in Figure 5-8, identify the investors along these curves. As the real interest rate on Euro-denominated securities increases, investors' demand for dollar-denominated securities declines. Therefore, the demand for the dollar declines. In terms of the supply of dollars, investors are inclined to sell their dollars in exchange for euros to buy euro-denominated securities. As Figure 5-8 shows, the supply curve for dollars increases. Both an increase in the supply curve and a decrease in the demand curve lead to the appreciation of the euro (or the depreciation of the dollar).

Government interventions

Assuming that trade and portfolio flows aren't restricted, domestic consumers and investors have a choice of which country's goods to consume and which country's currency to invest in. However, governments may be concerned about this freedom and may not like domestic consumers' and investors' demand for foreign goods or portfolios.

The previous exercises in this chapter explain why governments may feel this way. Favoring foreign goods and portfolios implies the exchange of the domestic currency for foreign currency, which depreciates the domestic currency. Therefore, sometimes governments implement restrictions on trade or portfolio flows to prevent the domestic currency from further depreciation. These restrictions are expected to appreciate the restriction-imposing country's currency.

Suppose that the U.S. starts imposing tariffs on some of the European Union's (EU) imports. To keep the exercise simple, assume that the EU doesn't retaliate. Figure 5-9 shows that trade restrictions imposed by the U.S. lead to a decline in the supply of dollars. The reason is that trade restrictions are prompting U.S. consumers to exchange fewer dollars for euros. The result is the appreciation of the dollar (or the depreciation of the euro).

Practicing government interventions

Many developing countries' governments resorted to government interventions during the 1960s through the mid-1980s. They adopted the import-substitution strategy to economic development, which implied the domestic production of some of the previously imported goods to strengthen domestic industry. In addition to trade restrictions, they imposed strong restrictions on portfolio flows. (See Chapter 13 for more information.)

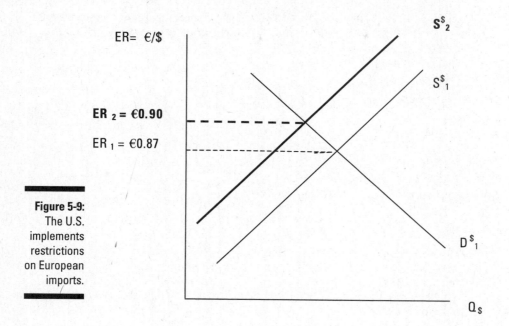

Figure 5-9:
The U.S.
implements
restrictions
on European
imports.

Figure 5-9 also illustrates government restrictions on capital flows. If the U.S. imposes restrictions on portfolio outflows, U.S. investors exchange fewer dollars for euros to put in a euro-denominated deposit. Therefore, the supply of dollars declines, and the dollar appreciates (and the euro depreciates).

Keeping It Straight: Using a Different Exchange Rate

You can repeat the entire analysis in the previous section using a different exchange rate. For example, we can invert the euro–dollar exchange rate, which implies the price of the dollar in euros. Now you have the dollar–euro exchange rate, which implies the price of a euro in dollars.

Since the price of a euro is given, on the x-axis of the model, you need to consider the quantity of euros. This time, the demand and supply curves indicate the demand for and supply of euros, which makes it the market for euros.

Figure 5-10 indicates this change. Note that the equilibrium exchange rate is the inverse of the euro–dollar rate of €0.87, or approximately $1.15 (1 ÷ 0.87).

ER= $/€

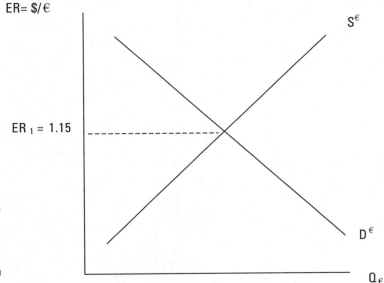

ER$_1$ = 1.15

S^ϵ

D^ϵ

Q_ϵ

Figure 5-10:
Market for
euros.

You can apply the same shocks that we applied to the dollar market, this time to the euro market. You'll be shifting different curves, but you should come to the same predictions in terms of the change in the exchange rate.

Take the increase in the U.S. inflation rate. Your argument remains the same. At the given exchange rate, American consumers will buy more goods from the Euro-zone countries, and Euro-zone consumers buy fewer goods from the U.S. Therefore, the demand for the euro increases and the supply declines, which increases the dollar–euro exchange rate. This situation shows a depreciation of the dollar (or an appreciation of the euro).

If the Euro-zone's real GDP growth rate is higher than that of the U.S., at the given exchange rate, European consumers buy more American goods. This scenario also increases the supply of euros and appreciates the dollar (or depreciates the euro).

If the real interest rate in the Euro-zone is rising, investors increase their demand for euro-denominated securities and, therefore, the euro, which then increases the demand curve for euros. With higher real interest rates on euro-denominated securities, investors sell fewer euro-denominated assets and, therefore, sell fewer euros, which decreases the supply curve of euros. These shifts lead to the depreciation of the dollar (or the appreciation of the euro).

In terms of government interventions, if the U.S. government introduces restrictions on the Euro-zone's goods or financial instruments, American consumers or investors buy less of them. This scenario then decreases the demand for euros, which leads to the appreciation of the dollar (or the depreciation of the euro).

Chapter 6

Setting Up the Monetary Approach to Balance of Payments

· ·

In This Chapter

▶ Examining the foreign exchange market from an international investor's point of view

▶ Relating the domestic money markets of two countries to the foreign exchange market

▶ Explaining how investors interpret the changes in monetary policy

▶ Explaining how investors' interpretation of monetary policy affects exchange rates

· ·

Chapter 5 covers the demand-supply approach to exchange rate determination. This chapter introduces an alternative theory of exchange rate determination. While the demand-supply model assumes that both international trade- and international investment-related factors change exchange rates, the Monetary Approach to Balance of Payment (MBOP) takes only international investment into account. In other words, the MBOP views the subject of exchange rate determination from the point of view of international investors.

In this chapter, you'll imagine investors trying to decide between two securities denominated in two different currencies. The answer to the question "How will they decide?" lies in the center of the MBOP's method of exchange rate determination. As investors favor one country's security over the other country's security, their decision affects the exchange of currencies and therefore leads to appreciation or depreciation of currencies.

You may be asking what the name *Monetary Approach to Balance of Payment* suggests. Here I break it down into two parts:

✔ **Monetary:** The term *Monetary* in the name of this particular approach to exchange rate determination reveals interesting insights regarding the decision-making process of international investors. It means that investors keep an eye on the interest rates in the money markets of two countries. Additionally, because changes in monetary policies of these countries change their interest rates, investors pay attention to changes in monetary policies of these countries as well.

✔ **Balance of Payments:** The *Balance of Payments* (BOP) indicates an account that keeps track of a country's transactions with other countries. The BOP captures trade in goods and services as well as the flow of funds (investment, loans, and so on) between the home country and the rest of the world. Historically, the Monetary Approach to Balance of Payments indicated the theory that explains the effects of the changes in a country's money market on its BOP or its transactions with the rest of the world. Then, the same name was used for the effects of the changes in the money market on exchange rates.

Combining these two points, you may view the name of the theory presented in this chapter (the Monetary Approach to Balance of Payments) as the Monetary Approach to Exchange Rate Determination.

Discovering the MBOP's Approach to Exchange Rates

This section provides a discussion regarding the assumptions and the general setup of the MBOP. It also compares the MBOP's approach to the demand–supply model (for more on the demand–supply model, see Chapter 5). In Economics, alternative theories explain the determination of a relevant variable. Looking at the approach of competing theories to a variable such as the exchange rate, you can see how and why each theory provides a certain prediction. Comparing the predictions of different theories and identifying the common factors in the determination of a variable, such as the exchange rate, is important for the empirical verification of these theories.

Viewing the basic assumptions

As in the case of the demand-supply model (see Chapter 5), the MBOP has its own assumptions:

✔ **No government intervention:** The MBOP assumes flexible exchange rates. In other words, the currencies in question are traded in foreign exchange markets with minimal or no government intervention.

The MBOP also provides insights into the credibility of currency pegs and the possibility of a currency crisis. Chapter 13 makes references to the MBOP in this context.

✔ **International investor behavior:** The most important characteristic of the MBOP is its exclusive focus on the behavior of international investors. The MBOP considers an international investor who is trying to decide between securities denominated in two different currencies. Therefore, it is not surprising that the MBOP is also called the Asset Approach to Exchange Rate Determination.

✔ **Changes in real returns:** The term *monetary* in the MBOP emphasizes the relevance of the changes in monetary policy and the resulting changes in real returns on securities denominated in different currencies. After investors observe these changes in real returns, they express their preference for a security, which leads to buying or selling certain currencies and, therefore, changes in the exchange rate.

Setting the MBOP apart

When comparing the assumptions of the MBOP to those of the demand–supply model (see Chapter 5), you notice that the MBOP focuses exclusively on investors' decisions between two securities. The MBOP considers investment-related factors in exchange rate determination compared to the demand-supply model, which considers both investment- and trade-related factors. Since the interest rate is an international investment-related factor, both theories use this factor in explaining the changes in exchange rates.

In fact, investors in both theories compare the real interest rates in two countries. The difference between these theories regarding real interest rates lies whether the source of the change in the real interest rate is explicitly discussed. The demand–supply model doesn't explicitly consider the source of the change in interest rates. It just assumes that the real interest rate in a country changes. However, as the beginning of this chapter notes, the MBOP relates the changes in the money markets of countries to the changes in exchange rates. Because money markets determine the real interest rates of countries in the MBOP, this theory explicitly shows how the changes in the market markets of both countries affect these countries' real interest rates and subsequently the exchange rate.

Therefore, in later sections of this chapter, you see that the MBOP consists of the combination of two models: the money market and the foreign exchange market. Basically, the changes in the money market lead to changes in real returns on securities denominated in different currencies. Then investors' subsequent reaction to the changes in real returns leads to changes in the relevant exchange rate. Therefore, this chapter develops the MBOP in three stages: the money market, the foreign exchange market, and the combination of the money and foreign exchange markets or the combined MBOP.

Explaining the Money Market

You may think of *money market* as a familiar term. A word of caution: sometimes the same term has a different content in Finance than in Economics. Money market is one of these terms. In Finance, the term money market is used to refer to securities whose maturity is one year or less (such as Treasury bills, commercial paper, and so on). In Economics, money market or orange market has essentially the same meaning. A market has a demand and a supply curve that shows the demand for and supply of the good in question.

As discussed in Chapter 5, when the market in question is the orange market, this market is illustrated by putting the quantity of oranges on the x-axis and the price of oranges on the y-axis. In this case, the curves of the model indicate the demand for and the supply of oranges. You consider the money market in the same way. The quantity of money goes to the x-axis and the price of money, which is the real interest rate, goes to the y-axis. The *money demand* represents people's liquidity preference. The *money supply* indicates the bills and coins issued by the country's central bank and various kinds of deposits held by public at depository institutions such as banks, credit unions, and so on. When the money demand and money supply are determined, an equilibrium real interest rate is reached in the money market.

This section also discusses the major sources of changes in the real interest rate. Identifying these changes in the real interest rate is important because later in this chapter you connect these changes in the money market to the changes in the exchange rate.

Demand for money

The demand curve for money is called the liquidity preference, for a good reason. This curve drawn in the real interest rate/real quantity of money space shows how much money you want to keep in your pocket or in a non-interest-earning account, such as your debit account. Of course, a good reason to keep money with you (or on your debit account) is the relevance of money as the *medium of exchange*. Every time you want to have pizza, you don't want to liquidate some of your assets, for example government bonds!

A standard money demand example

Figure 6-1 indicates the x-axis as the real quantity of money, where the nominal quantity of money (M) is divided by the average price level (P). For example, if you have $100 and tall lattes of $2 each are the only good you consume, your real money, or the purchasing power of your nominal money, equals 50 lattes ($100 ÷ $2).

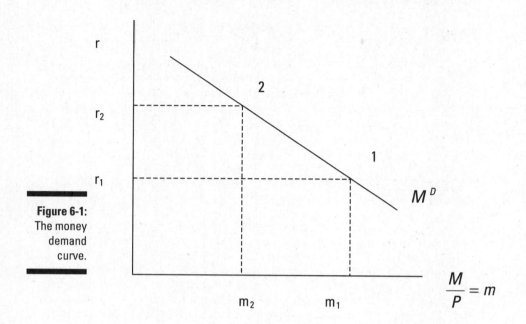

In Figure 6-1, the y-axis refers to the real interest rate (the nominal interest rate minus the inflation rate). You see that the money demand curve is a downward-sloping curve in the real interest rate-real money space. When the real interest rate increases (moving from Point 1 to Point 2 in Figure 6-1), the quantity of real money demanded declines. In other words, people carry less money to take advantage of higher real interest rates. Similarly, when the real interest rate is lower (moving from Point 2 to Point 1 in Figure 6-1), the quantity of real money demanded is higher because people are losing a smaller amount of interest income by keeping more money.

Drawing the money demand curve in the real interest rate-real quantity of money space is one of the alternative explanations of the money demand, which is commonly used in the MBOP. The money demand can also be derived in the nominal interest rate-nominal quantity of money space.

An example for the shift in the money demand

What would shift the money demand curve? To shift the money demand curve, or any curve in economics, you need to assume a change in the value of a *ceteris paribus* condition associated with this curve. *Ceteris paribus* translates to "all other things being equal or held constant." In other words, the assumption is that the values of certain variables are assumed to be constant along the money demand curve, no matter where you are on the curve, Point 1 or Point 2 on Figure 6-1.

In the case of the money demand curve, one *ceteris paribus* condition is worth mentioning: real income, which can be measured as real GDP or real income or output of a country (Y).

Figure 6-2 provides an example for a shift in the money demand curve. The shock associated with this shift is an increase in output. As output or real income increases, at the given real interest rate, the quantity of real money demanded increases as well. Because the value of the X variable increases at the given level of the Y variable, you refer to this shift as an increase in the money demand curve. Similarly, if a decline in the output of a country takes place, you decrease the money demand curve, which leads to a lower real quantity of money demanded at the given real interest rate.

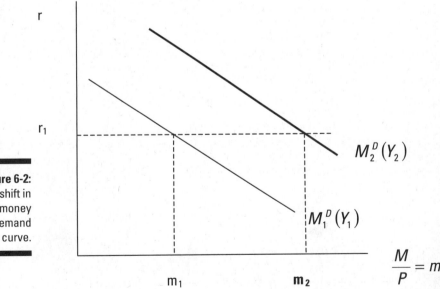

Figure 6-2:
A shift in the money demand curve.

Supply of money

In the money market of the MBOP, the central bank controls the nominal money supply (M^S). Given the average price level, the nominal money supply (M^S) divided by the average price level (P) defines the real money supply (m^S). Figure 6-3 shows the real money supply as a perfectly inelastic curve. Additionally, the central bank controls the nominal money supply. Therefore, the nominal money supply is one of the *ceteris paribus* conditions along the real money supply curve.

A *perfectly inelastic* (vertical) curve in Figure 6-3 indicates that the curve has an x-intercept. In other words, the curve is associated with a given level of the x- variable, in this case, the real quantity of money. A perfectly inelastic curve such as the real money supply curve in Figure 6-3 also indicates that the real quantity of money (m_1) does not vary with the real interest rate (r). The real interest rate can be higher or lower; the x-intercept or m_1 remains the same. In contrast, a *perfectly elastic* (horizontal) curve has a y-intercept. This time, there is a level of the real interest rate that doesn't respond to changes in the quantity of real money (m) on the x-axis.

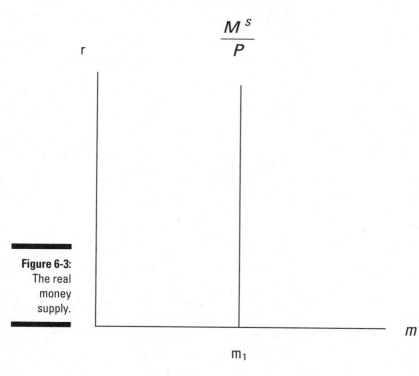

Figure 6-3:
The real
money
supply.

The perfectly inelastic (vertical) real money supply curve in Figure 6-3 may seem surprising. This particular real money supply curve implies that the central bank focuses on the quantity of money as the monetary policy tool. In recent decades, most central banks use a key interest rate (such as the Fed's Federal Funds Rate) instead of the quantity of money when conducting monetary policy. However, for our purpose it does not matter whether the real money supply curve is perfectly inelastic (the central bank's policy tool is the quantity of money) or perfectly elastic at the given interest rate (the central bank's policy tool is a key interest rate).

Another *ceteris paribus* condition along the real money supply curve is the average price level in a country. Changes in the nominal money supply lead to changes in the price level. The question is, when? To help answer that question, think about the predictions of two major schools of thought in economics (they coincide with the long-run and short-run analysis in economics):

- ✔ **The classical–neoclassical school:** This school relies on the Quantity Theory of Money. This theory predicts that the changes in the price level equal the changes in the nominal money supply. In this case, a positive relationship exists between the changes in the nominal money supply and the price level. Therefore, if a central bank increases the nominal money supply by 5 percent, it creates 5 percent inflation.

  The classical-neoclassical school relies on the long-run view. In economics, the long-run represents the run, during which all nominal variables adjust. Figure 6-4 illustrates the situation in which the nominal money supply has increased from M_1 to M_2. According to the long-run view, the average price level increases at the same rate from P_1 to P_2, leaving the real money supply unchanged (m_1).

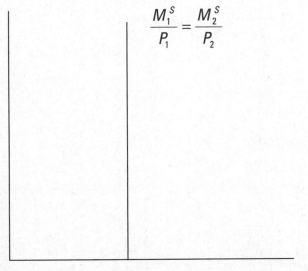

Figure 6-4:
An example of the increase in the nominal money supply (classical–neoclassical school; long-run view).

✔ **The Keynesian school:** You may have heard about Keynes's famous phrase: "In the long run, we are all dead." Clearly, Keynes did not care much about the long-run analysis that assumes that all nominal variables adjust. Instead, he introduced the notion of the short run, during which a nominal variable remains *sticky*. A sticky nominal variable is a variable that does not change, per definition, during the short-run. The MBOP assumes that prices of goods and services in an economy are sticky.

Various explanations seek to tell why prices are sticky. These explanations can be summarized as *menu cost*. Basically, menu costs imply the assumption that frequently changing prices of goods and services are annoying to consumers. Therefore, firms may not change the prices of their products every time their production costs change. They may wait until the current price is no longer sustainable at their new cost structure. However, note that when firms adjust their prices (upward or downward), the average price level remains sticky at a new level.

Assuming sticky prices, if a central bank increases the nominal money supply, the real money supply increases. Figure 6-5 shows this result. The initial nominal money supply, M_1, increases to M_2. Because prices are sticky in the short run, the initial price level, P_1, remains the same after the increase in the nominal money supply. Because you are dividing a larger number (M_2) by the same price level (P_1), there is an increase in the real money supply curve.

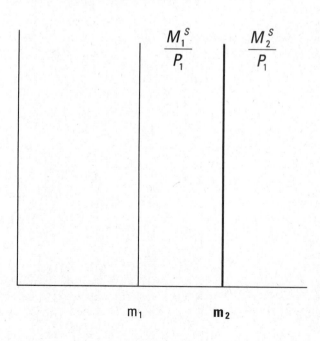

Figure 6-5: An example of the increase in the nominal money supply (Keynesian school; short-run view).

Similarly, if there is a decline in the nominal money supply, assuming sticky prices, this time the real money supply declines, decreasing the real money supply curve.

In the next section, both the short- and long-run analyses are applied when there is a change in the nominal money supply.

Money market equilibrium

When the money demand and supply curves are put together, you can view the money market. Figure 6-6 indicates the money market equilibrium, with the equilibrium real interest rate, r_1, and the equilibrium quantity of real money, m_1.

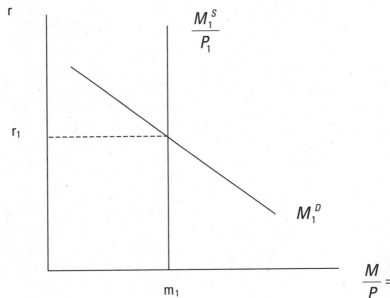

Figure 6-6:
The money market.

Remember the variables that can shift the money demand and supply curves. In the next example, a change in the country's output and nominal money supply is applied to the money market. You can predict how the real interest rate and the real quantity of money in the money market change.

We start with an increase in output. Figure 6-7 shows that an increase in output increases the money demand curve, which, in turn, increases the real interest rate without changing the quantity of real money.

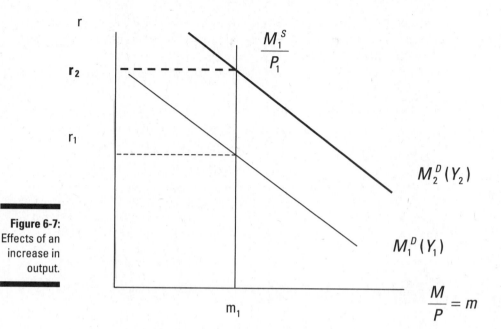

Figure 6-7:
Effects of an
increase in
output.

Now assume an increase in the nominal money supply, shown in Figure 6-8. Because there is a change in a nominal variable this time, the short- and long-run predictions differ.

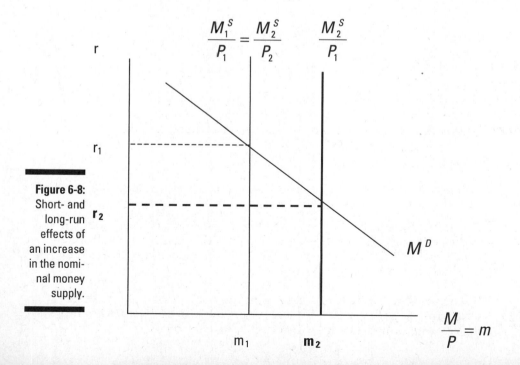

Figure 6-8:
Short- and
long-run
effects of
an increase
in the nomi-
nal money
supply.

In the short run, you assume sticky prices. At the same prices, if the initial nominal money supply of M_1 increases to M_2, the real money supply also increases. As a result, the real money supply curve increases (shifts to the right). Therefore, in the short run, you predict a lower real interest rate (r_2) and a higher quantity of real money (m_2).

To express your long-run predictions, make use of the Quantity Theory of Money. This theory states that, in the long run, the price level increases at the same rate at which the nominal money supply increased. Therefore, you expect the percent increase from P_1 to P_2 to match the increase in the nominal money supply from M_1 to M_2. In this case, the real money supply curve returns to its original position, indicating r_1 as the equilibrium real interest rate and m_1 as the equilibrium real quantity of money. The real quantity of money is the same as before m_1 because the price level and the nominal money supply have increased by the same proportion ($M_1/P_1 = M_2/P_2$).

Taking On the Foreign Exchange Market

Now the focus is on the foreign exchange market. The most important insight that you want to get from the foreign exchange market is the determination of the exchange rate. As discussed previously in this chapter, the approach to and the assumptions associated with exchange rate determination are the key to illustrating the foreign exchange market. Remember that the exchange rate determination based on the MBOP adopts an asset approach, which is based on the behavior of international investors contemplating investing in securities of different denominations.

Think of it this way: You are an American investor trying to choose between a dollar- and euro-denominated security of comparable risk and maturity. Suppose you observe that the annual real rate of return on comparable dollar- and euro-denominated securities is 5 percent and 6 percent, respectively. Are you thinking about picking the euro-denominated security? Hopefully not! You don't want to compare the real returns on securities that are denominated in different currencies; it's like comparing apples and oranges.

Therefore, this section first expresses the real returns on securities denominated in different currencies in a comparable format. After this discussion, grasping the meaning of the curves in the foreign exchange market is easier.

Asset approach to exchange rate determination

This section provides how-to information on comparing the real returns on dollar-denominated securities with the real returns on euro-denominated securities. The concept that makes this comparison possible is the expected change in the exchange rate.

For example, when you invest in a euro-denominated security, you hope to make money in two ways. First, you expect to earn a return on this security you are planning to hold. Suppose that r_ϵ is the real return on euro-denominated securities.

Second, you, the American investor, convert your dollars into euros, buy euro-denominated securities, earn returns in euros, and convert your euro earnings into dollars. Therefore, you care about the future exchange rate that you observe when you convert your earnings in euros into dollars. However, you are investing in euro-denominated securities now, and you don't know for sure what the dollar–euro exchange rate is going to be in the future — say, a year from now. Still, you need to have an expected dollar–euro exchange rate in mind.

Clearly, you can observe the current exchange rate. We can call the current time t. Suppose you have an expectation of what the dollar–euro exchange rate is going to be at a future date. You use the current and expected exchange rate to calculate the expected percent change in the exchange rate using the following formula:

$$\%\Delta ER_t^E = \left[\frac{\left(\overline{\frac{\$}{\euro}}\right)^E - \left(\frac{\$}{\euro}\right)_t}{\left(\frac{\$}{\euro}\right)_t} \right]$$

where:

ER = Exchange rate

$\left(\overline{\frac{\$}{\euro}}\right)^E$: expected Dollar-Euro exchange rate

$\left(\frac{\$}{\euro}\right)_t$: Dollar-Euro exchange rate at time t or current spot exchange rate

Note the line over the expected exchange rate, which indicates that you are holding its value constant. Later in this chapter, but especially in the next chapter (Chapter 7), you change this assumption.

Now you, the investor, can make the appropriate comparison between the real return on a risk- and maturity-comparable dollar- and euro-denominated security. You are indifferent between these securities if the following parity condition holds:

$$r_\$ = r_€ + \left[\frac{\left(\overline{\frac{\$}{€}}\right)^E - \left(\frac{\$}{€}\right)}{\left(\frac{\$}{€}\right)} \right]$$

Note that the previous formula drops the time subscript for simplicity.

where:

$r_\$$ = Real return on the dollar-denominated security (in dollars)

$r_€$ = Real return on the euro-denominated security (in euros)

The right side of the equation expresses the expected real returns on the euro-denominated security in dollars. By adding the expected change in the exchange rate to the real return on the euro-denominated security, you account for two possible sources of your return from a euro-denominated security: the interest rate on the euro-denominated security (r_e) and whether you will enjoy additional returns when you convert your earnings in euros into dollars. Now you can compare your earnings on a dollar-denominated security to your earnings on the euro-denominated security. In other words, you can compare the number of dollars you will have in the future from holding the dollar-denominated security to the number of dollars you will have in the future from holding the euro-denominated security.

Another way of expressing the parity condition is that the difference between the real return on a dollar-denominated security and that of a euro-denominated security in dollars must be zero:

$$r_\$ - r_€ - \left[\frac{\left(\overline{\frac{\$}{€}}\right)^E - \left(\frac{\$}{€}\right)}{\left(\frac{\$}{€}\right)} \right] = 0$$

Figure 6-9 shows four numerical examples to which you can apply the parity condition and decide which security gives you a higher real return. The second and third columns indicate the real return on the dollar- and euro-denominated securities, respectively. The fourth column shows the expected change in the exchange rate. The last column indicates the parity condition as the difference among these three variables, and the difference is zero. In other words, after adjusting for the expected changes in the exchange rate, a security denominated in euros offers the same (expected) real rate of return as the dollar-denominated security.

Example	$r_\$$ (%)	$r_€$ (%)	$\dfrac{\left(\dfrac{\$}{€}\right)^E - \left(\dfrac{\$}{€}\right)}{\left(\dfrac{\$}{€}\right)}$	$r_\$ - r_€ - \left[\dfrac{\left(\dfrac{\$}{€}\right)^E - \left(\dfrac{\$}{€}\right)}{\left(\dfrac{\$}{€}\right)}\right] = 0$
#1	10	6	4 %	$10 - 6 - 4 = 0$ %
#2	10	6	0 %	$10 - 6 - 0 = 4$ %
#3	10	12	-4 %	$10 - 12 + 4 = 2$ %
#4	10	6	8 %	$10 - 6 - 8 = -4$ %

Figure 6-9: Interest parity example.

For simplicity, the real returns on the dollar-denominated security don't change in Figure 6-9. However, you can see changes in the real returns on the euro-denominated security and the expected change in the exchange rate.

Take a look at Figure 6-9 and consider each example:

✔ **Example #1:** The real return on the dollar- and euro-denominated security is 10 percent and 6 percent, respectively. Additionally, the expected change in the exchange rate indicates 4 percent depreciation in the dollar. In other words, if you invest in the euro-denominated security, in addition to earning 6 percent interest on the security, you earn 4 percent by holding a security whose currency is expected to appreciate. In this case, you earn 10 percent real return in either security. Therefore, you are indifferent between the dollar- and euro-denominated securities.

✔ **Example #2:** The second example has the same real returns on the dollar- and euro-denominated securities, which are 10 percent and 6 percent, respectively. However, in this case, the expected exchange rate is the same as the current exchange rate, so the expected change in the exchange rate is zero. Now the real return on the dollar-denominated security exceeds that on the euro-denominated security by 4 percent. In this case, you want to invest in the dollar-denominated security.

✔ **Example #3:** This example indicates the real returns on the dollar- and euro-denominated securities as 10 percent and 12 percent, respectively. However, the expected change in the exchange rate is –4 percent, which indicates a 4 percent appreciation in the dollar. This reduces your real return on the euro-denominated security in dollars to 8 percent, which is lower than the real return on the dollar-denominated security. In this case, you want to invest in the dollar-denominated security.

✔ **Example #4:** The last example indicates that the real return on the dollar- and euro-denominated securities is 10 percent and 6 percent, respectively. The expected change in the exchange rate is 8 percent, which indicates a depreciation of the dollar by 8 percent. This means that your expected real return on the euro-denominated security is 4 percent greater than that on the dollar-denominated security. In this case, you want to invest in the euro-denominated security.

The next section derives the parity curve based on the discussion of the parity condition in this section, which is one of the curves in the foreign exchange market based on the MBOP.

The expected real returns curve

The aim is to develop the foreign exchange market. It means that there should be some curves describing the foreign exchange market. The discussion about the interest parity in the previous section provides a verbal description of one of the curves in the foreign exchange market. In this section, I show the transformation of explanations regarding the interest parity into a curve, called the expected real returns curve or the *parity curve*.

The foreign exchange market has the dollar–euro exchange rate on the y-axis and the real returns in dollars on the x-axis. Figure 6-10 illustrates the downward-sloping parity curve, which implies the expected real return on the euro-denominated security.

In all economic models, it's important to be mindful of which market is considered. This consideration is also important in the MBOP. Additionally, because this model deals with an exchange rate and two countries' real interest rates, you need to use the exchange rate and the real interest rates in a consistent manner. For example, in Figure 6-10, the foreign exchange market is in dollars. How do you know? Because the exchange rate on the y-axis implies the amount of dollars per euro, which is clearly in dollars. Also, if the exchange rate is in dollars, the x-axis has to indicate the real return in dollars, which can be the real return on the dollar-denominated security or the real return on the euro-denominated security in dollars. (There is another exercise at the end of this chapter, which helps you to keep the exchange rate and the real interest rates straight.)

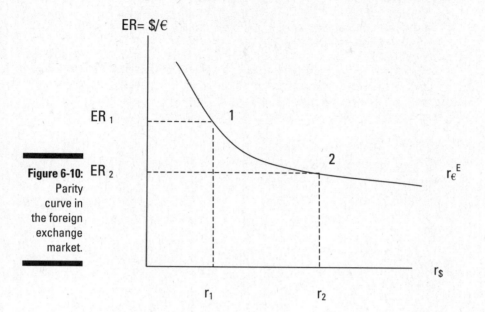

Figure 6-10: Parity curve in the foreign exchange market.

Now you know which variables are on the x- and y-axes of the model in Figure 6-10: the dollar-euro exchange rate and the real returns in dollars are on the y- and x-axis, respectively. But, remember from the discussion of the interest parity, you also need the information about the real returns on the euro-denominated security as well as its conversion into dollars. Therefore, the parity curve in Figure 6-10 indicates the right side of the parity equation:

$$r_\euro^E = r_\euro + \left[\frac{\left(\frac{\overline{\$}}{\euro}\right)^E - \left(\frac{\$}{\euro}\right)}{\left(\frac{\$}{\euro}\right)} \right]$$

Note that there is now an expectation superscript associated with the real returns on the euro-denominated security in dollars to emphasize the following idea. If you, an American investor, invest in dollar-denominated securities, you don't need to deal with the expected exchange rate. However, if you want to consider a euro-denominated security, its return has to be comparable to that of the dollar-denominated security. In this case, you need to consider the expected exchange rate, because the current exchange rate is likely to change while you are holding the euro-denominated security. This is why it is appropriate to explain this parity curve as the *expected* real returns on euro-denominated security in dollars.

Based on the parity equation, the expected real return on the euro-denominated security in dollars is equal to the addition of the real return on the euro-denominated security and the expected change in the exchange rate. At this point, it's important to recognize that the real return on the euro-denominated security is determined in the Euro-zone's money market, based on the discussion about the money market in the previous section. And the term in the bracket implies the expected change in the exchange rate, as you perceive it.

In Figure 6-10, it seems that a higher expected real return on the euro-denominated security in dollars is associated with a lower dollar–euro exchange rate. Similarly, a lower expected real return on the euro-denominated security in dollars is associated with a higher dollar–euro exchange rate. This means that the dollar appreciates from Point 1 to Point 2 in Figure 6-10. Why is the parity curve downward-sloping in the exchange rate-real return space?

The answer lies in the parity condition. Continue assuming real returns on the dollar- and euro-denominated security; also assume that the expected exchange rate does not change. Note that the current exchange rate $[(\$/\text{€})_t]$ is on the y-axis of the foreign exchange market. Because the aim here is to predict what the current exchange rate will be, it should be allowed to change. Also note that the same current exchange rate is used in the expected change in the exchange rate:

$$\%\Delta ER_t^E = \left[\frac{\left(\dfrac{\overline{\$}}{\text{€}}\right)^E - \left(\dfrac{\$}{\text{€}}\right)_t}{\left(\dfrac{\$}{\text{€}}\right)_t} \right]$$

If the expected exchange rate is assumed to be fixed and the current exchange rate can change, you can show that depreciation of a country's currency today lowers the expected real returns on the foreign security in domestic currency. Similarly, appreciation of the domestic currency today raises the returns on foreign currency deposits in domestic currency. Following are some numerical examples.

Suppose that the current dollar–euro exchange rate is $1.00 per euro, and the expected exchange rate next year is $1.05 per euro. Then the expected rate of depreciation in dollars is 5 percent ([1.05 – 1.00]/1.00 = 0.05, or 5 percent). This means that when you invest in a euro-denominated security, in addition to earning a return on this security, you receive an additional 5 percent return when you convert your euro earnings into dollars in the future.

Now suppose that current exchange rate suddenly depreciates to $1.03 per euro, but the expected exchange rate is still $1.05 per euro. You earn the same real return on the euro-denominated security. But what happens to your extra income that comes from the depreciation of the dollar? It's smaller now because the expected depreciation of the dollar declines from 5 percent to 1.9 percent ([1.05 − 1.03]/1.03 = 0.019, or 1.9 percent). Because the real return on the euro-denominated security, or r_ϵ, has not changed, the expected real return on the euro-denominated security in dollars declines as the current dollar–euro exchange rate increases or the dollar depreciates (which is a movement from Point 2 to Point 1 in Figure 6-10).

Therefore, when holding the expected exchange rate constant, a negative relationship exists between the current dollar–euro exchange rate and the real returns on the euro-denominated security in dollars.

The other real returns curve

Remember you are trying to construct a graphical representation of the foreign exchange market. The current exchange rate is on the y-axis. The real returns in dollars are on the x-axis. And the last section added the downward-sloping parity curve (the expected real returns on euro-denominated security in dollar curve). When you inspect Figure 6-10, you see that so far there is one curve in the foreign market and there is yet no equilibrium exchange rate. The reason is that you could be anywhere on the parity curve, at Point 1 or Point 2, but you don't know for sure. Therefore, you need another curve to complete the foreign exchange market.

At this point, it's helpful to consider the parity condition again:

$$r_\$ = r_\epsilon + \left[\frac{\left(\dfrac{\overline{\$}}{\epsilon}\right)^E - \left(\dfrac{\$}{\epsilon}\right)}{\left(\dfrac{\$}{\epsilon}\right)} \right]$$

Looking at the parity condition again makes you realize that the discussion until now focused on the right side of the parity equation, which is shown in Figure 6-10 as the parity curve. Therefore, all you know by now is the expected real return on the euro-denominated security in dollars. But how can you compare the euro-denominated security to the dollar-denominated security, if you don't know about the real return on the dollar-denominated security? The discussion needs to focus on the left side of the above parity equation.

As in the case of the euro-denominated security, the real return on the dollar-denominated security, $r_\$$, is determined in the U.S. money market based on the money demand and supply. Figure 6-11 illustrates the real return on the dollar-denominated security as a perfectly inelastic curve because the value of this variable is determined in the U.S. money market. Therefore, the real return on the dollar-denominated security doesn't vary with the exchange rate.

ER= \$/€

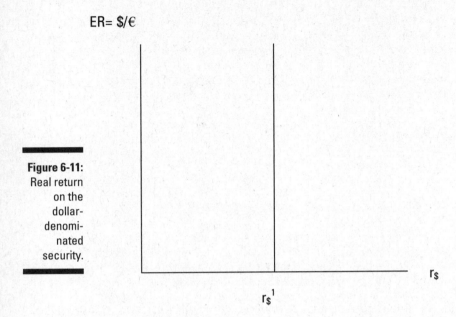

Figure 6-11:
Real return
on the
dollar-
denomi-
nated
security.

$r_\$$

$r_\$^1$

Of course, changes in the money market shift this curve. Figure 6-12 shows the effects of these changes in the money market on the foreign exchange market. Remember the variables that shift the curves in the money market, and try to explain the shifts in Figure 6-12.

\$/€

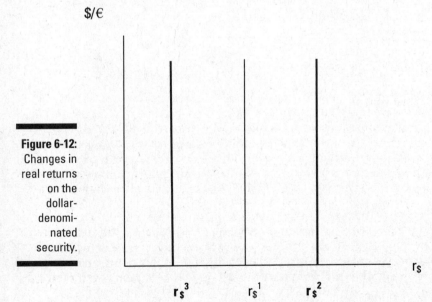

Figure 6-12:
Changes in
real returns
on the
dollar-
denomi-
nated
security.

$r_\$$

$r_\$^3$ $r_\$^1$ $r_\$^2$

In Figure 6-12, $r_\$^2$ indicates a higher real return on the dollar-denominated security. You can think about the following reasons for an increase in the real return of the dollar-denominated security:

- ✔ An increase in the real interest rate is consistent with a higher level of U.S. output. Everything else constant, a higher U.S. real GDP increases the money demand curve, resulting in a higher real interest rate.

- ✔ A higher real interest rate is also consistent with the short-run implication of a decline in the nominal money supply or a contractionary monetary policy. Note that the money market goes back to its initial position as the price level declines in the long run. Therefore, if the source of the shock lies in monetary policy, the real interest rate goes down to its initial level both in the money market and in the foreign exchange market ($r_\$^1$).

Also in Figure 6-12, $r_\$^3$ shows a lower real return on the dollar-denominated security. These are the possible reasons for the decline in real returns from $r_\$^1$ to $r_\$^3$:

- ✔ A decline in the real interest rate is consistent with a lower level of U.S. output. Everything else constant, a lower output decreases the money demand curve, resulting in a lower interest rate.

- ✔ A lower real interest rate is also consistent with the short-run implication of an increase in the nominal money supply or an expansionary monetary policy. Again, the money market goes up to its initial position as the price level increases in the long run. Therefore, the real interest rate goes back to its initial level both in the money market and in the foreign exchange market ($r_\$^1$).

Equilibrium in the foreign exchange market

Time to find our equilibrium! Now you can integrate the downward-sloping parity curve (expected real return on the euro-denominated security in dollars) and the perfectly inelastic curve (real return on the dollar-denominated security) into the asset approach to exchange rate determination. Figure 6-13 indicates the determination of the equilibrium exchange rate based on the MBOP.

Point 1 in Figure 6-13 shows the equilibrium exchange rate (ER_1), where the real return on the dollar-denominated security equals the expected real return on the euro-denominated security ($r_\$ = r_€^E$). At this point, you, the investor, are indifferent between the dollar- and euro-denominated securities.

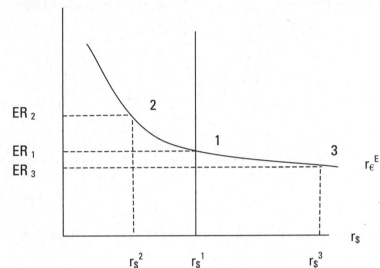

ER=$/€

Figure 6-13:
Foreign
exchange
market
(MBOP).

How do we know that the foreign exchange market settles at the exchange rate ER_1 at Point 1? Suppose that, for some reason, the market isn't in equilibrium, and the current exchange rate is ER_2. The associated point (Point 2) on the downward-sloping parity curve indicates that the expected real return on the euro-denominated deposit is less than that on the dollar-denominated security. As an investor, you're then inclined to sell your euros, buy dollars, and invest in the dollar-denominated security. The dollar appreciates, bringing the foreign exchange market equilibrium to Point 1.

Similarly, if the current exchange rate is ER_3, Point 3 indicates that the expected real return on the euro-denominated security is now higher than the real return on the dollar-denominated security. In this case, as an investor, you sell your dollars, buy euros, and invest in the euro-denominated security. The dollar depreciates, and the equilibrium in the foreign exchange market returns to Point 1.

In summary, when the parity condition holds, there's no excess supply of or excess demand for any security. Therefore, the foreign exchange market is in equilibrium when the parity condition holds. Investors are indifferent between dollar- and euro-denominated securities.

Changes in the foreign exchange market equilibrium

When you look at Figure 6-13, keep in mind that a number of money market-related variables in either the U.S. or the Euro-zone can change the equilibrium exchange rate. Following are some examples of the variables that can change the equilibrium:

✔ **The U.S. money market–related variables:** Figure 6-14 shows both an increase and a decrease in the real return on the dollar-denominated security ($r_\$^2$ and $r_\$^3$, respectively).

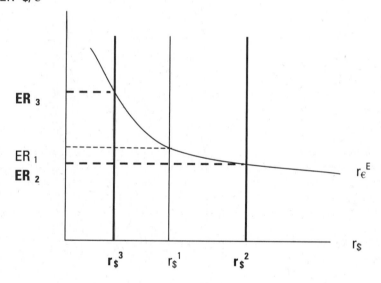

Figure 6-14: Shocks in the U.S. money market and the exchange rate.

- An increase in the real return on the dollar-denominated security ($r_\$^2$) may be the result of an increase in the money demand curve, due to an increase in the U.S. output or the short-run result of a decline in the nominal money supply. The changes in the money market that lead to a higher real return on the dollar-denominated security are associated with an appreciation of the dollar (ER_2).

- Conversely, a decline in the real return on the dollar-denominated security ($r_\$^3$) may be the result of decline in the money demand curve, due to a decline in the U.S. output or the short-run result of an increase in the nominal money supply. These changes lead to the depreciation of the dollar (ER_3).

✔ **The Euro-zone's money market-related variables:** In Figure 6-15, the downward-sloping parity curve shows the expected real return on the euro-denominated security. You know that this curve implies the money market conditions in the Euro-zone and is defined by the right side of the parity equation:

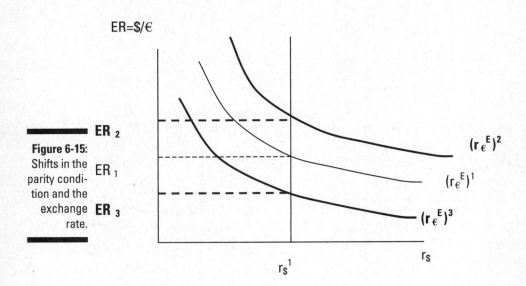

Figure 6-15: Shifts in the parity condition and the exchange rate.

In the following equation, r_ϵ indicates the real interest rate in the Euro-zone's money market. As in the case of the U.S. money market, a change in the money demand or supply in the Euro-zone can change the real return on the euro-denominated security.

$$r_\epsilon^E = r_\epsilon + \left[\frac{\left(\frac{\overline{\$}}{\epsilon}\right)^E - \left(\frac{\$}{\epsilon}\right)}{\left(\frac{\$}{\epsilon}\right)} \right]$$

• In Figure 6-15, $(r_\epsilon^E)^2$ indicates an increase in the parity curve. The reason for this shift can be an increase in the real interest rate in the Euro-zone (r_ϵ). Either an increase in the Euro-zone's output or the short-run effect of a decline on the nominal money supply increases the real interest rate in the Euro-zone and, therefore, increases the parity curve. This increase in the parity curve is associated with the depreciation of the dollar (ER_2) compared to the initial exchange rate (ER_1).

- Again in Figure 6-15, $(r_\epsilon^E)^3$ indicates a decline in the parity curve, which is related to a decline in the real interest rate of the Euro-zone. Either a decline in the Euro-zone's output or the short-run effect of an increase in the nominal money supply decreases the Euro-zone's real interest rate. The previous equation indicates that such a decline decreases r_ϵ, thereby decreasing the parity curve, which leads to an appreciation of the dollar (ER_3) compared to the initial exchange rate (ER_1).

For now, don't change the expected exchange rate in the bracket. That change happens in Chapter 7.

Combining the Money Market with the Foreign Exchange Market

This section discusses the capability to combine the money market and the foreign exchange market in the MBOP. Combining the two makes it possible to relate the change in the money market of one of the countries to the changes in the exchange rate.

The combined MBOP

At the beginning of this chapter, I mentioned that the MBOP model combines two models: the money market and the foreign exchange market. Figure 6-16 shows the combined MBOP model.

The combination of the money market and the foreign exchange market is possible because the y-axis of the U.S. money market (the real interest rate in the U.S.) is the same as the x-axis of the foreign exchange market (the real return on the dollar-denominated security). Note that the U.S. money market is rotated to take advantage of the common axes in separate models. Also note that Figure 6-16 explicitly shows the U.S. money market. The Euro-zone's money market is implied by the parity curve in the foreign exchange model (r_ϵ^E).

Figure 6-16 also makes it clear that, according to the MBOP, the exchange rate observed in the foreign exchange market has to be consistent with the money market equilibrium in both the U.S. and Euro-zone money markets. In other words, the current exchange rate observed on the y-axis of the foreign exchange market is determined based on the real return on the dollar- and euro-denominated securities. Of course, the real return on the euro-denominated security is transformed into the expected real return on the euro-denominated security in dollars so that the real returns on these two different securities are comparable.

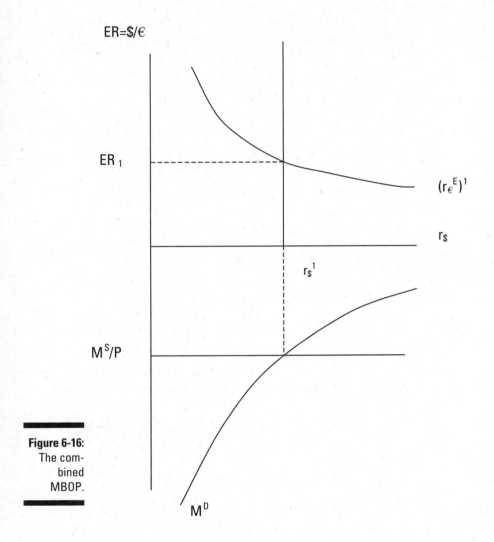

Figure 6-16:
The combined MBOP.

Changes in the exchange rate equilibrium in the combined MBOP

The variables that affect the current exchange rate remain the same as discussed in the previous section. The only difference in Figure 6-16 is that you can see the U.S. money market explicitly, and the Euro-zone's money market is implied by the parity curve in the foreign exchange market.

Therefore, shocks to output or nominal money supply (the latter has an effect only in the short run) either in the U.S. or the Euro-zone money market change the way investors compare dollar- and euro-denominated securities.

Chapter 7 provides examples for short- and long-run effects of changes in two countries' money markets on the current exchange rate.

Keeping It Straight: What Happens When You Use a Different Exchange Rate?

You must decide which money market you want to indicate as the explicit money market or which exchange rate you want to use in the MBOP. However, be careful about a few points so that the explicit money market correctly lines up with the exchange rate.

Consider Figure 6-16, in which the U.S. money market is the explicit money market:

- ✔ If you want to show the U.S. money market as the explicit money market, know that the y-axis of the money market becomes the x-axis of the foreign exchange market. Therefore, the real interest rate in the U.S. or the real return on the dollar-denominated security becomes your y-axis in the money market and your x-axis in the foreign exchange market.

- ✔ If the x-axis of the foreign exchange market is in dollars, you have to express the exchange rate on the y-axis in dollars as well. Therefore, you use the dollar–euro exchange rate. In this case, the downward-sloping parity curve in the foreign exchange market shows the expected real return on the euro-denominated security and, therefore, indicates the money market conditions in the Euro-zone.

Again, consider Figure 6-16. You can also start with the decision of which exchange rate to use:

If you want to use the dollar–euro exchange rate, the x-axis of the foreign exchange model has to be in dollars, indicating the real returns in dollars. Because the x-axis of the foreign exchange model implies the y-axis of the money market, the money market must indicate the U.S. money market. Therefore, the downward-sloping parity curve in the foreign exchange market shows the Euro-zone's money market.

Figure 6-17 gives a different example of a combined MBOP. Apply the previously mentioned considerations (in the bulleted list) to this figure.

In this model, the exchange rate is defined as the Australian dollar–dollar rate (A$/$). Thus, you must keep the foreign exchange market in Australian dollars. Therefore, the x-axis of the foreign exchange model must imply the real returns on the Australian dollar-denominated security. Because the x-axis of the foreign exchange model becomes the y-axis of the money market, the explicit money market shows the Australian money market. In this case, the downward-sloping parity curve in the foreign exchange market indicates the monetary policy of the U.S.

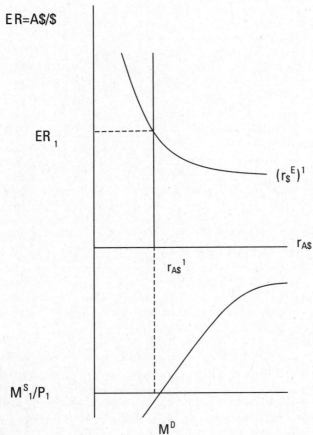

Figure 6-17:
Keeping it
straight.

Chapter 7

Predicting Changes in Exchange Rates Based on the MBOP

. . . .

In This Chapter

▶ Working with the combined MBOP model

▶ Understanding the difference between real and nominal shocks

▶ Predicting short- and long-run implications of nominal shocks

▶ Providing an explanation of exchange rate volatility through overshooting

. . . .

*T*his chapter uses the MBOP (the Monetary Approach to Balance of Payments introduced in Chapter 6) to predict the changes in exchange rates. You will see that there are real and nominal variables in the MBOP whose changes affect exchange rates. Real variables have no price effect in them. Real GDP is an example for a real variable, because it is adjusted for the changes in inflation. A nominal variable has price effect in it and therefore you'll see that a change in the nominal money supply affects exchange rates. Additionally, in terms of a change in a nominal variable such as the nominal money supply, I discuss how to make both short-and long-run predictions regarding the change in the exchange rate.

Applying Real Shocks to MBOP

The section starts with real shocks, because they are more straightforward than nominal shocks. What makes these shocks easier to handle is that real variables have no price effect in them. They are adjusted for the changes in prices. Therefore, they do not require a short-run and a long-run analysis, as nominal shocks do.

First, a shock implies a change in the value of one of the *ceteris paribus* conditions associated with a curve.

Chapter 6 introduces the term *ceteris paribus*. It means everything else equal or all else constant. These conditions (factors or variables) are important in economic analysis, because a change in one of them will shift a curve. And a shift in a curve will change the value of the variable that you want to predict.

Second, because this section deals with real shocks, think about which curve in the combined MBOP has a real variable as a *ceteris paribus* condition. Chapter 6 introduces output, or a country's real GDP, as a real variable and a *ceteris paribus* condition associated with the money demand curve. In other words, the level of output is held constant along any money demand curve.

Third, Chapter 6 offers information on how to construct the combined MBOP. But I want to give a short review here to help with the following sections. If you want to work with a specific exchange rate, such as the dollar–euro exchange rate, you put this exchange rate on the y-axis of the foreign exchange market. Because this exchange rate is expressed in dollars (amount of dollars per euro), the x-axis of the foreign exchange market should be in dollars as well, indicating the real returns in dollars. Because the x-axis of the foreign exchange market is the y-axis of the money market, the explicit money market has to be the U.S. money market. In this case, the downward-sloping parity curve in the foreign exchange market indicates Eurozone's money market.

Increase in U.S. output

The previous discussion identified output as the only real ceteris paribus condition in the MBOP. Because the MBOP includes two countries' variables, among them, their output, you can assume a change in U.S. or Eurozone output. This exercise assumes a change (an increase) in U.S. output, because the exchange rate is the dollar-euro exchange rate and therefore the explicit money market is the U.S. money market. As mentioned before, you'll apply the increase in U.S. output to the U.S. money demand curve, which provides an easier start.

Additionally, whenever a shock is introduced, it means that there are a variety of possible shocks happening both in the U.S. and in the Eurozone. But for simplicity you hold everything else constant and assume an increase in U.S. output.

Figure 7-1 shows the combined MBOP, where the exchange rate is expressed as the dollar–euro rate. In this model, changes in U.S. output are reflected in changes in the money demand curve in the U.S. money market.

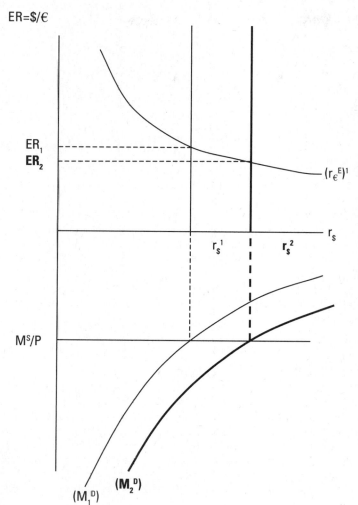

Figure 7-1:
Increase in
U.S. output.

Everything else constant, an increase in U.S. output or real income leads to an increase in the demand for money in the United States. As a result, the U.S. real interest rate increases.

Because of a higher real interest rate in the U.S. money market, you see an increase in the foreign exchange market in the perfectly inelastic curve that reflects the level of the real interest rate on the dollar-denominated security. This increase changes the equilibrium exchange rate from ER_1 to ER_2. Therefore, an increase in U.S. output with no change in the Eurozone leads to the appreciation of the dollar against the euro.

Increase in Eurozone's output

Continue working with the dollar–euro exchange rate. This exercise indicates the change in output as well, but this time, everything else constant, you assume an increase in Eurozone's output. Having an exercise with this assumption is important for the following reason: When you use the dollar-euro exchange rate, the explicit money market indicates the U.S. money market. Because the MBOP considers money markets of both the U.S. and the Eurozone, you may ask where the Eurozone's money market is, or which curve indicates the Eurozone's money market. This example is helpful in answering this question.

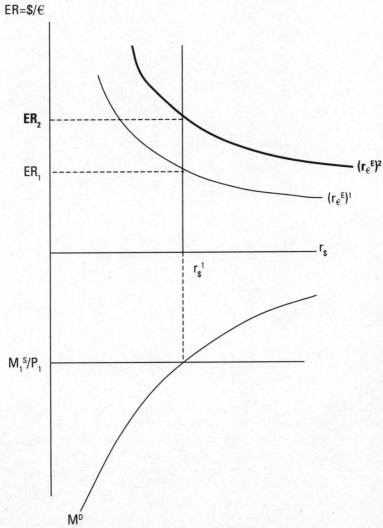

Figure 7-2:
Increase in Eurozone's output.

Remember, changes in any country's output in this model result in changes in the demand for money. In Figure 7-2, the explicit money market is the U.S. money market; the Eurozone's money market is reflected in the downward-sloping parity curve.

Also remember what the parity curve represents. In Figure 7-2, it implies the expected real return on the euro-denominated security in dollars. In other words, it shows:

$$r_\mathrm{\euro}^{E} = r_\mathrm{\euro} + \left[\frac{\left(\frac{\$}{\euro}\right)^{E} - \left(\frac{\$}{\euro}\right)}{\left(\frac{\$}{\euro}\right)} \right]$$

In this equation, $r_\mathrm{\euro}$ indicates the real interest rate in Euro-zone's money market, determined by the money demand and supply curves. If it's helpful for you, you can graph Euro-zone's money market, as in Figure 7-3. This figure shows that, because output is held constant along the money demand curve, an increase in output increases the money demand curve, thereby increasing the real interest rate in Eurozone.

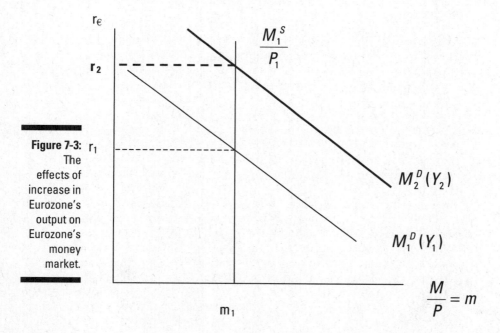

Figure 7-3: The effects of increase in Eurozone's output on Eurozone's money market.

Apply the increase in r_ϵ in the money market to the previous parity equation. r_ϵ in the equation increases, which increases the value of the parity curve. The parity curve in Figure 7-2 then also increases.

In this case, you predict that an increase in Eurozone's output leads to the depreciation of the U.S. dollar.

Applying Nominal Shocks to MBOP

Unlike real shocks, such as a change in a country's output, nominal shocks require you to conduct both short- and long-run analysis. Remember short-run refers to a period during which the value of a nominal variable is fixed or sticky. The long-run refers to a period during which all nominal variables change. (See Chapter 6 for discussions on the short- and long-run.)

The most important nominal variable in the MBOP is the nominal money supply. If a change in the nominal money supply occurs, the real money supply changes in the short run because of sticky prices. However, prices do not remain sticky in the long-run. They adjust in the direction proposed by the Quantity Theory of Money, and the money market goes back to its initial equilibrium.

As discussed in Chapter 6, the Quantity Theory of Money states that the percent change in the nominal money supply equals the percent change in the average price level in the same direction. For example, a 3 percent increase in the nominal money supply increases the average price level by 3 percent.

Suppose the central bank increases the nominal money supply. Assuming sticky prices (see Chapter 6), the real money supply increases in the short run. Because the Quantity Theory of Money implies that, in the long run, prices increase at the same rate as the increase in the nominal money supply, then as prices increase, the real money supply declines to its original level.

In the following, you analyze the short- and long-run effects of an increase in the nominal U.S. money supply on the dollar–euro exchange rate. This analysis is conducted first assuming no *overshooting* and then assuming overshooting. The term overshooting refers to a large, short-run change in the exchange rate (appreciation or depreciation) due to a nominal shock such as the change in the nominal money supply. Because overshooting indicates such a large increase or decrease in the exchange rate in the short-run, there will be some adjustments until the exchange rate settles at its long-run value.

You will see that the difference between the analysis with and without overshooting lies in the timing of changes in the expected exchange rate, which you hold constant until now. In the case of overshooting, you assume that investors adjust their expectations regarding the exchange rate in the short-run. If investors adjust their expectations regarding the exchange rate in the long-run, there will not be an overshooting.

Short- and long-run effects of a nominal shock — without overshooting

To start, I give you an example without overshooting because it's an easier start. Figure 7-4 shows both the short- and long-run effects of an increase in the U.S. nominal money supply on the dollar–euro exchange rate without overshooting. In Figure 7-4, the initial real interest rate in the U.S. money market is $r^1_\$$, and the initial dollar–euro exchange rate in the foreign exchange market is ER_1.

When the central bank increases the U.S. nominal money supply, assuming sticky prices in the short run, an increase in the nominal money supply leads to an increase in the real money supply (M^S_2/P_1). The resulting decline in the U.S. real interest rate (from $r^1_\$$ to $r^2_\$$) shifts the curve indicating the real return on the dollar-denominated security in the foreign exchange market to the left. As a result, in the short run, the dollar depreciates from ER_1 to ER_{SR}. Note that no change occurs in the parity curve; therefore, $(r^E_€)^1$ is still the relevant parity curve in the short run.

In the long run, prices adjust according to the Quantity Theory of Money. In this case, the rate of increase in prices equals the rate of increase in the nominal money supply. Therefore, the long-run real money supply (M^S_2/P_2) is the same as the initial real money supply (M^S_1/P_1). In other words, the U.S. money market goes back to its initial equilibrium, where $r^1_\$$ is the real interest rate.

Now you look at the foreign exchange market and determine where the long-run dollar–euro exchange rate is going to be. Consider the downward-sloping parity curve again. In Figure 7-4, the parity curve indicates the expected real return on the euro-denominated security in dollars.

In the next equation, $r_€$ indicates the real interest rate on the euro-denominated security and is determined by the Eurozone's money market. The term in brackets shows the expected change in the dollar–euro exchange rate. Therefore, the parity curve, or $r^E_€$, implies the expected real return on the euro-denominated security in dollars.

$$r_€^E = r_€ + \left[\frac{\left(\overline{\frac{\$}{€}}\right)^E - \left(\frac{\$}{€}\right)}{\left(\frac{\$}{€}\right)} \right]$$

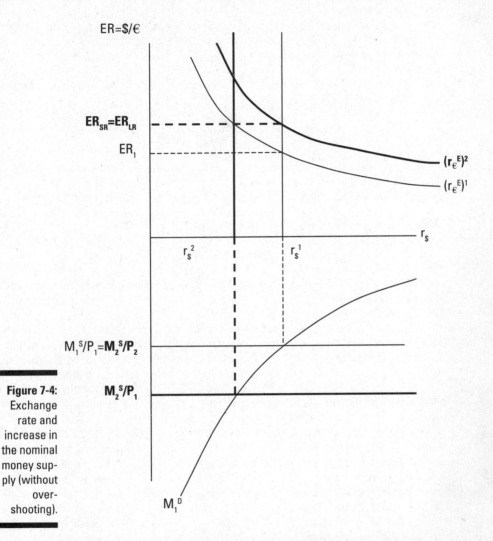

Figure 7-4:
Exchange
rate and
increase in
the nominal
money sup-
ply (without
over-
shooting).

Now focus on the expected dollar–euro exchange rate, which refers to the expected future spot rate some time from now. The MBOP without overshooting allows investors to change their expectation regarding the future spot rate only in the long run, after the adjustments in the price level take place.

Therefore, when the money market goes back to its initial equilibrium in the long run, investors in the foreign exchange market make an upward adjustment in the expected dollar–euro exchange rate. An upward adjustment in the expected dollar–euro exchange rate is consistent with the expected depreciation of the dollar. This adjustment increases the value of the bracket in the parity equation, thereby shifting the parity curve up from $(r^E_{\epsilon})^1$ to $(r^E_{\epsilon})^2$.

The shift in the parity curve brings the foreign exchange market into equilibrium, which is now consistent with the money market equilibrium. Note that, in terms of the level of exchange rate, the short- and long-run exchange rates are the same. This is shown as $ER_{SR}=ER_{LR}$ on Figure 7-4. However, while the short- and long-run exchange rates are the same, the long-run exchange rate is on the new parity curve, which is $(r^E_\text{€})^2$ on Figure 7-4.

In short, you predict depreciation in the dollar (or appreciation in the euro) when the U.S. nominal money supply increases.

Short- and long-run effects of a nominal shock — with overshooting

Figure 7-5 shows the short- and long-run effects of an increase in the U.S. nominal money supply on the dollar–euro exchange rate, now with overshooting. In Figure 7-5, the initial real interest rate in the U.S. money market and the initial dollar–euro exchange rate in the foreign exchange market still are $r^1_\$$ and ER_1.

The short-run analysis, assuming overshooting, starts just like the previous analysis without overshooting. Figure 7-5 indicates that following an increase in the U.S. nominal money supply, and assuming sticky prices in the short run, the real money supply increases from M^S_1/P_1 to M^S_2/P_1. Again, this change results in a lower real interest rate in the money market ($r^2_\$$).

In the case of overshooting, investors adjust their expectations regarding the future spot rate upward, and the parity curve increases in the short run. This adjustment creates a larger short-run depreciation of the dollar. Note that the short-run exchange rate that is consistent with the short-run equilibrium real interest rate in the money market ($r^2_\$$) is ER_{SR}. In other words, the exchange rate overshoots to ER_{SR}.

In the long run, prices adjust according to the Quantity Theory of Money. In the money market, the increase in prices is proportional to the increase in the initial nominal money supply. Therefore, the long-run real money supply (M^S_2/P_2) is the same as the initial real money supply (M^S_1/P_1). The U.S. money market goes back to its initial equilibrium, where $r^1_\$$ is the real interest rate.

As the money market returns in the long run to its initial equilibrium, ER_{LR} marks the equilibrium exchange rate. Note that the movement from ER_{SR} to ER_{LR} implies appreciation in the dollar; however, the dollar remains depreciated compared to the initial exchange rate ER_1.

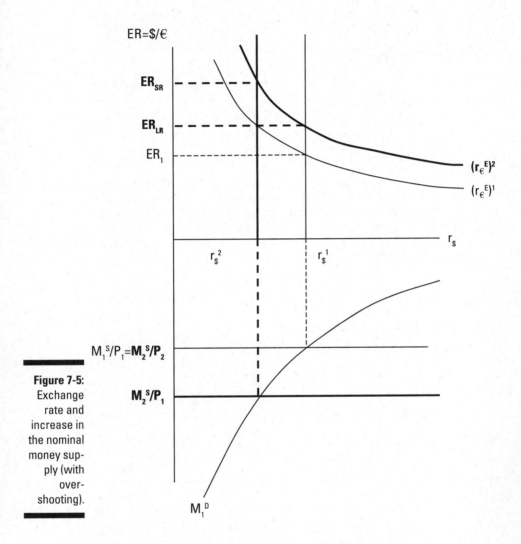

Figure 7-5:
Exchange rate and increase in the nominal money supply (with overshooting).

The concept of overshooting is one explanation for the surprisingly high volatility in exchange rates. Most short-term fluctuations in exchange rates don't reflect changes in fundamentals, such as changes in monetary policy or output. The overshooting argument indicates that short-run changes in exchange rates can result from adjustments. For example, as Figure 7-5 shows, appreciation in the dollar from ER_{SR} to ER_{LR} is not related to a change in monetary policy; instead, it reflects the adjustment in the real money supply when prices adjust.

Comparing MBOP with and without overshooting

Because Figures 7-4 and 7-5 are drawn separately, you may not realize the following. The only difference overshooting introduces is the difference in short-run exchange rates. The short-run exchange rate with overshooting (ER_{SR} in Figure 7-5) is higher than the short-run exchange rate without over-shooting (ER_{SR} in Figure 7-4). However, the long-run exchange rate (ER_{LR}) is the same in both figures.

Figure 7-6 shows Figures 7-4 and 7-5 side by side, to show that overshooting matters only in the short run. The model with overshooting implies a larger short-run response of investors to changes in monetary policy, indicated by the upward shift of the parity curve in the short run. In the model without overshooting, however, investors adjust their expected exchange rate when prices change in the long run.

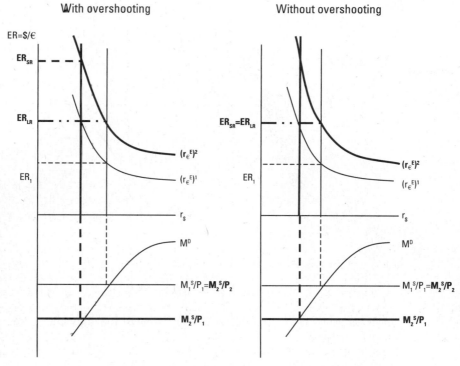

Figure 7-6: Exchange rate and increase in the nominal money supply (with and without overshooting).

In terms of the long run, Figure 7-6 indicates that, with or without overshooting, the long-run exchange rate settles at the long-run exchange rate of ER_{LR}. Note that, in both models, the ER_{LR} is on a higher parity curve, indicated by $(r^E_{\epsilon})^2$.

Keeping It Straight: What Happens When We Use a Different Exchange Rate?

This section introduces exercises with a different exchange rate. As discussed earlier, that the variables associated with the money and foreign exchange markets of the MBOP must be consistent with each other. Using a different exchange rate motivates you to consider the setup of the MBOP once again.

Additionally, the example for the nominal shock implies not only a different exchange rate, but also a different change in the nominal money supply than in the previous example.

Effects of a real shock

In this example, the real shock is a decline in U.S. output. You use the euro–dollar exchange rate.

Figure 7-7 indicates the exchange rate in the foreign exchange market as the euro–dollar exchange rate. Because the exchange rate is expressed as the number of euros per dollar (in other words, in euros), the x-axis of the foreign exchange model must be in euros as well, to indicate the real return on the euro-denominated security. Then the parity curve in the foreign exchange market shows the expected real return on the dollar-denominated security in euros, or $r_{\$}^E$.

In terms of the money market, the x-axis of the foreign exchange market becomes the y-axis of the money market. Therefore, the demand for and supply of money in Figure 7-7 are the Eurozone's.

The initial equilibrium in the foreign exchange is ER_1; it's r_{ϵ}^1 in the money market. Because the shock is a decline in U.S. output, you first want to identify what is affected by a change in U.S. output. Remember that a country's output is a *ceteris paribus* condition along the money demand curve. But the demand for money in the figure is the demand for euros in Eurozone, so it does not change when U.S. output changes. The demand for money in the Eurozone changes when Eurozone output changes. Because in this example the U.S. output changes and this change affects the U.S. money market, you need to locate where the U.S. money market is. In Figure 7-7, the U.S. money market is captured along the parity curve in the foreign exchange market.

In Figure 7-7, the parity curve implies:

$$r_\$^E = r_\$ + \left[\frac{\left(\frac{\overline{\text{€}}}{\$}\right)^E - \left(\frac{\text{€}}{\$}\right)}{\left(\frac{\text{€}}{\$}\right)} \right]$$

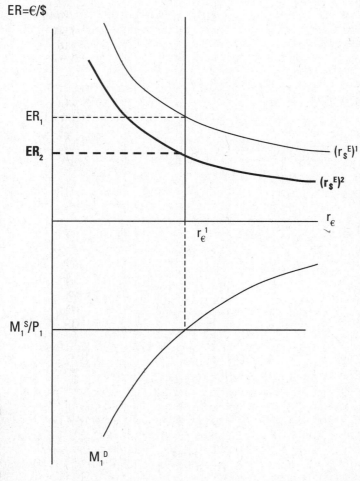

ER=€/$

Figure 7-7:
Decline in
U.S. output.

This parity curve indicates the expected real return on the dollar-denominated security in euros. The U.S. real interest rate ($r_\$$) that's determined in the U.S. money market is part of the parity curve. A decline in U.S. output decreases the money demand, thereby decreasing the U.S. real interest rate, which then decreases the value of this equation and shifts the parity curve down in Figure 7-7.

Based on this analysis, you predict the appreciation of the euro (or depreciation of the dollar).

Effects of a nominal shock

This nominal shock comes straight from the headlines. On October 7, 2009, *The Wall Street Journal* reported that the Australian Central Bank had raised its key interest rate ("Australia Rate Rise Poses a Global Policy Challenge," Section A14).

Note that the article mentions the key interest rate, not the nominal money supply. You can interpret the increase in the key interest rate as equivalent to a decline in Australia's nominal money supply (see Chapter 6).

Figures 7-8 and 7-9 show the effects of this monetary policy change without and with overshooting, respectively. In this example, you want to see the results of the changes in Australia's monetary policy explicitly in the Australian money market. Therefore, the explicit money market is the Australian money market, and the y-axis of the money market indicates the Australian real interest rate. In the foreign exchange market, the y-axis of the money market becomes the x-axis of the foreign exchange market. Because it is in Australian dollars, the exchange rate is in Australian dollars as well. This fact explains why you work with the Australian dollar–U.S. dollar exchange rate in this model.

Exchange rate without overshooting

Start with Figure 7-8, which shows the change in the exchange rate without overshooting. In the short run, a decline in the nominal quantity of money leads to a decline in the real quantity of money, assuming sticky prices. This increases the Australian real interest rate. In the foreign exchange market, you also observe a higher real interest rate, which is consistent with an exchange rate that's lower than the initial exchange rate ER_1. ER_{SR} indicates the short-run exchange rate, which implies an appreciation of the Australian dollar in the short run.

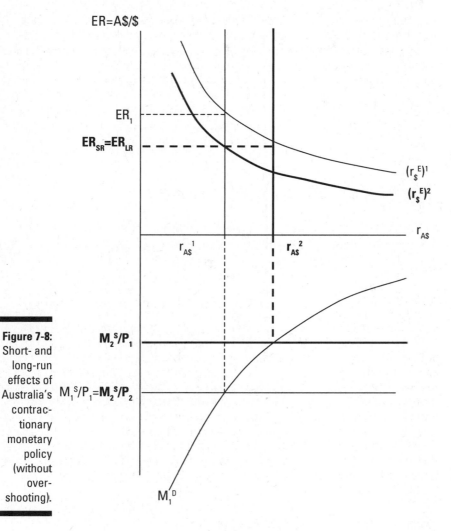

Figure 7-8:
Short- and
long-run
effects of
Australia's
contrac-
tionary
monetary
policy
(without
over-
shooting).

This term *contractionary* is generally used with respect to monetary policy,
where a contractionary monetary policy refers to a decline in money supply
and/or an increase in a central bank's key interest rate. This particular monetary policy makes money scarce, thereby increasing its price, which is the
interest rate. In contrast, expansionary monetary policy indicates an increase
in money supply and/or a decline in a central bank's key interest rate, which
makes money relatively more abundant, thereby decreasing its price (or the
interest rate).

In the long run, prices adjust downward at the same rate as the decline in the nominal money supply. Therefore, the money market returns its initial equilibrium, where the real interest rate is $r_{A\$}{}^1$. As the money market returns to its initial equilibrium, investors in the foreign exchange market make a downward adjustment in their expected exchange rate. Consider the parity curve that implies the expected real returns on a dollar-denominated security in Australian dollars:

$$r_\$^E = r_\$ + \left[\frac{\left(\frac{A\$}{\$}\right)^E - \left(\frac{A\$}{\$}\right)}{\left(\frac{A\$}{\$}\right)} \right]$$

A downward adjustment in the expected Australian dollar–U.S. dollar exchange rate implies an expected appreciation in the Australian dollar. This appreciation decreases the parity curve. Although the long-run exchange rate (ER_{LR}) is the same as the short-run exchange rate, the former is associated with a lower parity curve. And the long-run current exchange rate implies an appreciation of the Australian dollar (or depreciation of the U.S. dollar).

Exchange rate with overshooting

In Figure 7-9, you see the change in the exchange rate with overshooting. As discussed earlier, overshooting happens in the short run. Again, the Australian central bank decreases the nominal money supply and, assuming sticky prices, the real money supply declines. This leads to a higher real interest rate, $r_{A\$}{}^2$, in the Australian money market. Now investors in the foreign exchange market make a downward adjustment in their expected exchange rate in the short run, implying an expected appreciation in the Australian dollar. Therefore, the parity curve declines in the short run, causing an overshooting in the exchange rate to ER_{SR}.

As prices adjust downward in the long run, the real money supply goes back to its original position, bringing the real interest rate down to $r_{A\$}{}^1$. The real interest rate declines in the money market; in the foreign exchange market, the exchange rate increases to ER_{LR}. Although the change from ER_{SR} to ER_{LR} implies depreciation in the Australian dollar after an initial appreciation, ER_{LR} indicates that the net result is an appreciation in the Australian dollar compared to the initial exchange rate, ER_1.

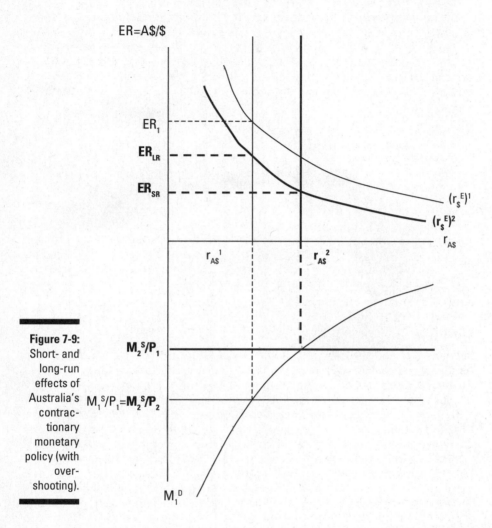

Figure 7-9:
Short- and
long-run
effects of
Australia's
contrac-
tionary
monetary
policy (with
over-
shooting).

Comparing Predictions of MBOP and the Demand–Supply Model

In economics, alternative theories seek to explain the determination of the same variable. And alternative theories apply to exchange rate determination as well. In Chapter 5, you predict the changes in the exchange rate according to the demand–supply model. In Chapters 6 and 7, the MBOP explains the changes in the exchange rate.

When you compare alternative theories, be aware of the differences in their approach to the subject:

- The demand–supply model considers both trade and portfolio flows. The MBOP considers only the portfolio flows and views the exchange rate determination exclusively from the viewpoint of international investors.

- As opposed to the MBOP, the demand–supply model does not explicitly deal with monetary policy; instead, it deals with its consequences, which imply the changes in the price level. The relevant shock in the demand–supply model is the changes in the inflation rate; the MBOP uses the changes in the nominal money supply as a nominal shock to the money market.

- Contrary to the MBOP, the demand–supply model does not explicitly refer to the short- and long-run analysis. However, throughout this chapter you read that a change in the nominal money supply will lead to a change in prices in the long-run. The fact that the change in the inflation rate is a shock in the demand–supply model indicates that this model implicitly considers the long run.

Despite differences in their approach to exchange rate determination, both theories generally provide the same prediction on the effects of similar shocks to the exchange rate.

In terms of the effects of changes in real interest rates, both theories offer the same prediction. First, the higher real interest country's currency is expected to appreciate. For example, Figure 5-8 in Chapter 5 shows that an increase in Eurozone's real interest rate leads to an appreciation in the euro against the dollar. You see the same result in this chapter in Figures 7-8 and 7-9. However, as indicated previously, the difference is that the demand–supply model doesn't indicate the source of the change in the real interest rate (it can be related to money supply or money demand). The MBOP, on the other hand, considers a shock to money supply or demand, which changes the real interest rate in the money market.

Second, both theories predict depreciation in the higher inflation country's currency. Again, these theories use different approaches when determining the effects of inflation on the exchange rate. Whereas the demand–supply model uses a trade-related explanation, the MBOP relates the change in the inflation rate to the change in the nominal money supply. In the MBOP, changes in the money supply lead to changes in the price level as proposed by the Quantity Theory of Money. Despite different theoretical framework, Figure 5-6 in Chapter 5 indicates that a higher U.S. inflation rate leads to depreciation of the U.S. dollar. Figures 7-4 and 7-5 predict the same result.

Empirical evidence verifies the predictions of both models with respect to the real interest rate and the inflation rate.

The only difference in these theories' predictions occurs in terms of the changes in output. Output is a trade-related factor in the demand–supply model. In this model, a higher output motivates a country's citizens to buy more foreign goods (at the given exchange rate). In Figure 5-7 in Chapter 5, you see that a higher output growth in the Eurozone leads to depreciation of the euro. In the MBOP, output is related to the money demand and affects the real interest rate. Higher output increases the money demand and, thereby, the real interest rate. Figures 7-2 and 7-4 indicate appreciation of the higher output country's currency. The predictions of these two theories regarding output are conflicting, and empirical evidence can help show which is correct. In this case, empirical evidence supports the predictions of the MBOP.

To conclude the theory part, the demand-supply model provides a simple model of the exchange rate determination. While the MBOP is more complex, it is a modern approach to exchange rate determination.

Part III
Understanding Long-Term Concepts and Short-Term Risks

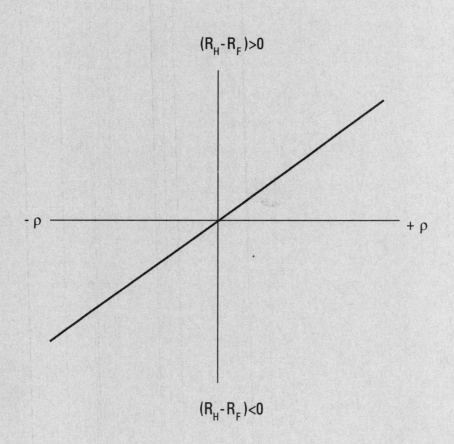

In This Part . . .

✔ You learn the concepts of the Interest Rate Parity and the Purchasing Power Parity. They enable you to tell not only which direction the change in the exchange rate will go, but how much the exchange rate is expected to change.

✔ You find out why you should not expect the dollar price of a Big Mac in Paris to be the same as in New York City.

✔ You get to see how foreign exchange derivatives help multinational companies to hedge against foreign exchange risk and help speculators to make a buck.

Chapter 8

Your Best Guess: The Interest Rate Parity (IRP)

· ·

In This Chapter

▶ Examining the relationship between interest rate parity and the MBOP

▶ Deriving the interest rate parity

▶ Estimating the forward rate

▶ Understanding the difference between covered and uncovered interest arbitrage

▶ Knowing when an arbitrage opportunity exists

· ·

*T*his chapter and Chapter 9 aim to accomplish similar goals. Whereas the theoretical models of Chapters 5, 6, and 7 predict the direction of the change in the exchange rate (appreciate or depreciate), the concepts of interest rate parity (IRP) in this chapter and purchasing power parity (PPP) in the next chapter seek to attach a number to the direction of change in the exchange rate. In other words, Chapters 8 and 9 help you not only identify appreciation of the dollar, for example, but also quantify that appreciation.

Although this quantification is an accomplishment, actual changes in exchange rates may not reflect the IRP-suggested changes every time you observe them. The same is true for the subject of Chapter 9, PPP. Therefore, both the IRP and the PPP give you a "best guess" regarding the direction and size of the change in the exchange rate.

This chapter's subject, the IRP, explains the changes in the exchange rate based on the interest rate differential between two countries. Understand that the IRP is a long-run relationship between nominal interest rates and changes in the exchange rate. Not every change in the exchange rate can be explained based on the interest rate differential.

This chapter also relates the IRP to the MBOP (monetary approach to balance of payments). The IRP and the MBOP involve different interest rates — nominal and real, respectively. A helpful guide to making the connection between the IRP and the MBOP is the International Fisher Effect (IFE).

Finally, this chapter examines the arbitrage opportunities based on the IRP. You can use the IRP to make profits, which is called the *covered interest arbitrage*. The concept of covered interest arbitrage is similar to the arbitrage examples in Chapter 3. This chapter helps you understand the difference between uncovered and covered interest arbitrage.

Tackling the Basics of Interest Rate Parity (IRP)

This section sets the stage for the IRP without explicitly talking about it. In fact, you need to be aware of three related subjects before you can understand the IRP and work with it. First, the general concept of the IRP relates the expected change in the exchange rate to the interest rate differential between two countries. This concept may ring a bell if you've already read Chapters 6 and 7. Therefore, this section examines the differences between the MBOP and the IRP at a general level. Second, understanding the concept of the International Fisher Effect (IFE) is helpful for understanding the IRP–MBOP relationship. Third, the IRP includes the concept of a forward rate as it is observed on a forward contract. This section discusses forward contracts and forward rates before moving on to the IRP.

Differences between IRP and MBOP

The IRP relates the interest rate differential to the change in the exchange rate. In Chapters 6 and 7, the MBOP seems to be doing the same. What's the difference?

Recall the parity condition in the MBOP (see Chapter 6 if you need a refresher):

$$r_\$ = r_€ + \left[\frac{\left(\frac{\overline{\$}}{€}\right)^E - \left(\frac{\$}{€}\right)}{\left(\frac{\$}{€}\right)} \right]$$

Here, $r_\$$, $r_€$,

$$\left(\dfrac{\overline{\dfrac{\$}{€}}}{}\right)^E$$

and

$$\left(\dfrac{\$}{€}\right)$$

denote the real interest rate on the dollar-denominated security, the real interest rate on the euro-denominated security, the expected dollar–euro exchange rate, and the spot dollar–euro exchange rate, respectively. The equation implies that the real return on the dollar-denominated security equals the expected real return on the euro-denominated security in dollars. When this equality holds, the foreign exchange market is in equilibrium. In other words, investors are indifferent between the dollar- and euro-denominated securities.

After this quick reminder, you can reorganize the parity equation so that its left side is the difference between the real interest rates in two countries:

$$r_\$ - r_€ = \left[\dfrac{\left(\overline{\dfrac{\$}{€}}\right)^E - \left(\dfrac{\$}{€}\right)}{\left(\dfrac{\$}{€}\right)} \right]$$

The IRP relates the interest rate differential to the expected change in the exchange rate, and this equation from the MBOP seems to do the same thing. At this point, the MBOP and the IRP sound similar. What's the difference between them?

First, when the MBOP talks about the interest rate differential, it means the difference in two countries' *real* interest rates. The IRP is also interested in the difference between interest rates as a predictor for changes in the exchange rate, but the IRP thinks in terms of *nominal* interest rates.

Second, whereas the MBOP uses the concept of an expected exchange rate, it doesn't specify how you can measure it. The IRP, on the other hand, uses the forward rate as indicated on a forward contract to get a numerical estimate for the expected change in the exchange rate.

Before introducing the IRP, the next two sections examine the International Fisher Effect (IFE) and forward contracts. The discussion of the IFE helps you understand the compatibility of real interest rates in the MBOP with nominal interest rates in the IRP. Having a basic knowledge of forward contracts is helpful for understanding the forward rate used by the IRP.

The International Fisher Effect (IFE)

The IFE is helpful in finding the relationship between the MBOP and its use of real interest rates, and the IRP and its use of nominal interest rates. Recall the Fisher equation (used in Chapter 5):

$$r = R - \pi$$

Here, r, R, and π imply the real interest rate, the nominal interest rate, and the inflation rate, respectively. According to the Fisher equation, the real interest rate equals the difference between the nominal interest rate and the inflation rate.

Therefore, if the MBOP and the IRP use the real and nominal interest rate differential in two countries, the difference between these two types of interest rates is the inflation rates in these countries.

The IFE suggests that investors expect the same real return in every country. To keep the real return the same in every country, nominal interest rates should adjust to the changes in the inflation rate. For example, as inflation rates increase, nominal interest rates increase as well, to keep real returns the same.

Suppose investors expect a 3 percent real return to domestic investment in all countries. Of course, the international comparison is based on a security of comparable risk and maturity. Suppose that the U.S. nominal interest rate and inflation rate are 5 percent and 2 percent, respectively. If the U.K.'s inflation rate is 1 percent and the exchange rate isn't expected to change, U.K. investors would look for a pound-denominated security whose nominal interest rate is 4 percent. (There's an exchange rate dimension in this example, which becomes important in the upcoming sections of this chapter. This exchange rate dimension implies that a real return of 3 percent to domestic investors does not necessarily imply a real return of 3 percent to foreigners in this example.)

Therefore, the discussion in this section shows that even though the MBOP and the IRP use the real and nominal interest rates, their approach to the interest rate differential between countries is related through the International Fisher Effect.

IRP and forward contracts

Another difference between the MBOP and the IRP is how they define the expected exchange rate. In the MBOP, the expected exchange rate is included in the parity equation. In Chapters 6 and 7, the expected exchange rate reflects investors' expectations regarding the exchange rate some time from now. In fact, in exercises provided in Chapter 7, investors adjust their exchange rate expectations upward or downward. However, the MBOP does not explicitly provide any tools that can quantify the expected exchange rate.

The IRP quantifies the expected exchange rate using *forward contracts*. Forward contracts are an example of *foreign exchange derivatives*. Chapter 10 examines foreign exchange derivatives in detail. But for now you can think of foreign exchange derivatives as financial contracts where you lock in a specific exchange rate today for a future transaction in currencies (buying or selling of currencies).

A forward contract is an example of a foreign exchange derivative. It allows you to trade one currency for another at some date in the future at an exchange rate specified today. Typically, you get a forward contract from a bank that is engaged in foreign exchange transactions. A forward contract includes the forward rate (the exchange rate on the forward contract), the amount of currency to be bought or sold, and the transaction date. Forward contracts are binding, in the sense that there is an obligation to buy or sell currency at the agreed price for the agreed quantity on the agreed transaction day.

The forward rate may be a good approximation of the expected exchange rate in the bracket of the parity equation in the MBOP. You might expect that a bank considers the current and expected values of the relevant variables for the exchange rate in both countries and quote a forward rate to you. Therefore, in the MBOP and in terms of the dollar–euro exchange rate, the percent change between the spot rate at time t and the expected exchange rate (or the i-period ahead future spot rate) at time $t+i$ is:

$$\left[\frac{\left(\frac{\$}{€}\right)^{E}_{t+i} - \left(\frac{\$}{€}\right)_{t}}{\left(\frac{\$}{€}\right)_{t}}\right]$$

If you use the forward rate instead of the expected exchange rate, the percent change in the exchange rate includes the forward rate and the spot rate:

$$\left[\frac{\left(\frac{\$}{€}\right)^{F}_{t+t} - \left(\frac{\$}{€}\right)_{t}}{\left(\frac{\$}{€}\right)_{t}}\right]$$

Working with the IRP

This section derives the IRP and shows how the relationship between the change in the exchange rate and the nominal interest rate differential is established. It also introduces the terminology of *forward discount* or *forward premium*, which implies the change in the exchange rate. I also give you numerical examples so you can work with the IRP.

Derivation of the IRP

Suppose that you consider investing in the home or foreign country for one period. It means that you have some amount of money now (present value or PV) and, given an interest rate, you want to make some amount of money in the future (future value or FV). Chapter 3 shows the basic relation between PV and FV for one period as:

$$\frac{FV}{PV} = (1+R)$$

Because you know how much money you have (PV) and what the interest rate (R) is now, the unknown is how much money you will make in the future (FV). You rewrite the above formula to have the unknown variable in the left-hand side and get:

$$FV_H = PV(1+R_H)$$

Here, R_H and $(1+R_H)$ are the nominal interest rate and the interest factor $(1+R_H)$ in the home country (H), respectively. For simplicity, assume a \$1 investment so that you can simplify your (dollar) earnings to the following:

$$FV_H = (1+R_H)$$

Similarly, your (euro) earnings in the foreign country by investing €1 in Eurozone are shown here:

$$FV_F = (1+R_F)$$

Here, R_F and $(1+R_F)$ imply the foreign country's (F) nominal interest rate and interest factor (in this case, Eurozone's), respectively.

You can't directly compare R_H and R_F or

$$(1+R_H) \neq (1+R_F)$$

because the home and foreign country's interest rates are denominated in different currencies. Therefore, you need a conversion mechanism.

You can convert your earnings in euro into dollars by multiplying the interest factor in foreign currency with the percent change in exchange rate. But in order to calculate the percent change in the exchange rate, you need to know the current exchange rate and the expected exchange rate. While the current exchange rate is observable, there is no explicit series called expected exchange rate. Therefore, you need a measure for the expected exchange rate. The exchange rate on a forward contract (namely, the forward rate) would be a good proxy for the expected exchange rate.

Therefore, express the nominal version of the MBOP's parity condition as follows:

$$(1+R_H) = (1+R_F) \times \left(\frac{F}{S}\right)$$

In this equation, F and S are the forward rate and spot rate, respectively. You can further write the forward rate (F) in a way that shows the relationship between F and S:

$$F_t = S_t(1+\rho)$$

This equation states that the difference between the forward rate and the spot rate is related to a factor ρ (rho). The variable ρ can be interpreted as the percentage difference between the forward rate and the spot rate. Inserting the previous definition of the forward rate

$$(1+R_H) = (1+R_F) \times \left[\frac{S(1+\rho)}{S}\right]$$

and eliminating the spot rate in the bracket of the equation, you have:

$$(1+R_H) = (1+R_F) \times (1+\rho)$$

This equation is a different way of expressing interest rate parity (introduced in Chapter 6). It implies that investors are indifferent between home and foreign securities denominated in home and foreign currencies if the nominal return in the home country equals the nominal return in a foreign country, including the change in the exchange rate.

Look at this equation also from the viewpoint of which variables are known and which variable should be calculated. In the equation, you observe the home and foreign nominal interest rates and want to know what ρ is. Therefore, you divide both sides by $(1+R_F)$ and find

$$(1+\rho) = \frac{(1+R_H)}{(1+R_F)}$$

or

$$\rho = \frac{(1+R_H)}{(1+R_F)} - 1$$

Conceptually, ρ implies the percent change in the exchange rate. Because the previous derivation was based on the change between the forward rate and the spot rate, you refer to ρ as a forward premium or forward discount.

The terms *forward premium* and *forward discount* refer to the other currency. You can explain this by considering the sign of ρ. Clearly, ρ can be positive or negative. If the home nominal interest rate (R_H) is larger than the foreign nominal interest rate (R_F), the ratio of the home and foreign interest factor $[(1+R_H)/(1+R_F)]$ becomes larger than 1, which makes ρ positive. Because higher nominal interest rate in a country is consistent with higher inflation rates, a positive ρ is *forward premium* on the foreign currency.

If the home nominal interest rate (R_H) is lower than the foreign nominal interest rate (R_F), the ratio of the home and foreign interest factor $[(1+R_H)/(1+R_F)]$ becomes less than 1, which makes ρ negative. Because lower nominal interest rates in a country is consistent with lower inflation rates, a negative ρ is *forward discount* on the foreign currency.

Calculation of forward discount and forward premium

Suppose that you observe T-bill rates in the U.S. and Turkey as 1.5 percent (R_H) and 11 percent (R_F), respectively. Plug in these rates into the IRP equation to calculate ρ.

$$\rho = \frac{(1+0.015)}{(1+0.11)} - 1 = \frac{1.015}{1.11} - 1 = -0.0856$$

Note that ρ is negative, and you interpret the result as 8.56 percent forward discount on the Turkish Lira.

Suppose you observe that the spot dollar–Turkish lira exchange rate is $0.43 per Turkish lira. Now you know ρ and the spot exchange rate. Therefore, you can calculate the IRP-suggested forward rate (F_{IRP}):

$$F_{IRP} = S_t(1+\rho) = 0.43 \times (1-0.0856) = \$0.39$$

The IRP-suggested forward rate implies an appreciation of the dollar against the Turkish lira, which makes sense. The Turkish T-bill rate is higher than that of the U.S., which implies a higher expected inflation rate in Turkey.

The previously mentioned forward rate is called the IRP-suggested forward rate for good reason. The concept of IRP enables you to come up with an expected change in the exchange rate (ρ) by looking at the interest rate differential between two countries. Then, when you apply the expected change in the exchange rate to the spot rate, you come up with your best guess of the expected change rate. You should go through these calculations and have your best guess regarding the expected exchange rate ready before you talk to a bank about the bank's forward rate. In the next section, you'll see the relevance of a discrepancy between the IRP-suggested forward rate and the bank's forward rate.

Now suppose that you observe T-bill rates in the U.S. and Japan as 1.5 percent and 0.13 percent, respectively. In this case, ρ is positive:

$$\rho = \frac{(1+0.015)}{(1+0.0013)} - 1 = \frac{1.015}{1.0013} - 1 = +0.0137$$

The result indicates a 1.37 percent premium on the Japanese yen. Suppose that you observe the spot dollar–yen exchange rate as $0.011 per yen. Plug in ρ and the spot exchange rate into the equation that indicates the IRP-suggested forward rate (F_{IRP}):

$$F_{IRP} = S_t(1+\rho) = 0.011 \times (1+0.0137) = \$0.0112$$

In this case, the IRP-suggested forward rate implies depreciation of the dollar because of higher nominal interest rate in the U.S.

Now you're a master at calculating and interpreting ρ! The next section focuses on applying this knowledge to speculation opportunities.

Speculation Using the Covered Interest Arbitrage

You can use the IRP to make profits — and everyone likes profits! Speculation involves buying and selling things to make profits. In this case, you are buying and selling currencies. Buying low and selling high is also the way to make money through currency speculation. Flip over to Chapter 3 and check out the speculation examples there.

To see the difference between the speculation exercises in Chapter 3 and the ones in this chapter, you have to understand the difference between covered and uncovered interest arbitrage.

Covered versus uncovered interest arbitrage

In Chapter 3's exercises, the speculator didn't have a forward contract to exchange currency at a future date. He just had his expectations regarding the future spot rate and used the future spot market to exchange currency.

Suppose that an American investor wants to make use of the differences in interest rates on the dollar and the euro, as well as the expected change in the dollar–euro exchange rate between now and sometime in the future by putting his money in a euro-denominated security. Therefore, he buys euros today, invests in the security, and, at maturity, sells his euros and converts them into dollars.

If this speculator relies on his expectations regarding the future spot rate to sell his euros and, therefore, sells those euros in the future spot market, he engages in an *uncovered interest arbitrage*: The future spot rate can be anything, and he's not hedged against possible changes in the future spot rate.

The IRP, however, assumes that the speculator gets a forward contract to exchange foreign currency in the future. Having a forward contract doesn't solve all his problems, as the discussion of foreign exchange derivatives shows in Chapter 10. Nevertheless, a forward contract can limit a speculator's exposure to unexpected and potentially large changes in future spot rates. When a speculator has a forward contract with a predetermined forward rate at which he'll sell currency in the future, this time he engages in *covered interest arbitrage*.

Now that you know about the difference between uncovered and covered interest arbitrage, there is one more topic to discuss before moving to numerical exercises. This topic is related to the question when a speculator makes a profit based on the covered interest rate arbitrage.

In order to think about your profit opportunities using the IRP or the covered interest arbitrage, consider the previous calculations of ρ and the IRP-suggested forward rate. ρ is calculated based on the interest rate differential between countries. When you plug your calculated ρ into the forward rate formula, to separate it from the bank's forward rate, you call it the IRP-suggested forward rate.

Suppose you collect data about the relevant interest rates and the spot exchange rate. You go to the bank and ask about its forward rate. If the IRP-suggested forward rate is the same as the bank's forward rate, the IRP holds; neither domestic nor foreign investors have an opportunity to engage in covered interest arbitrage and make profits. In other words, neither investor can use covered interest arbitrage to enjoy higher returns than the ones provided in their home countries. In this case, the change between the forward rate and the spot rate offsets the interest rate differential between two countries.

The IRP does not hold if the bank's forward rate does not reflect the interest rate differential. In other words, when you go to the bank and ask about its forward rate, its forward rate may be different than the IRP-suggested forward rate. In this case, either you *or* a foreign speculator can earn excess profits by investing in securities in the other country, but, under normal circumstances, not both of you.

Covered arbitrage examples

This section gives two numerical examples. The first one is related to the U.S. and Turkish T-bill example, for which you already calculated ρ. The second example looks at the covered interest arbitrage from both home and foreign investors' points of view. It also introduces a discussion about how you can decide which investor will have excess returns from a covered investment in foreign securities by observing the interest rate differential and the bank-suggested ρ.

The following numerical examples assume no transactions costs such as fees, bid-ask spreads, and so on.

Here you use the same example in terms of T-bill rates in the U.S. and Turkey. Suppose these are 52-week T-bill rates. In this example, you have the home and foreign interest rates, as well as the spot dollar–Turkish lira exchange rate: These rates are 1.5 percent, 11 percent, and $0.43, respectively. You already calculated ρ as –8.56 percent, and the IRP-suggested one-year forward rate is $0.39.

Now you go to the bank with this information and ask about its one-year forward rate. Suppose that the bank's forward rate is $0.41. Clearly, the bank's forward rate is higher than the IRP-suggested forward rate. The bank's forward rate implies a lower rate of appreciation in the dollar against the Turkish lira (TL). To see this clearly, calculate the bank-suggested ρ:

$$\rho_{BANK} = \left(\frac{F-S}{S}\right) = \left(\frac{0.41-0.43}{0.43}\right) = -0.0465$$

The bank's forward rate implies a forward discount of 4.65 percent on the Turkish lira, which is lower than the IRP-suggested forward discount of 8.56 percent. Because the IRP does not hold, you may have an opportunity to enjoy excess returns in this case. Assuming that you start with $100,000, you go through the following steps:

1. Get a forward contract to sell Turkish lira a year from now at the forward rate of $0.41.

2. Convert $100,000 into Turkish lira in the spot market: $100,000 / $0.43 = TL232,558.14.

3. Buy T-bills denominated in Turkish lira and hold them for a year: $232,558.14 \times (1.11) = TL258,139.53$

4. Sell $TL258,139.53$ on the forward contract: $258,139.53 \times 0.41 = \$105,837.21$.

Make sure that you make more money from covered interest arbitrage than you would have made in the home country. (Otherwise, why would you go through so much trouble?) You started with $100,000 and you made $105,827.21 by investing in Turkish securities. If you invested in U.S. securities, you would have made only $101,500 ($100,000 × 1.015). You can also calculate your rate of return from covered interest arbitrage and compare it to the home country's rate of return:

$$\left(\frac{105,837.21-100,000}{100,000}\right) = +0.0584$$

You can enjoy a return of almost 5.84 percent, which is higher than what you would have earned in the U.S. (1.5 percent). Now you've verified that covered interest arbitrage works for you (home country investor) in this example.

Suppose the following information is available:

- $S_t = (\$/\text{€})_t = \$1.31$

- $F_t = (\$/\text{€})_t = \$1.69$ (one-year forward rate)

- $R_{US} = 0.16$ percent (one-year nominal interest rate on a dollar-denominated U.S. security or R_H)

- $R_E = 0.60$ percent (one-year nominal interest rate on a euro-denominated Eurozone security or R_F)

Given this information, you can answer the question of whether the IRP holds. Then assuming an American and a European investor with $1,000,000 (the European investor has the euro-equivalent of $1,000,000 at the spot rate), you also can demonstrate which investor would be better off investing in foreign securities if the IRP doesn't hold.

Remember, covered interest arbitrage is profitable only when the IRP doesn't hold. To test whether the IRP holds, determine the IRP-suggested forward premium that should exist for the dollar–euro exchange rate:

$$\rho_{IRP} = \frac{(1+R_H)}{(1+R_F)} - 1 = \frac{1.0016}{1.006} - 1 = -0.0044$$

The sign of ρ is negative, and the calculation indicates a 0.44 percent discount on the euro. Therefore, we expect the forward rate to be:

$$F_{IRP} = S_t(1+\rho) = 1.31 \times (1-0.0044) = \$1.30$$

The IRP-suggested forward rate is $1.30, and it's lower than the actual forward rate of $1.69. In fact, the bank's forward rate-suggested ρ is:

$$\rho_{BANK} = \left(\frac{F-S}{S}\right) = \left(\frac{1.69-1.31}{1.31}\right) = +0.29$$

The bank's forward premium on the euro is about 29 percent, which contradicts the forward discount suggested by the IRP. Therefore, the IRP does not hold, and one of the investors has an opportunity to make excess profits based on the covered interest arbitrage.

First, look at it from the American investor's point of view. The American investor:

1. Gets a forwards contract to sell euros a year from now at $1.69.
2. Converts dollars to euros in the spot market: $1,000,000/$1.31 = €763,358.78.
3. Invests in a one-year euro-denominated security. In a year, he will have €763,358.78 × 1.006 = €767,938.93.
4. Sells euros at the forward rate and receives €767,938.93 × 1.69 = $1,297,816.79.

The American investor's rate of return in dollars is:

$$\left(\frac{1,297,816.79 - 1,000,000}{1,000,000}\right) = +0.2978$$

Covered interest arbitrage works for the American investor because his yield from investing in Euros is about 30 percent, which is much higher than the U.S. interest rate (0.16 percent).

Now look at the situation from the European investor's point of you. The European investor:

1. Gets a forward contract to sell dollars a year from now at $1.69.
2. Converts euros to dollars in the spot market: €763,358.78 × $1.31 = $1,000,000.
3. Invests in a one-year dollar-denominated security. In a year, he will have $1,000,000 × 1.0016 = $1,001,600.
4. Sells dollars at the forward rate and receives $1,001,600 / $1.69 = €592,662.72.

The European investor has a loss: €592,662.72 – €763,358.78= -€170,696.06.

The covered interest arbitrage does not work for the European investor.

Graphical treatment of arbitrage opportunities

You can use a graphical way to know which investor, home or foreign, can make use of the covered interest arbitrage to earn excess returns. Figure 8-1 illustrates this possibility.

In Figure 8-1, you see the approximate interest rate differential between home and foreign nominal interest rates on the y-axis, which can be positive or negative. Rather than using the formula for IRP, which is

$$\rho = \frac{(1+R_H)}{(1+R_F)} - 1$$

you can use the following approximation (preferably for small differences between two countries' interest rates):

$$\rho \approx R_H - R_F$$

In Figure 8-1, on the y-axis, you see the interest rate differential. The x-axis indicates the forward premium or discount, as measured by ρ. You also know that ρ can be positive (forward premium on foreign currency) or negative (forward discount on foreign currency), which is indicated by the positive and negative x-axis.

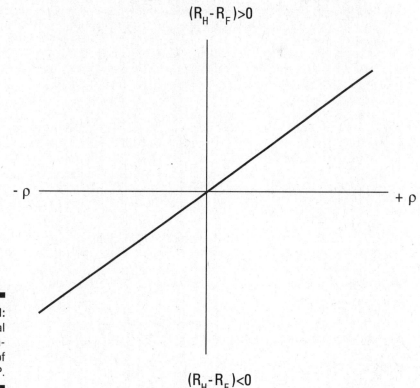

$(R_H - R_F) > 0$

$- \rho$

$+ \rho$

$(R_H - R_F) < 0$

Figure 8-1:
Graphical
representa-
tion of
the IRP.

The 45-degree line indicates when the IRP holds. Assuming no transaction costs, the IRP holds when the forward premium or discount equals the interest rate differential.

However, more clarity is needed on which forward premium or discount is relevant here: the one that reflects the bank's ρ. If the bank's forward rate reflects the IRP-suggested premium or discount, you're on the 45-degree line. This line indicates that the IRP holds; therefore, neither investor has an opportunity to make excess returns based on covered interest arbitrage.

What happens when the IRP doesn't hold? Look back to the last numerical example with American and European investors. In that example, the nominal interest rate differential between the dollar- and euro-denominated securities is -0.44 percent (0.16 – 0.60). However, you calculated the bank's implicit forward premium on the euro to be +29. Therefore, in terms of this example, you are certainly not on the 45-degree line in Figure 8-1: You're below this line and in the fourth quadrant (because of negative interest rate differential and positive ρ).

Generally, the area below the 45-degree line implies the area where the American investor (home country investor) earns excess profits from covered interest arbitrage. Note that this area includes parts of the first and third quadrants and the entire fourth quadrant. If the interest rate differential and ρ fall into the area above the 45-degree line, including the parts of the first and third quadrants and the entire second quadrant, the European investor (foreign country investor) earns excess profits.

A word of caution: Some of the examples show large rates of returns. The probability of enjoying such high returns in real life is small.

Determining Whether the IRP Holds

The IRP indicates a long-run relationship between interest rate differentials and forward premium or discount. Although at any given time this relationship may not hold, if appropriate estimation techniques are applied to long-enough data, you would expect the results to verify the IRP.

In reality, things don't work this smoothly. Factors interfere with the empirical verification of the IRP. In the following section, I show the interest rate–exchange rate relationship in reality.

Empirical evidence on IRP

The empirical verification of the IRP depends upon the approach. Empirical studies using forward rates seem to have a better chance of showing that the IRP exists. In other words, empirical results suggest that deviations from the IRP aren't large enough to make covered interest arbitrage profitable.

However, when empirical studies use interest rate differentials between two countries, the results suggest that interest rates aren't consistently good predictors of changes in exchange rates, especially larger ones.

The results also differ depending on whether we try to predict short- or long-term changes in exchange rates. Empirical evidence indicates that macro-economic fundamentals have little explanatory power for changes in exchange rates up to a year. In fact, random walk models of exchange rates seem to outperform macroeconomic fundamentals-based models of exchange rate determination. This is not very good news for macroeconomic models, if you consider what a random walk model is. A *random walk model* of exchange rates calculates the next period's exchange rate as today's exchange rate with some unpredictable error.

Factors that interfere with IRP

A variety of risks associated with a currency make a security denominated in this currency an imperfect substitute to another country's security.

The term *political risk* includes different categories of risks, which makes securities denominated in different currencies imperfect substitutes. Certain domestic or international events may motivate governments to introduce restrictions on incoming foreign portfolio investments. Or particular events or policies in a country may increase the country's default risk, as perceived by foreign investors. Likewise, differences in tax laws may cause concern among investors regarding their after-tax returns.

Other reasons also exist. Sometimes markets' observed preference for certain currencies cannot be explained based on interest rates differentials. The Swiss franc is a good example in this respect. Usually when most developed economies go through a recession, the Swiss franc appears to be the go-to currency, even though interest rate differentials suggest otherwise. This fact may reflect the liquidity preference of some international investors during periods of slower global growth.

Additionally, there is the so-called *carry trade*. It means borrowing in a low-interest-rate currency and investing in a high-interest-rate currency. Carry trade is very risky and is not consistent with the IRP. This kind of international investment appreciates the currency of the country with higher nominal interest rates, which goes against the predictions of the IRP.

All of these factors contribute to the weakening of the IRP-suggested relationship between interest rates and changes in the exchange rate.

Chapter 9

Taking a Bite Out of the Purchasing Power Parity (PPP)

....

In This Chapter

▶ Understanding the relationship between the PPP and the MBOP

▶ Exploring the relationship between inflation differentials and changes in exchange rates

▶ Deriving the PPP

▶ Estimating the PPP-suggested future spot rate

▶ Understanding the Big Mac standard

....

The models of exchange rate determination in Chapters 5, 6, and 7 predict the direction of change in the exchange rate in terms of appreciation or depreciation. This chapter aims to attach a number to the direction of change in the exchange rate. In other words, using the purchasing power parity (PPP), you can predict that, for example, the dollar will depreciate by 2 percent.

Whereas the interest rate parity (IRP; see Chapter 8) looks at the interest rate differential between two countries, the PPP considers the inflation rate differential to predict changes in the exchange rates. Therefore, as in the case of the IRP, the PPP also provides a "best guess" regarding the future spot rate.

In this chapter, using the PPP formula and the current spot rate, I show you how to calculate the estimated future spot rate. This chapter also discusses an interesting but sometimes misunderstood concept of the Big Mac Standard. This discussion focuses on different prices of Big Macs around the world and the interpretation of these differences.

Getting a Primer on the Purchasing Power Parity (PPP)

In this section, I cover the basics of the PPP. An important component is the connection between the PPP and the Monetary Approach to Balance of Payments (MBOP). As in the case of the interest rate parity (IRP), the PPP has a connection with the MBOP. It is important to think about these connections to realize that theories and concepts explaining the changes in exchange rates are connected.

Additionally, this section examines two approaches to the PPP: absolute and relative PPP. Distinguishing between absolute and relative PPP is important, especially when the discussion is about whether the PPP holds.

Linking the PPP, the MBOP, the IRP, and the IFE

The PPP implies the relationship between inflation differentials and changes in the exchange rate. This relationship is related to the monetary approach to balance of payments (MBOP), the interest rate parity (IRP), and the international Fisher effect (IFE). Chapters 6–8 predict the effect of inflation on exchange rates in the same way.

In Chapters 6 and 7 (the monetary approach to balance of payments), the focus is mainly on monetary policy. In these chapters, changes in monetary policy lead to changes in the price level in the long run. Those chapters show changes in the exchange rate following changes in the price level. The monetary approach to balance of payments predicts depreciation in the higher inflation country's currency and appreciation in the lower inflation country's currency.

Chapter 8 highlights the interest rate parity and the international Fisher effect. The interest rate parity relates the nominal interest rate differential to changes in the exchange rate. In this concept, higher nominal interest rates imply higher inflation rates because the international Fisher effect assumes that investors have the same real rate in all countries. Therefore, predictions of the interest rate parity are also such that the currency of the country with higher nominal interest rate is expected to depreciate.

A similarity between the interest rate parity and the purchasing power parity (PPP) is that the PPP also implies a long-run relationship between inflation differentials and changes in the exchange rate.

Figuring the absolute and relative PPP

The PPP implies that the changes in two countries' price levels affect the exchange rate. According to the PPP, when a country's inflation rate rises relative to that of the other country, the former's currency is expected to depreciate. In terms of the different PPP concepts, such as absolute and relative PPP, the nature of the change in the exchange rate is different.

The absolute PPP

The absolute PPP is similar to the Law of One Price. The concept of the Law of One Price means that the prices of the same products in different countries should be equal when they're measured in a common currency. Consider the dollar–British pound exchange rate. The absolute PPP indicates the following:

$$\frac{\$}{\pounds} = \frac{P_{US}}{P_{UK}}$$

where $\$/\pounds$, P_{US}, and P_{UK} indicate the dollar-British pound exchange rate, the price level in the U.S., and the price level in the U.K., respectively. Note that the absolute PPP can also be shown as the equality of the price levels in both countries where, using the dollar-British pound exchange rate (E), the U.K. price level is expressed in dollars:

$$P_{US} = P_{UK} \times E$$

Therefore, for the absolute PPP to hold, the dollar–British pound exchange rate should reflect the ratio of the price levels in the U.S. (P_{US}) and the U.K. (P_{UK}).

The relative PPP

The relative PPP, on the other hand, indicates that the changes in the dollar–British pound exchange rate reflect the changes in the ratio of the U.S. and U.K. price levels (P_{US} and P_{UK}):

$$\Delta\left(\frac{\$}{\pounds}\right) = \Delta\left(\frac{P_{US}}{P_{UK}}\right)$$

Note the difference between the absolute and relative PPP. The absolute PPP indicates that the exchange rate has to reflect the ratio of two countries' price levels. However, this is not easy. In reality, there are market imperfections such as nontransferable inputs, transportation costs, tariffs, quotas, and so forth. Therefore, the relative PPP takes these market imperfections in consideration and relaxes the relationship between the exchange rate and the price levels of two countries. It does so by considering the relationship between the changes in the exchange rate and the changes in the ratio of the price levels. All the relative PPP requires is the changes in the exchange rate equal the changes in the ratio of the price level.

From now on, when you read about the PPP in this chapter, it implicitly means the relative PPP, unless indicated otherwise.

Working with the PPP

This section explains how the PPP is derived. Understanding the relationship between inflation differentials and changes in the exchange rate enables you to attach a number to the change in the exchange rate, such as 2 percent depreciation. Then because spot exchange rates are observable, you can apply the expected change in the exchange rate to the spot rate, to predict the future spot rate.

Derivation of the PPP

Suppose that π_H and π_F indicate the home and foreign country's inflation rates, respectively. In the following equations, you work with inflation factors of home and foreign countries, $(1 + \pi_H)$ and $(1 + \pi_F)$, respectively.

Remember, the relative PPP implies that changes in an exchange rate follow the changes in both countries' price levels. You can express this relationship first by realizing that you cannot compare home and foreign country's inflation factors:

$$(1+\pi_H) \neq (1+\pi_F)$$

One way to express the relationship between the home and foreign countries' inflation factors is to adjust the foreign inflation factor with the expected change in the exchange rate. In this case, you have the following:

$$(1+\pi_H) = (1+\pi_F) \times (1+e)$$

Here, e indicates the percent change in the exchange rate and is defined as the number of home currency per foreign currency. You can solve this equation for e by dividing both sides of the equation by $(1+\pi_F)$ and moving 1 to the other side:

$$e = \frac{(1+\pi_H)}{(1+\pi_F)} - 1$$

This equation indicates that if the home inflation rate is larger than the foreign inflation rate, the ratio of the two inflation factors becomes larger than 1, making e a positive percent change in the exchange rate. This scenario implies a depreciation in the home currency.

On the other hand, if the home inflation rate is smaller than the foreign inflation rate, the ratio of the two inflation factors becomes smaller than 1, making e a negative percent change in the exchange rate. It implies an appreciation in the home currency.

The idea behind the relationship between the change in the exchange rate and the inflation differential is related to the exchange rate determination introduced in Chapter 5. For example, when home inflation rate is higher than foreign inflation rate, you are inclined to buy foreign goods, which leads to exchanging domestic currency for foreign currency. Therefore, domestic currency depreciates.

As an approximation, for a smaller inflation differential between home and foreign country, you can use this formula as the difference between the home and foreign inflation rates:

$$e \cong \pi_M - \pi_F$$

The previous equation means that the percent change in the exchange rate should approximately equal the difference between the home and foreign inflation rates.

In 2010, the inflation rates based on the Consumer Price Indices of the U.S. and Turkey were 1.64 and 8.52 percent, respectively. Based on these inflation rates, the PPP indicates an expected change in the exchange rate of:

$$e = \frac{(1+\pi_H)}{(1+\pi_F)} - 1 = \frac{1.0164}{1.0852} - 1 = -0.0634$$

The U.S. and Turkish inflation rates imply a 6.34 percent appreciation in the U.S. dollar. If you use the approximation ($1.64 - 8.52 = -6.88$), the appreciation in the U.S. dollar becomes 6.88 percent. These two rates of appreciation are considered as similar for most purposes.

Application of the PPP

If you know the current spot rate, you can use the expected change in the exchange rate given in the previous example to predict the next period's future spot rate. The dollar–Turkish lira exchange rate in 2009 was $0.67. Look at this rate as the spot rate in 2009, and suppose you want to guess the spot rate in 2010. For simplicity, further assume that the mentioned U.S. and Turkish inflation rates for 2010 reflect your expectations for 2010 in 2009.

The following equation connects the current and expected spot rate next period:

$$S_{t+1}^E = S_t \times (1+e)$$

Here, the components of the equation imply the expected spot rate at time *t+1*, the current spot rate at time t, and the change in the exchange rate. Using this formula, calculate your expected exchange rate for 2010:

$$S_{2010}^E = \$0.67 \times (1 - 0.0634) = \$0.63$$

Based on the inflation differential between the U.S. and Turkey, your expected dollar–Turkish lira exchange rate for 2010 is $0.63, which implies appreciation in the dollar. (By the way, the actual dollar–Turkish lira exchange rate in 2010 was $0.65.)

This numerical example doesn't constitute a test for the PPP. It aims to show the interpretation of the relevant equations. Clearly, you need to collect decades of data and apply suitable econometric techniques to test for the PPP or use the PPP for forecasting. Also, this example is closer to the future spot rate than what is often observed.

Deciding Whether the PPP Holds

As with the IRP, figuring out whether the PPP holds isn't exactly straightforward. Sometimes you have to be careful about what a certain test implies. Case in point: the Big Mac standard, a concept whose meaning is sometimes misinterpreted. Additionally, this section examines the factors that interfere with the empirical verification of the PPP.

The PPP and the Big Mac Standard

It's hard to believe, but we're talking here about McDonald's Big Mac. In 1986, a British magazine, the *Economist,* introduced the results of its worldwide survey at McDonald's restaurants regarding the prices of Big Macs, to make a case about the PPP (actually, a case against the absolute PPP, as you see later in this section).

In terms of selecting the Big Mac for this purpose, clearly the magazine picked a highly standardized good with little variation (bun, hamburger patty, onion, lettuce, ketchup, and so on) so that the differences in Big Mac prices aren't attributable to the differences in its content or quality.

After the *Economist* collected the prices of Big Macs around the world in local currency, it converted these prices into dollars at the market exchange rate. The results showed discrepancies of various sizes among the dollar prices of this seemingly standardized good.

The price of a Big Mac around the world

Think about the nature of the exercise. The *Economist*'s Big Mac standard is a test for the absolute PPP. The absolute PPP implies that the prices of similar goods around the world should be the same when their prices are expressed in a common currency.

However, the results indicated that Big Mac prices were much higher than in the U.S., especially in some of the European countries, such as France, and were lower in developing countries, such as Mexico.

Since 1986, the *Economist* has repeated this exercise every year, with similar results showing that the Law of One Price doesn't hold. As you will read later in this chapter, finding evidence even for the relative PPP is difficult. Therefore, the fact that the Law of One price doesn't hold isn't surprising.

Obviously, choosing a standardized good doesn't solve the problem. International price differences in the Big Mac stem from various circumstances. Based on tastes, demand conditions vary among countries. In some countries, eating at McDonald's may be a status symbol; in others, a stigma may be attached to it. Among other things, such attitudes may affect the manager's choice between a high volume/low margin and a low volume/high margin approach to profits.

Additionally, nonfood costs of production vary widely around the world. A variety of local taxes, labor laws and standards, government regulations of fast food, and costs of delivery, advertising, rent, electricity, and more certainly affect the prices of the Big Mac worldwide. These local conditions cannot be avoided by importing Big Macs from other countries: Big Macs are not a tradeable good.

Using the Big Mac standard to evaluate currencies

Every year, after reporting the worldwide dollar prices of Big Mac, the *Economist* attempts to examine whether currencies are trading at the "right" exchange rates. In other words, it asks whether currencies are overvalued or undervalued, based on the Big Mac standard.

This section first looks at the *Economist*'s approach to answering whether currencies are trading at the right exchange rates. Second, it raises a couple cautionary points regarding the use of the Big Mac standard for currency overvaluation or undervaluation.

For example, using the numbers from the Big Mac survey of July 2008, the price of a Big Mac was $3.57 in the U.S. and £2.29 in the U.K. Therefore, the implied PPP was calculated as:

$$\frac{\$3.57}{£2.29} = 1.56$$

In other words, the PPP-implied exchange rate was $1.56 per pound. At the time, the actual dollar–pound exchange rate was $2 per pound. Comparing the PPP-suggested exchange rate to the actual exchange rate, the *Economist* concluded that the pound was 28 percent overvalued against the dollar:

$$\frac{2.00 - 1.56}{1.56} = +0.28$$

The extent of other currencies' overvaluation and undervaluation against the dollar was calculated similarly based on the Big Mac standard. In these calculations, the Swiss franc appears one of the most overvalued currencies; the dollar price of a Big Mac in Switzerland is much higher than its U.S. price.

As another example, based in the 2004 Big Mac standard, the price of Big Mac in the U.S. and Switzerland was $2.90 and SFR3.92. Again, the PPP-implied exchange rate was this:

$$\frac{\$2.90}{SFR3.92} = 0.74$$

The PPP-implied exchange rate suggested $0.74 per dollar, but the actual dollar–Swiss franc exchange rate at the time of the publication was $1.25.

Therefore, according to the Big Mac standard, the Swiss franc was overvalued by 69 percent in 2004:

$$\frac{1.25 - 0.74}{0.74} = +0.69$$

According to the Big Mac standard, in most cases nominal exchange rates don't reflect the ratio of the price levels. And in terms of the cases mentioned, we were paying too much for a British pound and a Swiss franc. The market dollar price of a pound or a Swiss franc exceeded the Big Mac–based PPP rates.

Of course, in some countries, the dollar price of a Big Mac is much lower than the price in the U.S. One of these countries is China. In 2004, the price of a Big Mac in the U.S. and China was $2.90 and CNY10.41, respectively. Therefore, the PPP-suggested exchange rate should be $0.279 per Yuan:

$$\frac{\$2.90}{CNY10.41} = 0.279$$

In 2004, whereas the PPP-suggested dollar–yuan exchange rate was $0.279, the actual rate was $0.121 per yuan. According to the Big Mac standard, the yuan was undervalued by 57 percent:

$$\frac{0.121 - 0.279}{0.279} = -0.57$$

Therefore, the *Economist* concluded that we all should pay more dollars per yuan. The results from other developing countries, such as the Philippines, are similar to the results in China. Again in 2004, the Big Mac standard calculated the market dollar price of the Philippine peso to be about 58 percent below the level of the burger price parity!

The Big Mac standard implies that the Law of One Price, or the absolute PPP, doesn't hold. You can't go around the world and expect similar goods to be sold at the same price expressed in a common currency. The example countries in this section (the U.K., China, and the Philippines) widely vary in terms of their labor laws and standards, wage rates, and other possible nonfood production costs, so their Big Mac prices in dollars also vary.

Be careful when using the results of the Big Mac standard to comment on overvaluation or undervaluation. First, using the terms *overvaluation* and *undervaluation* in terms of (almost) freely traded currencies such as the British pound or the Swiss franc is misleading. Do you really want to conclude that foreign exchange markets cannot price them correctly?

Second, other factors are at work. Consider the Swiss case. In Chapter 8, I mention the fact that, especially in terms of short-term investment decisions, the Swiss franc is the go-to currency during global economic downturns. Additionally, the fact that the cost of living is higher in Switzerland has nothing to do with higher inflation rates. In fact, Switzerland is one of the lower-inflation countries with lower nominal interest rates. Therefore, there's no reason for the Swiss franc to be overvalued.

You can conclude from this examination that, in countries such the U.K. and Switzerland, higher nonfood production costs and various government restrictions are likely factors that increase the price of the Big Mac.

In China, the yuan is a pegged currency. The Chinese government implements extensive controls over the yuan and determines the yuan–dollar exchange rate. In this case, one can talk about overvaluation or undervaluation of the yuan. In fact, you know that the Chinese government has undervalued the yuan, to enhance the country's export performance.

Empirical evidence on the (relative) PPP

The PPP implies a long-run relationship between the changes in the exchange rate and inflation rate differential between two countries. The idea is that these variables should move together in the same direction. Generally, the evidence for the PPP isn't overwhelming because the empirical verification of the PPP seems to be sensitive to the choice of the base period and the size of the inflation differential between two countries. For example, everything else constant, a larger inflation differential seems to be helpful in verifying the PPP. This is because variation in inflation is necessary for inflation to be a helpful predictor. With low inflation that varies little, the forces assumed to be important in PPP are overwhelmed by tariff changes, changes in transportation costs and other real factors.

Other obstacles to finding empirical support for the PPP exist. These obstacles weaken the connection between the prices of similar goods in different countries, making it difficult for the PPP to hold. Some of these barriers are nontradable goods, government control of prices, restrictions on international trade, and transportation costs.

Some goods and services are called nontradables because their transportation costs are prohibitively high (housing and haircuts, for example). Prices of nontraded goods and services aren't linked among countries because domestic market conditions solely determine their prices. When the domestic market conditions change, prices of nontraded goods change. However, these changes in prices may not reflect the changes in the price of a similar nontraded good in other countries. This situation leads to deviations from the PPP.

Even if a good is tradable, a large increase in its transportation cost or the introduction of a government restriction on its trade in the form of tariffs, quotas, and so on increase the price of this good and, therefore, limit its trade. For example, in November 2012, the U.S. International Trade Commission decided to impose a tariff between 24 and 36 percent on Chinese-made solar panels. The reason was the government provided subsidy to solar panel production in China, which was believed to have provided an unfair advantage to Chinese suppliers. Any type of trade impediment as in this example weakens the relationship between changes in the exchange rate and inflation differential, which also leads to deviations from the PPP.

Chapter 10

Minimizing the FX Risk: FX Derivatives

. . . .

In This Chapter

▶ Defining FX derivatives

▶ Identifying who uses FX derivatives

▶ Determining the purpose of FX derivatives

▶ Spotting differences between FX derivatives

▶ Calculating gain or loss when using FX derivatives

. . . .

*Y*ou're likely happy to know that this chapter isn't about calculus! You don't have to take the derivative of a function. Whew! In finance, a *derivative* implies a contract to buy or sell a financial instrument at a future date and a price specified today. Because you get the contract today to engage in a future buying or selling activity, derivatives involve betting on the future price of a financial instrument.

In international finance, derivative instruments imply contracts based on which you can purchase or sell currency at a future date. In this chapter, I explore three major types of FX derivatives: forward contracts, futures contracts, and options. They have important differences, which changes their attractiveness to a specific FX market participant.

Note three points while reading through this chapter:

✔ As discussed in Chapter 3, spot FX markets are highly volatile. Because relying solely on the spot FX market is associated with higher risk, FX derivatives reduce some of the market participants' exposure to risk, among them, the MNCs (multinational companies).

✔ Every time a multinational company uses an FX derivative, the outcome will not be better than the alternative of using the future spot market. While numerical examples on this issue call this outcome an unsuccessful hedge, it doesn't reduce the usefulness of FX derivatives. A multinational company's losses would likely be higher, if the company relies exclusively on the spot market for all its FX transactions.

✔ The numerical examples in this chapter are all about shorter-term transactions for days or a couple months. Essentially, in an effort to reduce their exposure, market participants don't want to put their guess about the future exchange rates to a long-term test.

✔ For simplicity, we assume no transactions costs throughout this chapter, whereas, in real life, certain fees may be added to the price of an FX derivative.

Checking Out FX Derivatives

FX derivatives are contracts to buy or sell foreign currencies at a future date. Table 10-1 summarizes the relevant characteristics of three types of FX derivatives: forward contracts, futures contracts, and options. Because the types of FX derivatives closely correspond to the identity of the FX market participant, Table 10-1 is based on the derivative type-market participant relationship.

Table 10-1	An Overview of the Relevant FX Derivatives		
	Forward Contracts	Future Contracts	Options
Standardized regarding the amount of currency	No	Yes	Yes
Obligation to engage in the transaction on the specified day	Yes	Yes	No, but premium must be paid
Traded	No	CME Group GLOBEX OTC	CME Group GLOBEX ISE OTC
Useful for MNCs	Yes	Yes	Yes
Useful for speculators	No	Yes	Yes

CME Group: the leading derivative exchange formed by the (2007) merger of the Chicago Mercantile Exchange (CME) and Chicago Board Options Exchange (CBOT); GLOBEX: an international, automated trading platform for futures and options at CME; ISE: International Security Exchange, a subsidiary of EUREX, a European derivative exchange; OTC: over-the-counter.

Forward contracts and export–import firms

In the context of foreign exchange, forward contracts enable you to buy or sell currency at a future date. Then again, all foreign exchange derivatives do the same. As Table 10-1 indicates, there are differences among foreign exchange derivatives in terms of their characteristics. Forward contracts have the following characteristics:

✔ Commercial banks provide forward contracts.

✔ Forward contracts are not-standardized. This characteristic indicates that you can have a forward contract for any amount of money, such as buying €154,280.72 (as opposed to being able to buy only in multiples of €100,000).

✔ Forward contracts imply an obligation to buy or sell currency at the specified exchange rate, at the specified time, and in the specified amount, as indicated in the contract.

✔ Forward contracts are not tradable.

Who would use forward contracts? The non-standardized and obligatory characteristics of forward contracts work well for export–import firms because they deal with any specific amount of account receivables or payables in foreign currency. Additionally, these firms know their account receivables and payables in advance, so a binding contract isn't a problem.

Take a look at the following two examples, to get some insight:

✔ Suppose that you're an American importer, and you have to pay €109,735.04 to a German exporter on November 12, 2012. You get a forward contract today to buy €109,735.04 at the dollar–euro exchange rate of $1.10 on November 12, 2012. In this case, you're contractually obligated to buy €109,735.04 on November 12, 2012. On this date, you will pay $120,708.54 for it (€109,735.04 × 1.10).

✔ Or suppose that you're an American exporter, and you expect euro-receivables on November 12, 2012. Because an American firm cannot use euros in its daily operations, as soon as you receive euros, you sell them in exchange for dollars. Therefore, you get a forward contract to sell euros. Suppose that your firms' receivables amount to €246,947.40, and you get a forward contract today to sell €246,947.40 at the dollar–euro exchange rate of $1.10 on November 12, 2012. In this case, you will receive $271,642.14 on November 12, 2012 (€246,947.40 × $1.10).

As indicated in Table 10-1, forward contracts aren't tradable. This characteristic along with their non-standardized nature makes forward contracts unattractive to speculators. The next section examines the types of derivatives that are attractive to speculators.

Futures, options, and speculators

First of all, the term *speculators* implies a variety of people. They may be individuals who are trying to make a buck. In FX markets, they are individuals who represent financial firms, banks, or MNCs. Independent of their identity, speculators want to make a profit by buying or selling foreign currency using FX derivatives.

 Remember the golden rule of making money: Other than marrying into a rich family, if you want to make money through speculation, you need to buy low and sell high. No matter how sophisticated speculation may sound, it's always about buying low and selling high.

As forward contracts, futures and options are contracts enabling you to buy or sell currency on a future date at a price (exchange rate) specified today. While the main function of all FX contracts is the same, futures and options share common characteristics but also have differences.

Common characteristics of futures and options:

- These contracts are standardized. Their standardized nature implies that these FX instruments are denominated, for example, in multiples of $100,000.
- They are tradable, which make them attractive to speculators.

The main difference between futures and options:

- A futures contract implies that the holder of a futures contract has an obligation to fulfill the contract by buying or selling foreign currency at the specified exchange rate and at the specified date indicated in the contract.
- In contrast, when you hold FX options, well, you have an option. If you have an FX option, you have the right but not an obligation to buy or sell foreign currency. If this sounds too good to be true, yes, it is. Having a choice between exercising and not exercising the option is not free. The numerical examples later in this chapter show the associated cost with having an option.

Moving to Forward Contracts

In this section, the discussion on the forward premium and discount associated with forward contracts provides a first look at the relationship between the spot and the future spot rate. Additionally, numerical examples demonstrate successful and not-so-successful hedging against FX risk.

Forward premium or discount

Since banks provide forward contracts, you need to understand how to interpret a bank's forward rate. You also have to do your homework and gather some information before you talk to the bank. Therefore, this section is all about helping you put the bank's forward rate (the exchange rate on the forward contract) in perspective.

Suppose that you plan to buy some amount of Mexican pesos three months from now. Sure, you can buy pesos in three months whenever you need them. However, you know that spot markets are volatile, and a lot can happen between now and then in spot FX markets. Suppose that you're considering getting a forward contract from a bank to buy Mexican pesos. Before you talk to the bank, check out the spot dollar–Mexican peso rate, which tells you about today's exchange rate.

Clearly, neither the bank nor you know what the spot dollar–Mexican peso rate will be in the future. You and the bank have certain expectations regarding the future spot rate. Based on its expectations, the bank quotes you a forward rate.

The future spot rate doesn't have to equal the bank's forward rate. In fact, it rarely does.

Suppose you learn today that the spot dollar–Mexican peso exchange rate is $0.08. The bank tells you that the 90-day forward rate is $0.075. You notice that the bank's quote implies an appreciation of the dollar in 90 days. At this point, the question is about the extent of appreciation or depreciation implied by the forward rate. Therefore, it's necessary to come up with a formula that relates the bank's forward rate to the spot rate.

Assume the spot rate S and the forward rate F. If you think that the forward rate differs from the spot rate by some amount, you can call this amount ρ (the Greek letter rho) and express the relationship between the forward and spot rate as follows:

$$F = S(1+\rho)$$

Essentially, ρ implies some percentage and can be positive or negative. In other words, a forward rate can be larger or smaller than the spot rate. In the previous equation, the unknown is ρ because you can get the spot rate (S) from financial media, and the bank quotes the forward rate (F) to you.

To get ρ by itself, divide both sides of the previous equation by S:

$$\frac{F}{S} = (1 + \rho)$$

Then move 1 from the right side to the left as –1:

$$\frac{F}{S} - 1 = \rho$$

Now you know what ρ equals. But before plugging the exchange rates into the previous formula, the issue of the 90-day forward rate needs to be discussed. If the forward rate were annual (which means that the transaction will take place a year from now), you can use the previous equation. But because the example is about the 90-day forward rate, you need to make the appropriate adjustment. (It's customary to use a 360-day year in international finance.)

You can easily adjust the previous equation for 90 days (in fact, for any number of days). The adjustment is made by multiplying the percent change between the forward rate and the spot rate with $360/n$, where n stands for the number of days from now when the transaction will take place:

$$\rho = \left(\frac{F}{S} - 1\right) \times \frac{360}{n}$$

Now you're ready to plug the forward and spot rates ($\$0.075$ and $\$0.08$, respectively) into the previous equation:

$$\rho = \left(\frac{0.075}{0.08} - 1\right) \times \frac{360}{90} = -0.25$$

You interpret this result as –25 percent. Therefore, the percent change between the forward and spot rates is –25 percent. As mentioned before, this result implies an expectation that we need fewer dollars to buy one unit of Mexican currency in 90 days, which implies a depreciation of the Mexican peso. In this case, a negative ρ is interpreted as a 25 percent *forward discount* on the Mexican peso.

To provide an example for a forward premium, suppose the same dollar–Mexican peso spot rate of $\$0.08$. This time, the bank quotes you a 90-day forward rate of $0.085. Note that the forward rate is higher than the spot rate. Therefore, ρ must be positive. Plug in the numbers into the equation for ρ:

$$\rho = \left(\frac{0.085}{0.08} - 1 \right) \times \frac{360}{90} = +0.25$$

In this example, the percent change between the forward and spot rate is +25 percent. This result implies an expectation that we need more dollars to buy one unit of the Mexican currency in 90 days, which implies an appreciation of the Mexican peso against the U.S. dollar. We refer to this outcome as a *forward premium* on the Mexican peso.

Forward contracts that backfire

It's good to know how to interpret the relationship between the bank's forward rate and the spot rate (see the previous section). But the most important part of the story is coming up. How can you use this knowledge to hedge against FX risk? As indicated at the beginning of this chapter, you have a choice in buying Mexican pesos three months from now either at the future spot market or on a forward contact. The only reason to consider buying pesos on a forward contract is to avoid highly volatile spot FX markets.

Because you have an obligation to buy or sell currency on a forward contract, you don't need to check the spot rate every day until the contract is fulfilled. You are locked in the forward rate. On the transaction date, it would be interesting to look at the spot exchange rate, because no matter what you are buying or selling, you want to buy at a cheaper price and sell at a higher price. Therefore, compared to the forward contract, if the future spot market provides you with a lower price when you buy foreign currency or a higher price when you sell foreign currency, it's called *forward contract backfiring*.

Suppose you work for an American firm that exports backpacks. In a week, your firm will make a shipment to Germany, for which it will be paid €200,000 in 30 days. Therefore, you are planning to sell €200,000 in 30 days.

Surely you can wait until you receive €200,000 from Germany and exchange that sum for dollars in the future spot market. However, the idea is to avoid exposing the firm to excessive FX volatility between now and 30 days from now.

Assume that you get a forward contract from a bank to sell euros at $1.13 in 30 days. If you get this contract, you know that you will receive $226,000 (€200,000 × $1.13) in 30 days. Suppose further that the spot rate is $1.12.

Because you know the spot rate ($1.12) and the 30-day forward rate ($1.13), you figure that ρ is positive, meaning that there is a forward premium on the euro. In other words, the forward rate implies appreciation of the euro (or depreciation of the dollar).

You apply the equation for ρ:

$$\rho = \left(\frac{1.13}{1.12} - 1\right) \times \frac{360}{30} = +0.1071$$

You find that the forward contract implies a premium of about 11 percent on the euro.

What are you trying to avoid by getting a forward contract? Because your firm has account receivables denominated in euros, you are trying to avoid the depreciation of the euro, the very currency that you will be holding 30 days from now. With this contract, you will receive more dollars than at least what the current spot rate indicates. You may feel good about this, but not so fast.

What can go wrong here? The only reason the forward contract looks good to you is that, for some reason, you *do not* expect an appreciation of the euro more than 11 percent in the future spot market. But it can happen.

Suppose that the future spot rate is $1.21. Note that this rate implies an appreciation of the euro at a higher rate than what the bank's forward rate implies. In this case, without a forward contract, you sell your euros for $242,000 (€200,000 × $1.21) in the future spot market. This amount is clearly more than what you get on a forward contract ($226,000). In this case, your forward contract backfired.

As I mention at the beginning of this chapter, the fact that you would have received more dollars without the forward contract doesn't indicate the use-lessness of these contracts. If one considers many instances in which a firm buys or sells foreign currencies, you can lose more money if you rely exclusively on spot FX markets because of their highly volatile nature.

Finally, don't forget about the bank. What happens to the bank as the forward contract backfires for your firm? Think about the bank's motivation in providing you with a forward contract. If the bank buys euros from you on a forward contract, it plans to sell them at a higher rate in the future spot market. Therefore, the bank speculates. In fact, the bank may have expected a larger appreciation of the euro all along. The forward contract backfired for you, but the bank makes money. The bank pays you $226,000 for €200,000, sells €200,000 in the spot market for $242,000, and makes $16,000 ($242,000 – $226,000).

Forward contracts that work

Continuing with the previous example, your firm expects to receive €200,000 in 30 days, the current spot rate is $1.12, and the 30-day forward rate is $1.13. As discussed earlier, the forward rate implies an expected appreciation of the euro. Additionally, with the forward contract, you will receive $226,000 in 30 days.

Note that the spot rate, the forward rate, and the time horizon are the same here as in the previous example. Therefore, your calculations regarding the forward premium on the euro still apply.

Again, because your firm has account receivables denominated in euros, you are trying to avoid the depreciation of the euro 30 days from now. What if the outcome you are trying to avoid becomes a reality in 30 days? Suppose that the future spot rate turns out to be $1.11.

If you don't get a forward contract and you rely on the future spot market to sell your euros, you will receive only $222,000 (€200,000 × $1.11). Clearly, this is less than what you will receive on the forward contract ($226,000). In this case, you have a forward contract to sell currency, and the currency you sell depreciates in the spot market on the transaction day.

What happens to the bank as you hedge your firm's FX risk? The bank is still in the business of buying your euros low and selling them high in the future spot market. However, this time the bank loses. The bank pays you $226,000 for your Euros. Unfortunately, it can get only $222,000 (€200,000 × $1.11) for them in the spot market. This time, the bank loses $4,000 ($222,000 – $226,000).

Looking at Futures Contracts

As in the case of forward contracts, you can use futures contracts to buy or sell a specified amount of currency at a specified settlement date. Consider these differences between FX futures and forward contracts:

- ✔ While forward contracts can be obtained on any amount of money (non-standardized), futures contracts are standardized. For example, euro futures come in the multiples of €125,000.

- ✔ You can get forward contracts for any maturity; however, FX futures in the Chicago Mercantile Exchange (CME) have only a few maturity dates: every third Wednesday in March, June, September, and December.

✔ Forward contracts are provided by banks, whereas futures contracts can be obtained from brokerage firms. You tell a brokerage firm whether you would like to buy or sell currency futures and they will communicate your order to the CME. Then GLOBEX, a computerized platform, executes futures orders and matches buyers and sellers. This platform establishes bid and ask quotes for currencies for specified settlement dates. The difference between the ask- and bid-price is like a fee paid by the users of this platform.

✔ Although FX futures have a settlement date much like forward contracts, futures can be traded, which makes these contracts suitable for a multinational company hedging the exchange rate risk as well as for a speculator.

✔ On a forward contract, you have an obligation to buy or sell currency at a specified date. Because you are already locked in an exchange rate, you don't need to check the spot rate every day until the settlement date. While there is still a settlement date on FX futures, you keep an eye on the spot exchange rate between the day when you get a futures contract and the expiration date, because the value of your futures contract changes with the changing spot rate. This process is called *marking-to-market*.

The following two sections provide numerical examples related to FX futures. The first example is about the arbitrage opportunity between the forward and futures markets. The second exercise demonstrates how the marking-to-market process works in a speculation setting.

Finding arbitrage in FX derivative markets

Arbitrage implies taking advantage of price differences in the same or similar financial instruments. The golden rule of making money is also embedded in arbitrage: You want to buy low and sell high. Arbitrage opportunities may arise between different derivative markets. The next example implies that you observe a different exchange rate on forward and futures contracts and want to take advantage of it.

Suppose that September futures for the Mexican peso imply $0.08, while a forward contract implies $0.084. Clearly, the futures and forward contracts show a difference in the dollar price of the Mexican peso. You can buy pesos at the lower price of $0.08 on a futures contract and sell them at the higher price of $0.084 on a forward contract.

Now, suppose you want to buy and then sell MXP10,000,000. You pay $800,000 to buy MXP10,000,000 on a futures contract ($0.08 × MXP10,000,000) and sell them for $840,000 on a forward contract ($0.084 × MXP10,000,000). You make a profit of $40,000 by engaging in arbitrage ($840,000 – $800,000).

If something sounds too good to be true, it usually is. In the information age and today's well-connected financial markets, arbitrage opportunities don't appear around every corner. Additionally, when they become available, market participants recognize them and engage in arbitrage, which makes the arbitrage opportunity disappear. Here is why. In the previous example, as you buy pesos on the futures contract, the dollar price of pesos increases on these contracts. As you sell pesos on a forward contract, the dollar price of pesos declines in these contracts. The adjustment continues until the dollar–Mexican peso exchange rate is the same on futures and forward contracts — in other words, until no arbitrage opportunity exists. In fact, futures and forward prices of the same currency for similar maturity are very close.

Marking to market

As discussed previously in this section, after you get a futures contract, you need to keep an eye on the spot rate every day to see whether you want to close your FX position or wait until the settlement date. The value of a futures contract to you changes with two things: changes in the spot rate and changes in the expectations regarding the future spot rate at the settlement date. If the spot rate of a currency increases over a period, futures prices are likely to increase as well. In this case, purchase and subsequent sale of futures may be profitable. Conversely, if the spot rate declines, the futures rate would also decline, which would lead to a loss.

Before introducing the numerical example, you need to know about how FX futures work in reality:

- **Credit risk:** If you buy or sell futures, money is not exchanged until the settlement date. To keep the credit risk in check, the buyer or seller of a futures contract must deposit funds into a margin account. In other words, there is an initial *margin requirement*. This requirement is typically between $1,000 and $2,000 per currency contract.

- **Marking-to-market:** After the futures contract is obtained, as the spot exchange rate changes, the price of the futures contract changes as well. These changes result in daily gains or losses, which they are credited to or subtracted from the margin account of the contract holder. This is called the *marking-to-market process*. This process reduces the credit risk to brokerage firms as well as to the CME.

- **Maintenance margin:** Holders of FX futures are required to maintain a minimum level of margins. If their margin accounts are below the maintenance margin, they receive a *margin call* from their brokers to increase their funds on their margin account.

In the numerical example, you consider British pounds. As indicated before, futures contracts are standardized, which mean that the number of currency units per contract is predetermined. For example, a futures contract on the euro and the Mexican peso has 125,000 and 500,000 units, respectively. In the case of the British pound, there are 62,500 units per contract.

Suppose in May you buy a June futures in British pound, which means "going long in June British pound." While you'll gain from the appreciation of the British pound against the dollar, you'll take losses if the British pound depreciates.

Table 10-2 summarizes the changes in the spot rate for a couple days and the associated gains/losses. Time *t* on the table indicates the day when you buy the British pound futures. t+1, t+2, and so on, shows the subsequent days afterwards. Futures price indicates the daily exchange rate that settles the futures market. As indicated before, changes in the spot rate derive the changes in the futures price. Suppose an initial margin of $2,000 and a maintenance margin of $1,500.

Table 10-2		FX Futures: A Marking-to-Market Example			
Time	Futures Price ($/€)	Change in $/€	Gain/Loss	Cumulative Gain/Loss	Margin Account
t	1.5712				$2,000
t+1	1.5736	+$0.0024	+$150	+$150	$2,150
t+2	1.5710	−$0.0026	−$162.5	−$12.5	$2,137.5
t+3	1.5675	−$0.0035	−$218.75	−$231.25	$1,906.25

Time *t* indicates the time when you buy a futures contract at the futures rate of $1.5712 per British pound. Next day, t+1, the futures price increases to 1.5736, which gives you a change in the futures price of $0.0024 (1.5736-1.5712). Considering the fact that your contract has 62,500 units of British pound, your gain is $150 ($0.0024 × 62,500), which is also your cumulative gain at time t+1. The gain of $150 increases your margin account to $2,150 ($2,000+$150). At t+2, there is a decline of $0.0026 in the futures price (1.5710-1.5736), which leads to a loss of $162.5 (−$0.0026 × 62,500) and a cumulative loss of $12.5 ($150–$162.5). This reduces your margin account to $2,137.5 ($2,150–$12.5). At t+3, the change in the futures price is −$0.0035 (1.5675-1.5710). In this case, your losses are $218.75 (−$0.0035 × 62,500). Your cumulative losses are $231.25 (−$218.75–$12.5). Your margin account is declined to $1,906.25 ($2,137.5–$231.25). However, the maintenance margin has not been reached in this example.

The marking-to-market process implies that, rather than directly purchasing or selling currency, the holder of a futures contract considers whether to maintain his long or short position everyday as the spot exchange rate changes. You can end this if you sell a contract with the same maturity, in which case your net position will be zero. This is how futures contracts are closed out in most cases.

Just Say "No" to Obligation! Looking at Options

As discussed in the section "Checking out FX derivatives," FX options imply no obligation to buy or sell currency, which distinguishes them especially from forward contracts. This particular characteristic is attractive to speculators who don't want to be stuck with an obligation to buy or sell currency. Additionally, in terms of MNCs, when uncertainty surrounds an international project, options make sense, to hedge against the FX risk. For example, if an American firm wants to pursue a joint venture with a Mexican firm, regulations in either country (among other issues) may make this idea an uncertain project. However, if both sides see a chance of the joint venture materializing and the American firm is expected to provide pesos to the Mexican partners, say, three months from now, the American firm wouldn't want to buy pesos on a forward contract, where pesos must be bought. In this case, FX options work better.

Two types of options exist:

- ✔ **Call option:** If you buy a call option, you have the right (but not the obligation) to buy foreign currency.

- ✔ **Put option:** If you have a put option, you have the right (but not the obligation) to sell foreign currency.

The buyer of a call or put option is also called the *holder* of the option. The seller of an option is called the *writer* of the option.

Note the following characteristics of call and put options:

- ✔ The exchange rate on an option contract is called the *strike* or *exercise price*.

- ✔ The day of the transaction is called the *expiration* or *maturity date.*

- ✔ There are different types of options regarding the exercise flexibility at the maturity date. A *European-type option* can only be exercised at the maturity date. An *American-type option* can be exercised any time after purchasing the option until the maturity date.

✔ The CME Group and the ISE (see Table 10-1 for descriptions of these names) are the leading international exchanges for options (as well as futures). The electronic platforms of these exchanges are used by brokers who buy or sell options for their clients for a commission. As in the case of futures contracts, clients have to maintain a margin for the life of the option contract.

✔ Options are also provided by commercial banks and brokerage firms. Banks trade options either in the interbank market or as OTC transactions with their clients. While typical OTC options are the European-style options (can only be exercised at the expiration date), they can be bought and sold prior to expiration.

On an option contract, you may or may not exercise your right to buy or sell currency, which sounds too good to be true. And it is. Therefore, before discussing call and put options in more depth, the next section focuses on the price of having a choice, which is the option premium.

Paying the price for having an option: The option premium

The option premium (hereafter, the premium) is also called as the price of an option. The buyer of the call or put option has the right but not obligation to buy or sell currency, respectively. Therefore, the premium is the price of having a choice. In fact, for both types of options, call or put options, the premium is paid at the time of buying these options (actually agreed to be paid, because it's credited or debited two working days following obtaining an options contract.) I show in the upcoming numerical exercises, the premium is expressed in dollars per unit of currency.

Now you know why the premium is called the option price: you pay the premium upfront when you get a call or put option. You can look at the premium as a sunk cost (a cost that already incurred and cannot be recovered), especially when exercising or not exercising your right to buy or sell currency. However, as some of the upcoming numerical exercises will show that, especially in speculation, the premium is not a sunk cost when it comes to calculating your profit or payoff.

When you look at the financial media, such as the *Wall Street Journal*, you'll see that the premium is expressed in so-called *pips*. (In finance, a pip is 1/100th of one percent.) When you read about, for example, the premium of a call option being 3.94 per euro on the dollar-euro exchange rate, it means that you have to pay for each euro $0.0394 as a premium. The upcoming numerical exercises express the premium in the latter format, not in pips.

Option premiums aren't the same for all currencies or maturities. The valuation of an option is mathematically complex. A number of variables, such as the forward rate, the current spot rate, the strike price, the time to maturity, the volatility of currencies, and the home and foreign interest rates are included in the valuation of FX options. The upcoming numerical exercises assume a certain premium without discussing how this particular premium is calculated.

Table 10-3 summarizes the characteristics of FX options. As discussed previously in this section, the buyer or the holder of a call or put option pays the premium for having a choice between exercising and not exercising the option. While the seller or the writer of a call or put option receives and keeps the premium, he has obligations toward the buyer of the option, if the buyer decides to exercise the option. In the case of a call option, these obligations imply that, once the buyer decides to exercise the option, the writer has to sell to the buyer of the call option a specified amount of currency at the specified strike price. In the case of a put option, once the buyer decides to exercise the option, the writer has to buy from the buyer of the put option a specified amount of currency at the specified strike price.

The following two sections focus on call and put options. For each option type, you'll have a numerical example regarding the use of options by MNCs and speculators.

Table 10-3	Characteristics of FX Call and Put Options	
	Call Option	*Put Option*
Definition	Right to buy currency	Right to sell currency
Who pays the premium?	The buyer (holder) of the call option, because he has the right to buy currency	The buyer (holder) of the put option, because he has the right to sell currency
Who receives the premium?	The seller (writer) of the call option	The seller (writer) of the put option

Employing your right to buy: Call options

Having an FX call option means that you have the right to buy foreign currency. If you represent a multinational company, the company may have account payables in foreign currency, which would motivate the company to hedge against foreign exchange risk. In this case, the exchange rate risk is a possible appreciation of the foreign currency. If you are a speculator, you plan to buy foreign currency at a cheaper price on the option contract and sell it at a higher price in the future spot market. In this case, you'd like to take advantage of a possible appreciation of the foreign currency.

As an MNC or a speculator, a call option locks you in a maximum price to be paid for a currency in the future. The future spot market is your benchmark for exercising the call option or not. If the spot exchange rate is larger than the exercise price (the exchange rate on the options contract), the holder of a call option exercises the option to buy the currency. If the spot rate is lower than the exercise price, the holder lets the call option expire without exercising it. Now I show these ideas in numerical examples. This section has three numerical exercises. The first two show how to decide whether to exercise your right to buy foreign currency as an MNC and a speculator. The third exercise uses a speculation setting and is about selling a call option.

Using a call option: To exercise or not to exercise

A U.S. firm imports cheese from a Swiss firm for SFR100,000, which has to be paid in Swiss francs upon delivery in March. In this case, the American importer has future payables in Swiss francs and faces the risk of appreciation of this currency.

Suppose the American importer buys a call option with a premium of $0.0125 per Swiss franc and the exercise price of $1.10. The U.S. firm pays a total premium of $1,250 upfront ($0.0125 × 100,000) and if it decides to exercise the option, it will buy SFR100,000 for $110,000 (SFR100,000 × $1.10).

If the Swiss franc appreciates over the strike price during the contract period, the U.S. firm will exercise the call option and buy Swiss francs cheaper on the call option. For example, if the spot rate is higher than $1.10 (the exercise price), for example $1.13, the U.S. importer will exercise the call option and buy Swiss francs on the option contract. However, if the spot rate is $1.06 (lower than the exercise rate), the U.S. firm will let the option contract expire and buy Swiss francs in the spot market, paying only $106,000 (SFR100,000 × $1.06).

FX options can be used in currency speculations, when market participants expect changes in the exchange rate in the future. As indicated before, speculation implies profiting from buying low and selling high. Therefore, if a speculator buys a call option, say, in pesos, he must be expecting an appreciation of the peso in the future spot market. His plans are to buy pesos at a lower price on a call option and sell them at a higher price at the future spot market.

Suppose you expect an appreciation in the peso in a month. You buy a call option for MXN1,000,000 with a premium of $0.0014 per unit and a strike price of $0.083. The expiration date is a month from now. Your decision whether to exercise your option depends on the dollar–Mexican peso rate that you observe in the spot market. When the future spot rate exceeds the exercise price, you'll exercise the call option. Suppose the spot rate one month from now is $0.086. Your per-unit revenue is $0.003 ($0.086 – $0.083) because you'll buy pesos on the option contract for $0.083 and sell them at the spot market for $0.086. Your total revenue from this transaction is $3,000 (MXN1,000,000 × 0.003).

Now consider a situation where the future spot rate is lower than the exercise price, for example, $0.080. In this case, you wouldn't exercise the call option, because your per-unit revenue from buying pesos on a call option and selling them at the future spot market is negative ($0.080 – $0.083 = –$0.003). Now you let the call option expire.

Note that until now you consider your "revenue" from buying currency on a call option and selling it at the future spot market. Your payoff or profit is different than your revenue. Starting when you buy the option until and including the time of your decision to exercise or not exercise, the premium remain a sunk cost, an already paid and unrecoverable cost. However, when you consider your payoff or profit, you need to consider the premium. In a call option, your profit/loss is indicated by:

profit/loss = selling price – buying price

In the previous formula, the selling price implies the spot exchange rate. The buying price consists of the addition of the exercise price and the premium. In other words:

profit/loss = spot exchange rate – (exercise price + premium)

Consider the case when you buy a call option for MXN1,000,000 with a premium of $0.0014 per unit and a strike price of $0.083. You exercise your option when the current spot rate is $0.086. In this case, your per-unit profit is:

profit/loss = $0.086 – $0.083 – $0.0014 = +$0.0016

Considering the fact that you buy MXN1,000,000, your total profit is $1,600 (MXN1,000,000 × $0.0016).

Selling a call option

When you sell a call option, you are selling the right to buy foreign currency. Therefore, you no longer have an option. The buyer of your call option has the option to buy currency from you. In other words, you become the seller of foreign currency. You collect the premium, but need to accommodate the decision of the buyer regarding exercising his option. The buyer decides whether to buy foreign currency from you, and you don't have any say in the matter.

Suppose the previous example. You sell a call option on MXN1,000,000 with a premium of $0.0014 per unit and an exercise price of $0.083. The expiration date is a month from now.

As in the previous example, if the future spot rate of $0.086, the buyer exercises the call option and buys pesos from you on the option contract. Of course, you have to sell pesos to the buyer. In this case, you have to buy pesos at the future spot market at $0.086 and sell them for $0.083. In terms of revenues, you lose $0.003 per peso. In terms of your payoff:

profit/loss = selling price – buying price

In the case of the seller of a call option, the selling price consists of the addition of the exercise price and the premium. Because the seller buys the currency at the spot market, the buying price is the spot exchange rate:

profit/loss = (exercise price + premium) – spot exchange rate

Using the previous example:

Profit/loss = $0.083 + $0.0014 – $0.086 = –$0.0016

Note that the buyer's loss is limited to the premium, and his profits are unlimited. You, the seller of a call option, face unlimited loss, and your profits are limited to the premium.

Applying your right to sell: Put options

An FX put option gives you the right to sell foreign currency. As in the case of call options, put options can be used by MNCs and speculators alike. An American exporter may have account receivables in a foreign currency. In this case, the exchange rate risk is a possible depreciation of the foreign currency and the MNC would like to hedge against this risk. If you are a speculator, you plan to buy foreign currency at a cheaper price at the future spot market and sell it at a higher price on the put option. In this case, you'd like to take advantage of a possible depreciation of the foreign currency.

As an MNC or a speculator, a put option locks you in a minimum exchange rate to be received in the future. As in the case of the call option, your benchmark for exercising the put option or not is the future spot market. If the spot exchange rate is lower than the exercise price, the holder of the put option exercises the option to sell currency on the put option. If the future spot rate is higher than the exercise price, the holder of the put option lets the option expire without exercising it.

Three numerical exercises are provided: the use of put options by MNCs and speculators as well as selling a put option.

Using a put option: To exercise or not to exercise

A U.S. firm exports backpacks to Germany and expects to be paid €100,000 upon delivery in March. The American exporter has future receivables in euros and faces the risk of depreciation in the euro.

The American firm buys a put option with a premium of $0.021 per euro and the exercise price of $1.31. Therefore, the American exporter pays a total premium of $2,100 upfront ($0.021 × 100,000). If the firm decides to exercise the option, it will sell €100,000 for $131,000 (€100,000 × $1.31).

The exchange rate risk faced by the American exporter is depreciation of the euro. If in fact the euro depreciates in the future spot market, the American firm will exercise the put option and sell the euros at a higher rate on the put option. Suppose the future spot rate is $1.29. In this case, the American exporters exercises the put option and sells €100,000 for $131,000 (€100,000 × $1.31) instead of the spot market, which would give the firm only $129,000 (€100,000 × $1.29).

What if the future spot rate is $1.36? This time the American exporter has the opportunity to sell its euros for $136,000 (€100,000 × $1.36) at the spot market. Compared to the revenue from the put option ($131,000), using the spot market provides more dollars. Therefore, the firm lets the put option to expire.

In terms of speculating with put options, your goal is the same: you want to buy currency at a lower price and sell it at a higher price. Using a put option, you are planning to buy currency cheaper at the future spot market and sell it at a higher price on the put option. You must have an expectation of depreciation of the foreign currency.

Suppose you expect depreciation of the euro in a month. You buy a put option for €100,000 with a premium of $0.021 per unit and a strike price of $1.32. Again, you pay a total premium of $2,100 upfront ($0.021 × 100,000). The expiration date is a month from now. The dollar–euro exchange rate that you'll observe in the future spot market is the benchmark for your decision for exercising or not exercising the put option. When the future spot rate is lower than the exercise price, you'll exercise the put option. Suppose the spot rate one month from now is $1.31. In this case, your per-unit revenue is $0.01 ($1.32 – $1.31) because you'll buy euros at the spot market for $1.31 and sell them on the put option for $1.32. Your total revenue from this transaction is $1,000 (€100,000 × $0.01).

If the future spot rate is higher than the exercise price, you wouldn't exercise the put option. Suppose the future spot rate is $1.33. In this case, your per-unit revenue from buying euros at the spot market and selling them on a put option is negative ($1.32 – $1.33 = –$0.01). Now you let the put option expire.

In terms of your payoff or profit, in a put option, your profit/loss is indicated by:

profit/loss = selling price – buying price

Your selling price corresponds to the exercise price at which you sell currency on the put option. The premium that you paid upfront and the spot exchange rate at which you buy currency are subtracted from the exercise price. In other words:

profit/loss = exercise price – (spot exchange rate + premium)

Consider the case when you buy a put option for €100,000 with a premium of $0.021 per unit and a strike price of $1.32. You exercise your option to sell euros when the spot rate is $1.31. In this case, your per-unit loss is:

profit/loss = $1.32 – $1.31 – $0.021 = –$0.011

Considering the fact that you sell €100,000, your total loss is $1,100 (€100,000 × $0.011).

Selling a put option

When you sell a put option, you are selling the right to sell currency. Therefore, you become the buyer of currency and have no option. The buyer of the put option has the right to sell currency to you. You collect the premium and need to accommodate the decision of the buyer regarding exercising his option.

Suppose that you sell a put option with a premium of $0.019 per euro and an exercise price of $1.32. If the transaction amount is €100,000, you collect a premium of $1,900. Suppose the expiration date is a month from now.

If the future spot rate is $1.30, the buyer exercises the put option, because he buys euros at the spot market for $1.30 and sells them on the put option to you for $1.32, making $0.02 per euro ($1.32 – $1.30). But his gain is your loss. You have to buy euros from him at a higher rate ($1.32) and sell them at a lower rate at the spot market ($1.30).

Consider your payoff. The premium that you collect and the spot exchange rate at which you sell euros are your total selling price or what you receive in these transactions. The exercise price on the put option is the exchange rate at which you buy euros. Therefore:

profit/loss = selling price − buying price

profit/loss = (spot exchange rate + premium) - exercise price

profit/loss = $1.30 + $0.019 − $1.32 = −$0.001

Your per-unit loss is $-0.001 and your total loss is $100. In the case of selling the put option, the buyer of the put option can limit his loss to the premium, while his profits have no limits. You, the seller of the put option, can make a maximum per-unit profit that equals the premium; however, your loss has no limits.

Part IV

Conducting a Background Check: Changes in Currency through the Years

Checking Out Euro Exchange Rates

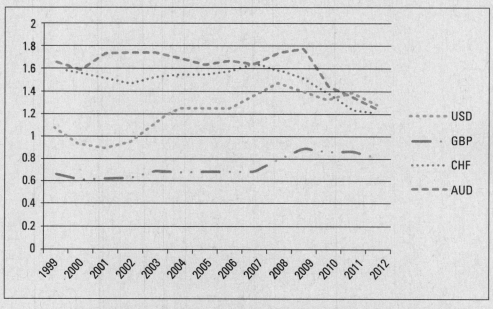

Data available at http://www.ecb.int/stats/exchange/eurofxref/html/index.en.html. Annual averages are calculated from daily data.
USD, GBP, CHF, and AUD represent the U.S. Dollar, British Pound Sterling, Swiss Franc, and Australian Dollar, respectively.

Learn how a common currency works and the effort that goes into creating one in the article "Creating a Common Currency" at www.dummies.com/extras/internationalfinance.

In This Part . . .

- I give some background on how the type of money has changed around the world through the ages.

- You'll be able to examine the close relationship between the type of money (fiat money vs. metallic standard) and the resulting exchange rate system.

- I share information on the Bretton Woods era (1944-1971). You'll learn that the reserve currency system of the Bretton Woods era was a specific type of metallic standard.

- I uncover the post-Bretton Woods era during which a variety of exchange rate regimes appeared. You'll understand why most developed countries adopted floating exchange rates, while developing countries opted out for unilaterally pegged exchange rates.

- You'll discover what the Optimum Currency Area (OCA) is and review its characteristics through the example of the euro.

Chapter 11

Macroeconomics of Monetary Systems and the Pre-Bretton Woods Era

....

In This Chapter

▶ Understanding the relationship between types of money and exchange rate regimes

▶ Examining the feasibility of independent macroeconomic policies under a metallic standard

▶ Reviewing the metallic standard years prior to 1944

....

This chapter is the first of three chapters that focus on the international monetary system from a historical perspective. The term *international monetary system* refers to (implicit or explicit) arrangements that govern exchange rates between currencies. The first three chapters in Part IV (Chapters 11–13) tell the story of various exchange rate regimes that defined the international monetary system between the 19th and 20th centuries. The last section of this chapter starts with the golden days of the gold standard during the mid- and late-1800s and ends right before the start of World War II. Chapter 12 covers the Bretton Woods era (1944–1973). Finally, Chapter 13 examines the exchange rate regimes of the post–Bretton Woods era.

While it is informative to examine historical episodes of the international monetary system, one needs quite a bit of background information to understand monetary systems. Therefore, this chapter provides this much-needed macroeconomic background organized under three categories:

✔ Types of money

✔ Relationship between the type of money and exchange rate regimes

✔ Macroeconomics of a metallic standard

This sequence indicates that the type of money affects the type of the exchange rate regime. When examining the types of money and the relationship between the types of money and exchange rate regimes, examples are provided from various eras.

Additionally, it's important to understand whether macroeconomic policies can be implemented under different exchange rate regimes. This discussion focuses particularly on macroeconomic policies under a metallic standard, because the historical episodes under review in this (up to 1939) and the next chapter (Chapter 12, 1944 – 1973) imply various types of a metallic standard. In terms of macroeconomic policies, I discuss how the exchange rate regime can be maintained and, at the same time, how policy makers can achieve price stability, growth, and full employment in a country.

In addition to giving you a fundamental understanding of the relationship between money types, exchange rate regimes, and macroeconomic policies, this chapter (along with Chapters 12 and 13) examines the history of international monetary systems. The monetary systems discussed in Chapters 12, and 13, give fundamental relationships that this chapter discusses further. Not surprisingly, the discussion of the history of international monetary systems reflects their chronological order. In terms of exchange rate regimes, this chapter starts with the earliest period and covers the pre–Bretton Woods era. In other words, it covers the period until the Bretton Woods conference of 1944, which aimed to introduce a new international monetary order after WWII.

Reviewing Types of Money through the Ages

Money is defined as a token that is generally accepted as payment for goods and services. The first examples of money in history as well as the changes in the type of money used around the world show the importance of its role as a medium of exchange. In fact, the definition of money implies the medium of exchange function of money: money is used to pay for goods and services.

The following three sections provide a short overview of the types of money in the past 3000 or more years.

Pure commodity standard

If there had been no money, trade would have been by barter. You can imagine how ineffective the barter system would have been. In a barter system, people exchange goods and services for other goods and services. Therefore, the barter system requires the double coincidence of wants. What if we had a barter system now? Suppose you want to learn about international finance, and I know something about international finance. In a barter system, we would have met in the market, with you carrying a sign stating, "I need lessons in international finance, and, in exchange, I can cook for whoever would teach me the subject," and me carrying a sign stating, "I can teach international finance, in exchange for cooking." It's a good thing we have money and you can just buy this book!

Why was there a change from the barter economy to an economy with money? When you note the places where the first examples of money appeared, it is clear that societies that were engaged in regional and even international trade must have realized the inefficiencies of the barter system. Among these societies with early examples of money are civilizations of Asia Minor, China, the Indus valley, and the Nile valley. A common characteristic of most of these early civilizations were that they were located in fertile regions and enjoyed surplus agricultural production. Their increasing exchange of agricultural goods with other types of goods (spices, textiles, metals, and so forth.) in a barter setup may have motivated the idea how efficient a monetary economy could be.

The first examples of money were coins of precious metals, such as gold or silver coins, which may date back to seventh century BC in Asia Minor and China. The first metallic standard is also called the pure metallic standard (gold or silver specie standard*).

Note that, even 3,000 years ago, civilizations understood that you shouldn't grow money in your backyard. If you did, rapidly increasing money supply would lead to higher inflation rates, thereby decreasing the purchasing power of money. Therefore, instead of using beans or olives as money, civilizations used precious metal coins, because the supply of precious metals is limited.

Sometimes people are nostalgic and think that monies of yesteryears were more reliable. For example, you may think that having coins in circulation made of precious metal would make an economy inflation-proof. However, the rulers understood how to create income for themselves even in a pure metallic standard. Whenever the ruler's treasury needed extra funds (for example, to finance a war) it reduced the precious metal content of coins and replaced it with an inexpensive metal, which is called *debasement*. If the initial gold content was 99 percent, the ruler decreased it to 75 percent, for example, and used the difference to buy whatever he needed to buy.

Rulers of these early civilizations were also clever enough to keep the look of the debased coins the same as the good ones. Early bankers or businessmen could put the coins to some tests, such as weighing them, and determine which ones were debased, but simple folks couldn't do so. Gresham's Law states that bad money drives out good money, meaning that people who knew the difference between good and debased coins used the debased ones as payments for goods and services and saved the good coins. Good coins disappeared from circulation, and bad coins in circulation drove up prices.

In addition to debasement, new gold mines may have been discovered. Such a discovery then increased the amount of gold in circulation, thereby increasing the price level and creating inflation. This exact scenario happened in Spain when expeditions to new continents brought back gold and silver in the late 15th and 16th centuries. Therefore, even in a pure commodity standard, inflation is possible.

Convertible paper money and gold standard

Another type of money appeared toward the end of the Middle Ages (about the 15th century), coinciding with expeditions to distant regions of the world that monarchs financed. These expeditions led to a significant increase in international trade at that time. Along with international trade, the flow of money among countries, which we would today call international capital flows was also increasing, contributing to globalization starting in the 15th century. To handle the increasing international trade, banks and bankers appeared on the scene. Double-entry bookkeeping also was introduced in medieval times, which made it easier to keep track of bank balances. Some meticulously kept business documents from mostly Italian businessmen have survived to our time and show sophisticated business practices and financial schemes.

This increase in the volume of economic activity required a different type of money to increase the efficiency of goods- and money-related transactions. Convertible bank money appeared around the 15th century and slowly replaced commodity money. Suppose you were a merchant in 15th-century Venice. You deposited your 50 gold coins with a banker, and he gave you a certificate that you could use in your transactions as money. Therefore, at the beginning, convertible bank money was based on precious metal coins.

At the time when convertible paper money appeared, there was no monetary authority. Bankers created deposits that were convertible to gold. While the Bank of England is the oldest central bank and has been around since the 17th century, many central banks started in the 19th and 20th centuries. Convertible bank money went through some changes after its introduction in the 15th century.

In the earlier periods of convertible paper money, banks promised to pay precious metals but generally held fractional reserves of precious metals, lending out some of the precious metals. On occasion, more depositors would want to withdraw metal than the actual stock of precious metals held by banks, which led to bank runs. Major countries used silver, gold, or both to back their money.

Despite its variations, convertible paper money lasted until 1973. Therefore, you may think that a metallic standard in some shape or form was the only type of money until 1973. This thinking isn't entirely correct. In one of the upcoming sections "Understanding the macroeconomics of the metallic standard," I discuss the fact that a metallic standard does not allow monetary policy to be used to address a country's economic problems or create additional funds. Therefore, the metallic standard didn't continuously last until 1973.

During the world wars in the 20th century, many other wars, civil wars, and revolutions, countries went off the metallic standard, printed money without backing, created inflation, and paid for the expense of armed conflicts. The history is full of examples where countries dropped the metallic standard during wars and revolutions to be able to raise revenues. Examples of the suspension of the gold parity include France during the French Revolution (1789), Great Britain during the Napoleonic wars (1803-1815), the U.S. during the Civil War (1861-1865), and many countries during WWI (1914-1918) and WWII (1939-1945).

Fiat money

The Bretton Woods era (1944-1973) was the last period with a metallic standard. Since the end of the Bretton Woods era in 1973, money is the fiat money. Whenever paper money is just paper and has no convertibility to something of value and is therefore not backed by a precious metal such as gold, it is called fiat money.

Fiat money was nothing new to the world when it was introduced in 1973. The French Revolution probably was the first widespread issuance of paper money. As indicated previously in the section on convertible paper money, countries abandoned the metallic standard during wars, revolutions, and other armed conflicts. Until 1973, whenever paper money wasn't backed by a previous metal, such as during a war, it was fiat money.

Clearly, fiat money has no intrinsic value, which means that it cannot be converted into a specific amount of precious metal. Nevertheless, fiat money is legal tender. It's also valuable because other people are willing to take the money in exchange for goods and services. Otherwise, it would be worth the value of paper on which it is printed.

Because fiat money isn't convertible into a precious metal, monetary policy affects the purchasing power of fiat money. In the fiat money system, central banks have the responsibility to promote price stability and, therefore, maintain the purchasing power of money.

Examining the Relationship between Types of Money and Exchange Rate Regimes

A close relationship exists between the types of money and the types of exchange rate regimes. This section provides information about the fundamentals of this relationship.

Exchange rates in a commodity standard system

A metallic standard in more than one country implies a fixed exchange rate. For example, if the international monetary system is a gold standard, each country defines the price of its currency in gold or silver, which is called *parity*. Suppose that the gold parity in the U.S. and the U.K. is $35 and £17 for an ounce of gold, respectively. This leads to the dollar–pound exchange rate of $2.06 per British pound ($35 = £17).

In Chapter 12, you see that there are variations of metallic standards. For example, the Bretton Woods system introduced in 1944 was also called the *reserve currency standard* or *dollar exchange standard*, in which the dollar was pegged to the gold and all other currencies were pegged to the dollar. This particular international monetary system also leads to fixed exchange rates.

For most of the Bretton Woods years (1944–1973), the gold parity in the U.S. was $35 for an ounce of gold. In terms of other currencies being pegged to the dollar, suppose that the pound–dollar and the German mark–dollar exchange rates were £0.49 and DM1.7 per dollar, respectively. Then the pound–German mark exchange rate would be £0.29 per German mark (£0.49 = DM1.7).

Later in this chapter, and in the next chapter, you'll read about the suspension of the metallic standard during wars. In these times, there was no metallic standard existed for anchoring exchange rates.

Exchange rates in a fiat money system

As discussed earlier in this chapter, a fiat currency has no intrinsic value. In other words, its value is not based on a precious metal. Monetary policy determines the purchasing power of the currency. The exchange rate regime involving fiat currencies is called a flexible or floating exchange rate regime, where the exchange rate is determined in international foreign exchange markets. Chapters 5–7, which cover exchange rate determination, implicitly assume that the currencies in question are fiat currencies and that exchange rates between fiat currencies are determined in foreign exchange markets, as they are today. These chapters of exchange rate determination emphasize the relevance of monetary policy for explaining the changes in exchange rates.

An international monetary system in a fiat currency world is characterized by floating exchange rates. In fact, most developed countries' exchange rates are characterized as such. Chapter 12 examines floating or flexible exchange rate regimes and examines the possibility of government as well as central bank intervention in exchange rates under the floating exchange rate regime.

Fiat currencies do not necessarily lead to a flexible exchange rate regime. Although almost all developed countries adopted a floating exchange rate regime starting in 1973, most developing countries adopted pegged exchange rate regimes, where governments unilaterally decide what the exchange rate is going to be.

Chapter 13 examines the different types of pegged regimes during the post–Bretton Woods era, the reason for their implementation, and their consequences. Dollarization and currency board are examples of hard pegs. *Dollarization* involves replacing the domestic currency with another country's currency. A *currency board* indicates the commitment of a central bank to a certain exchange rate by being willing to trade domestic currency for foreign currency at a fixed rate. In the pure case, a currency board keeps 100 percent reserves of the foreign currency. In this case, the central bank doesn't conduct monetary policy to address the country's economic problems; monetary policy maintains the peg. In addition to hard pegs, countries can implement soft pegs that overvalue or undervalue the domestic currency, in an attempt to make either imports or exports cheaper or attract foreign portfolio investment.

Understanding the Macroeconomics of the Metallic Standard

To understand why certain problems appear under certain exchange rate regimes, you need to discover the macroeconomic fundamentals of the metallic standard. This section does precisely that; it shows what kind of macroeconomic objectives countries can have under a metallic standard. Remember, a metallic standard leads to a fixed exchange rate regime. So in addition to whatever countries want to achieve in their domestic economies, they need to uphold the fixed exchange rate. As you can guess, doing so isn't easy because countries' domestic economic policies may exert pressure on the fixed exchange rate to the direction of devaluation or revaluation. Therefore, in this section, I discuss maintaining internal and external balance to see whether a country can achieve its domestic economic goals while preserving the fixed exchange rate.

As if the difficulty of achieving the internal and external balance isn't enough, two additional challenges make maintaining internal and external balance even harder under a metallic standard. First, interdependence between countries' macroeconomic policies comes into play because fixed exchange rates enable a country to export its current macroeconomic problems to other countries. Second, the so-called trilemma in international finance implies that some of the components of the internal and external balance aren't compatible.

The following sections delve into the internal and external balance, the interdependence between macroeconomic policies, and the trilemma.

Maintaining internal balance

The term *internal balance* refers to full employment with price stability, which is a tall order. Full employment does not refer to 0 percent unemployment. It implies a positive unemployment rate at which the country uses its available human and physical resources and produces output at its long-run capacity consistent with a well-functioning labor market. Therefore, the full employment level of unemployment (also called the natural rate of unemployment) mainly consists of frictional unemployment (people looking for better-paying or more suited jobs, or people between jobs).

The one piece of the internal balance is full employment, the other is price stability. Price stability implies that the changes in the price level are small, gradual, and expected, so that the financial decisions of households and businesses aren't materially affected by the changes in the average price level. In other words, the country sees no substantial amount of expected or unexpected inflation (an increase in the average price level), disinflation (a decline in the inflation rate), or deflation (a decline in the average price level).

Monetary policy can be used to stabilize prices and affect employment. However, a metallic standard makes monetary policy useless for both of these purposes. Suppose a country is under the gold standard and the central bank of the country wants to decrease unemployment and promote growth. An increase in the money supply might achieve this goal by raising prices. But if prices rise in the country, gold is worth less in that country and gold would flow out, lowering the money supply and the price level. In short, the central bank cannot change the money supply to pursue domestic goals.

Whenever you read about a change in monetary policy, you should understand the kind of monetary policy that can have an effect on the price level.

Because monetary policy is ineffective under a metallic standard, the burden of promoting economic growth and full employment falls on fiscal policy. This task is no easy one, either. Policy makers have to be aware of the fact that tax or expenditure policies can improve the country's productive capacity. Therefore, in a fixed exchange rate system, the government needs to focus on policies that increase the productivity of the country, such as education reform, tax reform, and, generally speaking, incentive-compatible institutions.

The fact that monetary policy isn't effective under a metallic standard may be helpful in achieving price stability. Avoiding large changes in the growth rate of money supply also avoids large changes in the average price level, unless changes in the supply of the precious metal change the average price level.

This section concludes that monetary policy under a commodity standard is useless for maintaining internal balance with a fixed value of the money in terms of a precious metal. The next section adds to the challenge of achieving internal balance by introducing the maintenance of a fixed exchange rate, which indicates external balance.

Maintaining external balance

External balance implies that the fixed exchange rate is maintained. The most important variable that may prevent the maintenance of the fixed exchange rate is the current account. Because the discussion about the external balance under a metallic standard involves the balance of payments, you first need some basic knowledge about the major components of the balance of payments.

The balance of payments (BOP) contains a country's transactions with the rest of the world. These transactions include international trade (exports and imports) and the flow of short- and long-term capital. Therefore, the BOP has two main components: current and financial accounts:

- **Current account:** Includes mainly exports and imports (as well as items called invisibles, such as tourism and workers' remittances).

- **Financial account:** Contains purchases and sales of foreign and domestic assets as well as investments.

In a metallic standard such as the gold standard, the BOP has a prominent role. In this particular monetary system, the central bank fixes the gold parity (the relationship between the price of gold and the currency). But to establish the gold parity, the central bank needs adequate gold reserves to maintain the gold parity. Maintaining external balance means trying to avoid significant changes in these gold reserves. Under a metallic standard, safeguarding the fixed exchange rate and maintaining the stability of gold reserves — in short, maintaining external balance — is accomplished by the BOP with the help of the *price–specie–flow mechanism*.

Here is the definition of this mechanism and how it helps achieving the external balance. First of all, the term *specie* refers to the precious metal — for example, gold. Therefore, the price–specie–flow mechanism explains the relationship between money as a precious metal, prices, and international transactions such as trade and capital flows. Second, the mechanism implies that money supply (as specie), prices, and the BOP are related. If a country runs a current account surplus and accumulates specie, prices in the country will increase, making this country's goods more expensive to foreigners. This situation will then reduce the current account surplus in the home country and the current account deficit in the foreign country.

Under the classical gold standard and without a central bank (as in the U.S. until 1913 when Congress created the Federal Reserve System), the price–specie–flow mechanism did work pretty much this way. People took gold to the government and got money, then spent it. However, it worked this way less in the U.K. because the Bank of England could accumulate reserves and not increase the money stock.

In a metallic system, some countries may face persistent current account surpluses or deficits. For example, if a country runs persistent current account surpluses (exports exceed imports), its central bank accumulates gold, which revalues the currency. But under the fixed exchange rate regime, this situation can't be allowed. One way to reduce the amount of reserves is to engage in international lending. On the other hand, if a country runs persistent current account deficits (imports exceed exports), its central bank would lose gold reserves, leading to devaluation. To avoid devaluation, this country either attracts funds or borrows.

Even though borrowing (in times of current account deficit) and lending (in times of current account surplus) is assumed to reduce the pressure on the fixed exchange rate, they could be problematic as well. Suppose a country with large and persistent current account deficits tries to avoid devaluation of its currency by borrowing. Increasing borrowing may lead to payment difficulties, which in turn would increase the cost of borrowing (with higher interest rates on loans). Such problems may even lead to the country's exclusion from international capital markets. Large and persistent current account surpluses are not desirable either. In this case, international lending may adversely affect domestic investment by decreasing it.

Checking out the interdependence of macroeconomic conditions

Maintaining internal and external balance is challenging under a metallic standard. In addition to the difficulty of maintaining the internal and external balance, a metallic system has other challenging characteristics. One is the interdependence of macroeconomic conditions under a fixed exchange rate system.

The interdependence of macroeconomic conditions implies that the fixed exchange rate regime allows countries to export their macroeconomic problems to other countries. The main channel of interdependence is international trade. A country experiencing lower growth and higher unemployment doesn't import as much from other countries. The decline in other countries' exports sectors can create lower growth and higher unemployment in the exporting countries.

If a country experiences higher inflation compared to its trade partners, other countries' goods become less expensive to domestic consumers (at the given exchange rate). And increased demand for other countries' goods increases trade partners' inflation as well.

Note that the only reason for the ability to export one's own problems to other countries is a fixed exchange rate. The interdependence of macro-economic conditions is possible because the exchange rate isn't allowed to change. Consider the example of the lower-growth country. If exchange rates are flexible and not fixed, the lower-growth country's exchange rate depreciates, making its exports less expensive and its imports more expensive. This situation then increases the country's exports and decreases its imports. In the case of the higher-inflation country, and assuming a flexible exchange rate regime, the same events (starting with the depreciation of the currency) happen.

The moral of the story is that if there's a fixed variable and changes in the economic environment aren't allowed to affect the fixed variable, frictions will occur. Therefore, the spread of economic problems through international trade can be viewed as a friction that occurs under the fixed exchange rate regime.

Finding compatibility: The trilemma

The *trilemma* is a three-faceted dilemma faced by small and open economies under any fixed exchange rate regime. (A small economy is an economy that cannot influence the world interest rate. An open economy allows international trade, as well as international flows of capital.) This concept shows the limits on economic policy under a commodity standard.

The trilemma implies that, under the fixed exchange rate regime, the simultaneous implementation of the following three items isn't possible:

- ✔ Internal balance
- ✔ External balance
- ✔ Free capital flows

It means that all three items cannot be manipulated simultaneously by the government and a government can choose at most two of these three items.

Suppose the government wants to determine all three items independently. In other words, a country aims to maintain the internal and external balance while opening the country to free capital flows. If the country implements an expansionary monetary policy in an attempt to increase output and employment, the increase in the money supply decreases the domestic interest rate. Because the country doesn't have any capital controls, both domestic and foreign investors move funds abroad to receive higher interest rates in other countries. They would sell domestic currency in exchange for foreign currency, which would devalue the domestic currency. To prevent the currency from devaluating, and to maintain the fixed exchange rate, the central bank intervenes in the foreign exchange market by selling some of its foreign currency reserves to buy its own currency.

If the government continues in its expansionary monetary policy, investors will also continue to move funds out of the country and the central bank's foreign exchange reserves will eventually be exhausted. Chapters 12 and 13 show that this is a speculative attack, or a run on a currency. At the end, the fixed exchange rate is broken, and a large devaluation of the domestic currency follows.

Okay, so all three items can't be simultaneously possible. You can pick any two from the previous list and think about what you can accomplish and what you need to let go. For example, if you want to focus on maintaining internal and external balance, you need to implement some capital controls. Otherwise, whenever you implement a monetary policy change, it will end up pressuring the fixed exchange rate to change.

If you prefer maintaining external balance and free capital movement, then internal balance (full employment with price stability) can't be achieved through domestic monetary policies. In this case, you need to revamp the country's fiscal policy framework.

If you keep internal balance and free capital movement, and forgo external balance (in other words, the fixed exchange rate), this system becomes a lot like the current flexible exchange rate system examined in Chapter 13. You can use monetary policy to your heart's content to address the domestic economic situation of the country and allow international capital movements, which changes the exchange rate. Chapters 5, 6, and 7 discuss that, under flexible exchange rates, an expansionary and contractionary monetary policy leads to the depreciation and appreciation of the currency, respectively.

Discovering the Monetary System of the Pre–Bretton Woods Era

The macroeconomic fundamentals of a metallic standard and the resulting fixed exchange rates in the previous sections lay the groundwork for understanding the various periods of fixed exchange rate regimes.

In this chapter, you'll read about the historical periods of fixed exchange rate regimes until the Bretton Woods conference of 1944. One reason to use this conference as a benchmark is that the Bretton Woods era (1944-1971) had a stronger multilateral characteristic than the preceding fixed exchange rate systems. In fact, by reading about the international monetary order of the pre-Bretton Woods era in this chapter you'll understand the efforts of the Bretton Woods conference to introduce a multilateral international monetary order in Chapter 12.

This section starts with the heyday of the gold standard in the 19th century and ends right before the start of World War II. The reason for calling the period 1870–1914 the heyday of the gold standard is that, during this period, the international financial system was rapidly integrating. The historical accounts reflect the difficulties associated with maintaining the internal and external balance, the interdependence of macroeconomic problems in countries connected via international trade, and the trilemma.

In terms of the historical episodes, this section includes the bimetallic era (until 1870), the pre–World War I era (1870–1914), and the interwar years

(1918–1939). As mentioned previously, because monetary policy isn't effective under a metallic standard, countries went off the gold standard during the World War I (1914–1918) and World War II (1939-1945), to pay for war expenses.

The bimetallic era (until 1870)

Although the gold standard dates back to 1821 in the United Kingdom as a legal institution, until the early 1870s, many countries had a bimetallic standard by pegging their currency to both silver and gold. In this case, countries had to maintain parity between gold and silver money as well. Not surprisingly, gold was generally worth several times more per ounce than silver.

Here are advantages and disadvantages of the bimetallic system:

- **Advantage:** When the relative market price of gold and silver changed, the use of gold and silver dollar coins was adjusted. Whichever metal's price was rising, coins made of this metal were disappearing from circulation. For example, when the gold price rose relative to that of silver, gold coins were used to buy silver coins and gold coins went out of circulation. The fact that coins made of scarce (therefore more expensive) metal disappeared from circulation may have reduced the inflation rate and acted like insurance for price stability.

- **Disadvantage:** What was described as an advantage may turn out to be a disadvantage. The flexibility in the use of gold or silver coins can lead to instability, especially when the relative price of these metals change frequently and substantially. As discussion in this section shows, frequent wars, revolutions, and so on may have magnified this particular disadvantage of the bimetallic standard.

The U.S. and the bimetallic standard

After the American War for Independence, the U.S. introduced the bimetallic standard in 1792 and continued to be on it until the Civil War. The bimetallic system required adequate amounts of gold and silver to back paper currency. It also required establishing parity between gold and silver. In the 18th century, for example, parity was 1 ounce of gold for 15 ounces of silver.

The bimetallic standard in the U.S. went through various changes. The Independent Treasury Act of 1840 allowed the Treasury to do business only in gold or silver coins, in an attempt to take the fiscal authority out of the banking system. The government's attempt to use specie (gold or silver coins) in its transactions reduced the increase in credit using paper money. However, specie payments to and from the government affected the amount of specie in circulation and therefore the money market.

In the late 1840s, silver became overvalued relative to gold. Hoarding of silver led to a reduction of gold in circulation and caused a search for gold, which led to the California Gold Rush of 1849. Later in 1853, in an attempt to keep silver coins in circulation, the U.S. reduced the silver weight of coins.

The later part of the bimetallic era coincides with the Free Banking Era (1837–1862). During the Free Banking Era, the U.S. had no central bank. In fact, until 1863, only state banks existed. These banks issued money backed by specie (gold and silver coins). However, they were short-lived, and about one third of banks went out of business because of losses on their assets.

During the final crisis of the Free Banking Era in 1857, the U.S. suspended payments in silver. Nevertheless, the bimetallic standard was used until the Civil War (1861–1865). As in the case of every armed conflict, the bimetallic standard was abolished in 1861 to print money and finance the war. Greenbacks introduced during the Civil War were fiat currency (see the section "Fiat money," earlier in this chapter), which led to higher inflation rates during the war years. After a decade following the Civil War, the U.S. introduced the gold standard in 1875.

The bimetallic standard around the world

Britain was one of the first countries to leave the bimetallic standard, and it introduced the gold standard in 1844. In addition to the fact that the Napoleonic Wars had left Britain in serious silver shortage, Britain's wars with China reduced the amount of silver-based money.

As in the case of Britain, one of the problems of the bimetallic era was that it coincided with a period of world history filled with wars and revolutions. Especially in Europe, frequent armed conflicts reflected the pain of getting out of the empire setting and establishing nation states. The following example looks at Austria, a country that was involved in many military conflicts during the bimetallic era. The example shows that it's no wonder countries sacrificed the metallic standard and fixed exchange rates to finance wars.

Between the late 18th century and the late 19th century, Austria's monetary history was one of printing money and then promising to exercise budgetary discipline. For example, the government announced its intention in 1811 to stop printing money and issue a new currency, to decrease the amount of paper money in circulation. However, the renewal of the Napoleonic war in 1812 prompted Austria to again print too much of the new currency. At the end of the Napoleonic wars, France made reparations payments to Austria, and the Austrian government promised to use those payments to retire some of the money in circulation. However, when the Hungarian revolt against the Austrian rule began in 1848, the government suspended silver redemption and banned the export of gold and silver. Then the Crimean War (1853–1856), wars against the Italian nationalists in northern Italy, and a devastating war with Prussia (1866) followed. Only after the Prussian War in 1866 did Austrian governments exercise discipline on their budget and stop printing money. Eventually, the then-Austrian currency (florin) had a premium against silver. Even though Austria had been on a silver standard since 1816, armed conflicts didn't allow the country to effectively implement the metallic standard for half a century.

The later parts of the bimetallic era coincided with important developments in financial markets. During the 19th century, developed countries started introducing their central banks. Additionally, the connection between financial markets of developed countries was strengthening, which led to various monetary unions between countries. The next section discusses these unions.

Gold standard of the pre–World War I era (1870–1914)

The period 1870–1914 is considered the heyday of the international gold standard. The reason for the successful maintenance of fixed exchange rates for about four decades is that internal balance generally was sacrificed to maintain external balance, or the fixed exchange rate, during this period. The success of the pre–World War I gold standard is important when you consider the fact that no multilateral agreement enforced the system. It is equally important to realize that the commitment to the gold standard came with the cost of lower growth rates.

In the late 19th century, the main benefit of joining the gold standard was to gain access to capital markets such as London, Paris, or Berlin. The tradeoff was the requirement to acquire gold reserves. However, many countries were ready to pay the price of access to capital markets. Coordination was achieved by maintaining convertibility, which fixed exchange rates between national monetary units within narrow limits.

A small number of countries also developed monetary agreements. In fact, one of the remarkable developments of this period was the emergence of regional monetary unions. Although no multilateral agreements were struck, countries' actions implied loyalty to the metallic standard. Consider two examples:

- Belgium, Italy, Switzerland, and France developed the Latin Monetary Union, starting in 1866. It lasted until the start of WWI in 1914.

- Denmark, Norway, and Sweden established the Scandinavian Monetary Union between 1873 and 1914.

These monetary unions allowed their members to treat each other's currency as legal tender. Central banks in these monetary unions accepted each other's money and established a clearinghouse to settle balances.

However, problems were also brewing in the background. Whereas Britain was having large and persistent current account surpluses, other countries were running deficits. Remember that the price–specie–flow mechanism should have taken care of these imbalances. This mechanism implies that when surplus countries lend and deficit countries borrow, this reduces the pressure of imbalances on the fixed exchange rate. However, surplus countries that were accumulating gold reserves were not lending to deficit countries. Central banks of countries with current account deficits were losing their gold reserves fast.

Especially toward 1914, the price-specie-flow mechanism ceased to function properly: The responsibility fell almost solely on deficit countries, while surplus countries continued accumulating their current account surpluses (and, therefore, gold reserves). As a result, deficit countries felt the need to implement increasingly contractionary monetary policies that raised interest rates in these countries. Deficit countries did so to attract foreign capital flows into these countries. However, contractionary policies and higher interest rates led to decreasing growth and increasing unemployment.

As World War I started in 1914, countries abolished the gold standard. The world went back to the fiat currency system until 1918.

The interwar years (1918–1939)

As in the case of other wars, governments suspended the gold standard during World War I, to increase the money supply and pay for the war. Therefore, as in the case of all post-war eras, many countries faced much higher inflation rates at the end of World War I.

The U.S. returned to the gold standard in 1919, and other European countries and Japan reinstated the gold parity a couple years later. Considering the limited gold supply of the early 1920s, the European countries and Japan decided on a partial gold standard, where reserves consisted of partly gold and partly other countries' currencies. This standard is known as the *gold exchange standard*.

These countries attempted to restore the gold standard in 1918 at the end of World War I, but for the most part, their attempts remained unsuccessful. One reason for the lack of success is that efforts were mostly unilateral. It means that countries decided about post-WWI parities without consulting each other. This tendency to unilateralism had its own reasons. Post–World

War I inflation rates varied among countries, depending on how much they inflated the economy during the war. But some countries chose their pre–World War I gold parity even though their post–World War I inflation rates were much higher than those of the prewar period.

Trying to move back to the gold standard

Britain was one country that went back to its pre–World War I parity, even though the post-war price level was higher than the prewar price level. The British government made this decision to maintain its credibility as the world's superpower. However, maintaining the unrealistic prewar parity meant that the British pound was overvalued. To avoid further problems with the gold parity, Britain implemented a monetary policy of higher interest rates (or lower quantity of money, essentially a contractionary monetary policy), which led to a weak output performance and unemployment in the years following the end of World War I.

Another important event after World War I later affected the decisions made during the Bretton Woods conference of 1944. As in the case of other countries, Germany suspended gold convertibility in 1914. However, unlike other countries, it couldn't return to the gold standard after World War I. Heavy reparations payments imposed on Germany forced the country to continue having a fiat currency and to print German marks, which created hyperinflation in Germany in the 1920s. Even though Germany recovered from hyperinflation during the National Socialist regime, that very regime led to World War II in 1939. In Chapter 12, I state that the imposition of heavy reparations payments on Germany was noted as a mistake during the Bretton Woods conference in 1944.

Therefore, as far as the gold standard is concerned, the interwar period started on the wrong foot. Three fundamental problems characterized the interwar era from the beginning:

- The post–World War I gold parities weren't consistent with the post-war price levels.

- Aware of the first problem, and in an attempt to maintain the external balance (to keep the fixed exchange rates and not lose gold reserves), central banks in many countries implemented contractionary monetary policies, which led to output decline and unemployment.

- Despite the fact that a metallic standard requires a good amount of cooperation, the international monetary system of the interwar years cannot be described as such a system. The international disagreements ranged from disputes over Germany's reparation payments during the early post–World War I years to trade restrictions during the Great Depression.

During the Depression era (1925–1931), a series of disastrous financial events affected almost all major countries. Examples of such events are the October 1929 New York stock market crash and bank failures around the world, especially in Austria and Germany in the early 1930s.

Additionally, Britain paid the price of an overvalued pound, and the currency was attacked in 1931. In other words, investors who were holding British pounds converted them into gold. The Bank of England lost a substantial amount of its gold reserves during this attack. This situation worsened bank failures around the world because banks in other countries were holding pound reserves, and suddenly the value of their foreign currency reserves substantially dropped.

Nevertheless, the 1931 attack on the British pound may have had an upside. Not only Britain, but also Australia, New Zealand, and Canada left the gold standard and both implemented expansionary monetary policies and lowered interest rates to promote growth and employment. These countries experienced the Great Depression as a severe recession, but other countries — including the U.S., France, and Switzerland — remained committed to the gold standard and, therefore, experienced the Great Depression.

Holding the gold standard in the U.S.

This section focuses on what it meant for the U.S. to hold on to the gold standard during the Depression years.

Because a metallic standard requires maintaining the external balance, the U.S. was trying hard to prevent fluctuations in its gold reserves. In fact, the dangerous direction at that time was to lose a substantial amount of gold reserves. To avoid losing gold reserves and promote incoming capital flows, the U.S. tried to keep interest rates higher through contractionary monetary policies.

Declines in the money supply led to deflationary pressures, which created considerable problems for the banking system. Similar to the British pound, the dollar experienced a speculative attack in 1931. Foreign and domestic investors and U.S. banks were converting paper money into gold, depleting the Fed's gold reserves.

Some economists blame the Fed's insistence on the gold standard for the long duration and the severity of the Great Depression. Holding on to the gold standard prevented the Fed from implementing expansionary monetary policies to stimulate the economy and act as a lender of last resort during the time of bank runs.

By the way, the tendency toward contractionary monetary policy to maintain the external balance had been a problem of the metallic standard since the 19th century. Some economists call this race to higher interest rates under a metallic standard a *deflationary vortex*.

As previously mentioned in this section, the lack of international coordination continued throughout the interwar period. It started with unilaterally determined gold parities following World War I and continued with disputes over Germany's reparations payments. The lack of international coordination reached its height during the Great Depression, when countries started using trade restrictions to prevent the loss of gold reserves. Especially deficit countries were imposing trade restrictions to favorably affect their current account and, therefore, their external balance.

Even though the fixed exchange rate normally implies the effect of external imbalance on the exchange rate (which, in turn affects the demand for foreign goods), during the 1930s, policymakers reversed the direction of causality and used trade restrictions to improve their current account. For example, the U.S. introduced the infamous Smoot–Hawley tariff in 1930. Along with trade restrictions, strong capital controls led to a drastic decline in capital flows starting in the late 1920s.

In 1932, Roosevelt ran successfully against President Hoover, who held on to the gold standard. However, in 1934, the gold parity implied an over 40 percent devaluation of the dollar, from \$20.67 to \$35 to the troy ounce (a measure that is used to weigh precious metals, 1 troy ounce = 31.1034768 grams). When the last countries with a gold standard left the gold parity in 1936, the metallic standard was gone and the world was preparing to go to war.

Despite differences among the metallic standards of the pre-Bretton Woods episodes (up to 1944), one of their common characteristics seems to be the lack of international cooperation when identifying parities. Another one implies the impossibility of conducting monetary policy to promote growth and employment.

At another's expense

Attempts to improve one's own economic outcome at the expense of other countries are called beggar-thy-neighbor policies. These policies not only worsen economic conditions in other countries, but they also lead to retaliatory actions by injured countries, which ultimately makes all countries worse off.

Chapter 12

The Bretton Woods Era (1944–1973)

In This Chapter

▶ Understanding the purpose of the Bretton Woods Conference

▶ Identifying the international monetary system that came out of the conference

▶ Pinpointing what did and didn't work during the Bretton Woods era

The Bretton Woods era has a unique position among the historical experiences with an international monetary system. One of the reasons that made this era so special was the fact that the Bretton Woods system was much more multilateral than any of the previous international monetary systems. Forty-four countries attended the Bretton Woods Conference in 1944, but the number of countries in the system toward the end of the era was more than double that number. However, the system's highly multilateral nature wasn't enough for it to enjoy success: The Bretton Woods era lasted less than 30 years and it wasn't very successful while it lasted.

This chapter covers the Bretton Woods era from start to finish. It shows the characteristics of the post-WWII international monetary system until the early 1970s. As Chapter 11 indicates, wars, revolutions, and so on, interrupted the metallic standard and WWII was not different in this regard. The Bretton Woods conference of 1944 marked the time when countries were trying to select a viable post-war international monetary system. In this chapter, I talk about the alternative proposals made during the conference, which proposal was accepted, and how the Bretton Woods system worked (or didn't work).

Gaining Insight into the Bretton Woods System

By the time the Bretton Woods Conference started, participating countries were aware of the decisions and policies of yesteryears, especially the ones made during the interwar years (1918–1939) that led to the demise of the previous international monetary systems. As Chapter 11 explains, the tendency toward contractionary monetary policies to maintain the fixed exchange rates and toward trade restrictions to reduce persistent and large current account deficits had disastrous consequences during the 1920s and early 1930s. The Bretton Woods system sought to avoid protectionist trade policies and competitively contractionary monetary policies that led to deflation during the Great Depression. It wanted to reestablish the metallic standard after WWII without repeating the mistakes of the previous metallic standard periods.

However, pinpointing past mistakes wasn't helpful in identifying and avoiding the mistakes associated with the new system. As Chapter 11 explains, the Bretton Woods Conference introduced a variation of the gold and gold exchange standard called the reserve currency system. Because the U.S. emerged from World War II as the new military and economic superpower, the dollar became the reserve currency. The special position of the dollar helped the U.S. afford autonomous macroeconomic policies, to some extent — and the very countries the U.S. helped rebuild (mainly Western European countries and Japan) later resented those policies.

Other reasons were to blame for the weakening of the Bretton Woods system. Among them was this one: Things change. One of the important changes in the external environment was rapidly developing and integrating financial markets. As Chapter 11 explains, the trilemma in international finance implies that maintaining internal and external balance in a fixed exchange rate system is impossible while capital flows freely. Therefore, at the beginning, the Bretton Woods system allowed capital controls. However, in the second half of the 1960s, it was clear that rapidly developing, highly liquid, and fast-integrating financial markets were reducing the efficiency of capital controls. The U.S., along with other countries, tried to intervene in some of the markets, such as the gold market, with little success.

The end of the Bretton Woods system came in the early 1970s, when another fixed exchange rate regime was dissolved. In 1944, the U.S. was a military and economic power whose currency seemed to be as good as gold. At the end of the era, the U.S. was fighting against large current account deficits, disappearing gold and foreign currency reserves, higher inflation rates, and constant pressure to devalue the dollar.

Attending the Bretton Woods Conference in 1944

In July 1944, more than 700 delegates from 44 nations attended the United Nations Monetary and Financial Conference in Bretton Woods (New Hampshire), which later became known as the Bretton Woods Conference. The purpose of the conference was related to one of the facts of the metallic standard that Chapter 11 explores. A metallic standard doesn't allow monetary policy to be conducted, which becomes a serious limitation during wars. As in the case of all wars and revolutions, the metallic standard was also abandoned during World War II in most countries. Therefore, the main objective of the Bretton Woods Conference was to establish a new post-war international monetary order.

This section provides information about the agenda of the Bretton Woods Conference. The relevance of the conference agenda lies in the fact that this conference was very different from the previous monetary arrangements that aimed to bring countries back to a metallic standard following a war. First, the sheer amount of participation made the Bretton Woods Conference a strongly multilateral setting. Second, more than ever before, and probably due to the extent of destruction during World War II, the participants were keen to make a list of all previous efforts toward establishing a metallic standard and to identify what worked and what failed in the past.

Lessons learned from the past and new realizations

The collective awareness among the participants of the Bretton Woods Conference had two main dimensions. First, many countries realized that certain past decisions weren't particularly helpful for a successfully functioning international monetary system. Second, in the light of the new developments, there were also some new realizations. Following is an explanation of each of these dimensions.

Lessons learned from the past:

- ✓ The conference participants wanted to avoid repeating the same mistake following World War I. In an attempt to punish Germany, countries had imposed large reparation payments starting in 1918. These payments were supposed to cover the debt accumulated by Allied forces during the war and help them pay to rebuild their countries. However, because of the heavy burden of these payments, Germany never recovered from World War I. To make reparation payments, Germany printed money and created hyperinflation. Especially during the Weimar Republic (1921–1924) in Germany, hyperinflation worsened: One pound of bread cost DM3 billion.

- ✓ One of the responses to the Great Depression was to implement trade restrictions (see Chapter 11). Starting in the late 1920s, most countries introduced trade restrictions (tariffs, quotas, and so on) to improve their current account deficits and stop the reserve loss. Additionally, retaliation against trade restrictions only pushed the level of restrictions to international trade higher and further suppressed output and employment in many countries.

Meeting of the minds

Aware of the limitations of trade restrictions during the Great Depression years, when President Roosevelt and British Prime Minister Churchill met on a ship in the North Atlantic in 1941, free trade was on their minds. The resulting Atlantic Charter emphasized the right of all nations to equal access to trade.

New realizations:

✔ Despite cooperation, the tensions between the Western Allies and the Soviet Union became increasingly visible. By the way, the Soviet Union didn't attend the Bretton Woods Conference. The conference participants declared their ideological views so that they would rely on capitalism to solve the economic problems of the post–World War II era. Despite their differences in views regarding the desired extent of government interventions in markets, the countries represented in the conference were dedicated to capitalism.

✔ The then-flourishing Keynesian ideas implied specific expectations from governments. In his *General Theory of Employment, Interest, and Money* (published in 1936), Keynes prescribed during recessions an increase in government spending, to prevent aggregate spending from falling. Reflecting the Keynesian ideas, the welfare state emerged out of the Great Depression. The experience of the Great Depression promoted the expectation that governments actively try to improve the outcomes related to employment and growth.

Clashing ideas at the conference

The two major personalities at the conference reflected the leading countries of the Western world at the time: Britain as the previous world power and the U.S. as the emerging world power. Therefore, the ideas of John Maynard Keynes, an economist representing Britain, and Harry Dexter White, an economist and a senior Treasury official representing the U.S., dominated the Bretton Woods Conference.

The most important item on the agenda was the shape of the upcoming international monetary system. All participants wanted to establish a new metallic standard. However, disagreements arose regarding the format and the administration of the new metallic system. Memories of the adverse effects of current account imbalances on the gold standard were still fresh, so discussions centered on how to avoid such imbalances.

Checking out the British plan

Keynes proposed an International Clearing Union (ICU) as a way to addressing current account imbalances. He wanted to avoid the reappearance of persistent and large current account deficits that happened during the interwar years (1918–1939), which increased countries' debt and debt payments and decreased growth at the global scale. Keynes thought of the ICU as a bank with its own currency (called Bancor), exchangeable with other currencies at a fixed rate. He proposed using Bancor to measure countries' trade deficits or surpluses.

According to Keynes, countries with current account deficits would have an overdraft facility in their Bancor account with the ICU. He worked out specific numbers regarding the size of the overdraft facility. His proposal implied a maximum overdraft of half of the country's average trade size over five years. If a country needed funds higher than the overdraft, it would be charged interest, thus motivating the country to devalue its currency.

Keynes also had an idea for countries with large and persistent current account surpluses. (See Chapter 11 for more on this topic.) One of the problems of the interwar years was that surplus countries didn't do much to reduce their current account surplus. Then the pressure was all on countries with large and persistent current account deficits. During the interwar years, and especially around the times of the Great Depression, Keynes observed these deficit countries implementing increasingly contractionary monetary policies and increasing interest rates in an attempt to prevent funds from leaving these countries. However, as Chapter 11 shows, this led to deflation, lower output, and higher unemployment. Therefore, Keynes's plan implied an interest charge of 10 percent if a country's current account surplus was more than half the size of its permitted overdraft; this solution would motivate these countries to lend more. At the end of the year, if the country had a current account surplus that was half the overdraft, the ICU would confiscate the surplus.

Taking a look at the American plan

The American plan differed from that of the British. As indicated before, Harry Dexter White represented the U.S. at the Bretton Woods Conference. Even though Keynes objected to White's ideas, at the end of the conference, the post–World War II international monetary system reflected almost exclusively the ideas of the U.S.

The U.S. agreed on the necessity of an agency to manage current account imbalances, but Keynes's idea of the ICU was too interventionist for the American side. Additionally, the U.S. saw itself as a surplus country in terms of its current account in the years to come and didn't want such interventionist ideas to be practiced on the U.S. Therefore, the White Plan emerged with two key components. First, White proposed the International Stabilization

Fund (which later became the International Monetary Fund, or the IMF), which placed the burden of balancing current accounts on deficit countries and imposed no limits on surplus countries.

Since the international monetary system wasn't the only item on the American agenda, White included a second aspect to the plan. After earlier wars, the aggressors were made to provide reparation payments. This time, however, the U.S. wanted to lead the reconstruction efforts. Therefore, the White Plan included a new multilateral development agency that would plan and finance economic reconstruction in all war-torn countries, allied or aggressor. The International Bank for Reconstruction and Development (IBRD, part of today's World Bank) emerged from the American ideas about reconstruction.

The economic and military power of the U.S. at the end of World War II was extremely influential on countries choosing between the two alternative plans for the post–World War II international monetary system. The White Plan emerged as the winner.

Judging the Outcome of the Bretton Woods Conference

Three multilateral organizations were born at the Bretton Woods Conference: the International Monetary Fund (IMF), the International Bank for Reconstruction and Development (IBRD), and the General Agreement on Tariffs and Trade (GATT). These institutions were created based on the need for increased post–World War II international economic cooperation in issues related to international finance and international trade, as well as economic reconstruction of war-torn Europe and Japan. The U.S. was very interested in multilateral organizations because these organizations were considered insurance against economic nationalism that had proved extremely harmful during the Great Depression.

General Agreement on Tariffs and Trade

The General Agreement on Tariffs and Trade (GATT) was a multilateral treaty that was the predecessor of the current World Trade Organization (WTO). As a Bretton Woods organization, the GATT's objective was to reduce or eliminate trade restrictions such as tariffs and quotas. The GATT was replaced by the WTO in 1995.

This section mostly focuses on the structure of the post-war international financial system. First, I discuss the version of the gold standard that the Bretton Woods system introduced. Second, I examine the role assigned to the IMF as the manager of fixed exchange rates.

Setting the reserve currency system

The reserve currency system that was established at the Bretton Woods conference is a version of the gold standard. In this system, one of the world currencies is identified as the reserve currency, and the reserve currency is pegged to gold. Then all other currencies are pegged to the reserve currency. Between the end of World War II and the end of the Bretton Woods system in the early 1970s, the dollar was the reserve currency; almost every country pegged its currency to the dollar.

In this system, even though the U.S. had to have gold reserves, other countries could do so but didn't *have* to. However, nonreserve currency countries had to keep sufficient dollar reserves in order to intervene in their currencies by buying or selling the dollar to maintain the fixed exchange rates. Central banks of nonreserve currency countries held a large portion of their international reserves in U.S. Treasury bills, as well as short-term dollar deposits, which were (and are) highly liquid.

As in the case of any metallic standard, the reserve currency system also implies fixed exchange rates. Because under this system the dollar was convertible into gold and other currencies were pegged to the dollar, all cross rates (see Chapter 2) were automatically fixed as well.

This example is based on the discussion of cross rates in Chapter 2. Suppose that the French franc–dollar and German mark–dollar exchange rates are FFR2 per dollar and DM1.5 per dollar. The French franc–German mark exchange rate thus would be FFR1.33 per German mark (2 ÷ 1.5). If the French franc–German mark exchange rate were any different than FFR1.33, arbitrage would eliminate any exchange rate other than the fixed cross rates. Suppose that the French franc–German mark exchange rate is FFR1.60. In this case, you could sell $100 to the Bundesbank in Germany for DM150 ($100 × 1.5), sell your German marks to the Bank of France for FFR240 (DM150 × 1.60), and sell your French francs to the Fed for $120 (FFR240 ÷ FFR2), making $20 in the process. (However, this was not possible because the U.S. didn't buy or sell gold at the Bretton Woods price.)

Time to take the lead

In the reserve currency system, the reserve currency country has a special position: It has more room to conduct monetary policy to achieve the internal balance. Therefore, the reserve currency country can attempt to maintain its internal balance through monetary policy without affecting its external balance. However, other countries that peg their currency to the reserve currency cannot change their monetary policy without affecting their reserves and messing up their external balance. Therefore, whenever the reserve currency country changes its monetary policy objectives, all other countries have to accept it.

For example, if a non-reserve currency country increases its money supply, it will lead to a decline in its international reserves. The reason is that an increase in the money supply decreases the interest rate in this country relatively to that of other countries. As investors flee this country in search for higher interest rates, an excess demand arises for foreign currencies, which revaluates the other countries' currencies. But such a change in the exchange rate goes against the fixed exchange rates and maintenance of the external balance. Therefore, countries whose currencies are revalued engage in interventions in foreign exchange markets, where they can buy the assets of the reserve country with their own currency. This situation then increases the supply of these currencies, decreases interest rates, and devalues these currencies.

Power has its privileges

In fact, in a reserve currency system, the reserve currency country doesn't have to intervene in the foreign exchange market to maintain the fixed exchange rate. Unlike in other countries, the central bank of the reserve currency country doesn't have to buy or sell currencies in the foreign exchange market. The objective of the reserve currency country is to peg the reserve currency to gold. For example, the Federal Reserve was responsible for holding the dollar price of gold at $35 an ounce. Therefore, although the U.S. had more freedom to conduct monetary policy as the reserve currency country, its freedom had limits. For example, excessively expansionary monetary policy in the U.S. would make the gold parity of $35 for an ounce overvalued and pressure the gold parity to increase. A speculative attack on the dollar then would ensue. To avoid a possible decline in the value of their dollar reserves, other countries would attempt to sell their dollars in exchange for gold, depleting the gold reserves of the Federal Reserve Bank.

Clearly, the reserve currency system put the U.S. in a privileged position. The U.S. got away with the reserve currency system for essentially three reasons:

- ✔ The basic gold standard, in which all countries peg their currency to gold and hold gold reserves, wasn't attractive during the Bretton Woods conference because the Soviet Union was one of the major gold producers in the world.

- ✔ The Soviet Union did not attend the Bretton Woods conference, and the wedge between the Soviet Union and the West was growing.

- ✔ The U.S. emerged as the new superpower, taking the place Britain had occupied for so long. With the U.S. as the new economic and military power, the dollar became the reserve currency.

IMF: Manager of fixed exchange rates

The IMF's Articles of Agreement implied both discipline and flexibility, to avoid the mistakes of the interwar period.

The discipline part of the agreement implied that the value of the dollar was to be pegged to gold and that all other currencies were to be pegged to the dollar, which led to fixed exchange rates. The flexibility part ensured that countries having trouble with keeping the fixed exchange rate would receive financial assistance. This was supposed to work as a remedy to the mistakes during the interwar period, when countries tried to maintain fixed exchange rates at the expense of free trade and employment.

Because unilateralism caused so many problems during the interwar years, the IMF, as a multilateral institution, had to offer facilities to assist countries with external balance problems. The lending facilities of the IMF aimed to reduce member countries' current account problems by providing additional liquidity. However, if the IMF were to provide liquidity to member countries, the organization needed funds. Therefore, a subscription system was created in which IMF members were assigned quotas that reflected the countries' relative economic power. This subscription was to be paid 25 percent in either gold or the reserve currency (dollar) and 75 percent in the member's own currency. The quota system helped the IMF establish a pool of gold and currencies.

Now with funds at its disposal, the IMF was charged with managing current account deficits to avoid large currency devaluations. To make substantial changes in the exchange rate, a member country needed the IMF's determination and approval that the country was suffering from a fundamental disequilibrium. However, no explicit definition was drafted for what constitutes a fundamental equilibrium. Clearly, what constitutes a fundamental disequilibrium would change from country to country as well as over time.

Even though international trade was a major headache in maintaining the external balance, the IMF promoted free international trade and urged its members to make their currencies convertible. Convertibility in currencies, also called current account convertibility, means that all currencies can be acquired and exchanged with other currencies. Clearly, if a country's currency isn't traded, it discourages trade with that country. U.S. and Canadian dollars became convertible as early as 1945. Most European countries restored convertibility in 1958, and Japan joined later, in 1964.

In addition to current account convertibility, capital account convertibility implies the free flow of capital between countries. As Chapter 11 discusses, capital account convertibility is part of the trilemma in international finance.

Maintaining internal balance (full employment level of output) and external balance (fixed exchange rate) while capital freely moves between countries is called the trilemma because you cannot achieve these three goals simultaneously. Therefore, the IMF allowed restrictions on capital flows, which gave countries more freedom to use monetary policy to address internal imbalances. Based on the experience during the interwar years, in an attempt to attract investors in their countries, countries with current account deficits implemented contractionary monetary policies to keep their interest rates higher. As Chapter 11 shows, this particular policy decision led to lower output, higher unemployment, and deflation in a deficit country. Additionally, as other countries felt compelled to do the same, severe recessions simultaneously happened in many countries. To avoid such an outcome, the IMF allowed restrictions to be placed on capital flows so that countries could use their monetary policy to address domestic macroeconomic problems.

Marking the Decline of the Bretton Woods System

Britain, the world's financial and military superpower until World War II, emerged from the war as a weaker country. The U.S., on the other hand, became the new superpower. The U.S. economy was strong, and the dollar became the reserve currency. The gold parity, $35 for an ounce of gold, was credible because the U.S. economy was strong, and the U.S. was committed to converting dollars into gold at this price. The dollar was about to play the same role as gold during the gold standards of previous decades. In terms of its political role, the U.S. was to help war-torn countries with their economic recovery, which implied a large outflow of dollars through grants, loans, military spending, and private investment.

Despite a promising start at the Bretton Woods conference, this section aims to show that the cracks in the Bretton Woods system appeared as early as 1947. In a way, the system died a slow death in the early 1970s.

Dollar shortage and the Marshall Plan (1947)

In the immediate aftermath of the Bretton Woods Conference, the problem of a dollar shortage emerged. During the late 1940s, the U.S. was running large current account surpluses, and its gold reserves were growing. At the same time, especially Western European countries were running large deficits. If the U.S. were to support the rebuilding efforts in war-torn countries, it was necessary to reverse this flow and make more dollars available for other countries' use. The U.S. had to reverse the process and run current account deficits.

Even though the IMF and the IBRD were introduced to finance current account imbalances and reconstruction, respectively, it became apparent soon after the Bretton Woods Conference that these multilateral organizations didn't have sufficient funds to do the job. By 1947, the IMF and the IBRD were admitting that they didn't have enough funds (dollars) to fulfill their functions.

Therefore, in 1947, the U.S. introduced the European Recovery Program, also known as the Marshall Plan, which provided large grants to European countries. Between 1947 and 1958, the U.S. tried to encourage the outflow of dollars to improve liquidity around the world. Not only the Western European countries, but also the strategically relevant Mediterranean countries (such as Greece and Turkey) and other developing countries, received grants from the U.S. In the late 1940s, the Cold War had already started, and it was important for the U.S. to suppress the Soviet Union's political influence. Not surprisingly, starting in 1950, large current account surpluses in the U.S. changed to large deficits.

The Bretton Woods system gave the U.S. a special place as the engine of stability. The U.S. was engaged in trade with developing countries, resulting in trade surplus. Then the U.S. sent these surplus dollars to Europe to be used in rebuilding their economies so that they could sell their goods to the U.S. In turn, European countries' export earnings from the U.S. allowed them to trade with developing countries. To support Western European countries' economic recovery, the U.S. did not retaliate against the protectionist trade practices of these countries. It seemed that the U.S. was the coordinator of these trade flows for the good of all parties involved. However, the successful working of this scheme depended upon the ability of the U.S. to keep having current account surpluses and using them in providing financial aid to Europe and Japan. During the 1950s, the system started showing signs of destabilization.

Systems getting out of hand (1950s and 1960s)

As early as 1950, the U.S. current account balance showed a deficit. Until John F. Kennedy won the presidential election in 1960, the U.S. response to the increasing current account deficit was to introduce trade restrictions, which was exactly what the Bretton Woods Conference had tried to avoid. The struggle to maintain the gold parity of $35 per ounce intensified during the 1960s.

As indicated earlier, the Bretton Woods system forced the gold convertibility on the reserve currency country. However, gold convertibility wasn't required for all countries, so that they could hold dollars instead of gold. The problem was, there was a gold market. If the dollar was pegged to gold at $35 per ounce, the market price of gold had better be $35 per ounce. Persistent and large U.S. current account deficits indicated that the dollar was overvalued and the parity should be something higher than $35 per ounce of gold. This situation tempted investors into buying gold at the Bretton Woods price and selling at a higher price in the gold market. If you think about what investors are using to buy gold, the answer is the dollar. All this further enlarged the discrepancy between the gold parity and the market price of gold, which fed the frenzy of selling dollars and buying gold. Of course, certain events during the Cold War, such as the Cuban Missile Crisis in 1962, fueled increases in the gold price as well.

The U.S. found itself in a situation called Triffin's dilemma. On one hand, the U.S. current account deficit was helping mainly European countries and Japan grow. Therefore, if the U.S. eliminated its current account deficit, these countries would be adversely affected. On the other hand, persistent and large current account deficits were contributing to the increasing discrepancy between the gold parity and the market price of gold.

In an attempt to strengthen the Bretton Woods system, two ideas were introduced: the London Gold Pool and the Special Drawing Rights.

The London Gold Pool

Apparently, the U.S. wasn't willing to give up its support to Europe and Japan. Instead, it tried to affect the market price of gold. In 1961, eight countries (the U.S., the U.K., Germany, France, Italy, Belgium, the Netherlands, and Switzerland) came together and created the London Gold Pool, in which the U.S. initially contributed 50 percent of the gold in the pool. The aim of the Gold Pool was to affect the gold price set by the morning gold fix in London. Because most of the time the gold price was increasing, the Gold Pool sold gold in the market to counteract the increases in the price of gold.

The U.S. was also looking into domestic policy options to strengthen the economy and its export potential. The new Kennedy administration was considering a tax reform to increase productivity and promote exports, which would have helped prevent an increase in the gold parity (in other words, a devaluation of the dollar). However, such attempts were unsuccessful. Finally, the Gold Pool disintegrated in 1968. Congress revoked the 25% requirement of gold backing of the dollar. Countries in the pool suspended the exchange of gold with private entities. Additionally, the U.S. suspended its gold sales to countries that were known to participate in the gold market by selling dollars in exchange for gold. However, these efforts didn't stop the depletion of the U.S. gold reserves.

The Special Drawing Rights

In an attempt to create liquidity, in 1969, the IMF introduced the Special Drawing Rights (SDR) as a supplementary reserve asset. Basically, the SDR represented a claim to currency that IMF member countries held. When the SDR was introduced, its value was equivalent to 0.888671 grams of fine gold, which was also equivalent to one U.S. dollar. IMF members were required to accept SDR holdings equal to three times their share. The main objective of the SDR was to prevent nations from buying gold at the Bretton Woods price and selling at the higher free market price. Another objective was to limit the amount of dollars that could be held.

Current account deficits weren't only a U.S. problem. In 1964, a large current account deficit initiated a speculative attack on the British pound, eventually devaluating the currency. Another attack on the pound followed in 1967. Other countries faced the effects of these speculative attacks on the pound. Some European countries with current account deficits devalued their currencies, and countries with surpluses revalued their currencies, which also affected capital inflows and outflows to and from these countries.

Consequently, parity changes became increasingly unilateral decisions. Countries with strong exports postponed revaluation of their currencies, and countries with larger imports postponed devaluation. Frequently used national discretion made the Bretton Woods system even weaker.

Nailing the coffin in 1971 (and then again in 1973)

The U.S. accumulated persistent current account deficits to provide loans, grants, aid, and troops to Allied countries. During the 1960s, it became clear that the U.S. was putting the Bretton Woods system and its reserve currency status in danger. Still, the U.S. continued on the path designed in the late 1940s until the system broke down completely.

While the U.S. remained insistent on continuing its mission described by the Bretton Woods system, the world was changing. Throughout the 1960s and 1970s, important structural changes were taking place that also contributed to the breakdown of the Bretton Woods system:

✔ **The increasing monetary interdependence between countries.** Most Western European currencies and the Japanese yen became convertible in 1958 and 1964, respectively. The return to convertibility led to an increase of international financial transactions, which strengthened monetary interdependence.

✔ **Due to the aftermath of World War II, a rapid development and integration of international financial markets was introduced.** Starting in the mid-1960s, banks formed international syndicates. By 1971, most of the world's largest banks became shareholders in these syndicates. These multinational banks moved around large amounts of funds for investment purposes, as well as for speculation and hedging against exchange rate fluctuations. These developments in financial markets made large capital flows possible.

✔ **The economies that the U.S. helped rebuild were becoming economic powers themselves.** By the mid-1960s, the European Economic Community (EEC) and Japan were on their way to becoming international economic powers. Their total reserves exceeded U.S. reserves, they had higher growth rates, and their per-capita income was approaching that of the U.S. In fact, the international landscape of economic power in the mid-1960s looked very different than at the time of the Bretton Woods Conference in 1944. In a world with multiple economic powers, the privileged role of the dollar was being questioned. The U.S. was determining the level of international liquidity for all, which caused dissatisfaction among other countries. As the 1970s approached, the U.S., the reserve currency country, didn't look the part.

Another reason lay behind the dissatisfaction of Europe and Japan with the system. U.S. policies were influencing not only economic conditions; some of these countries resented the military conflicts such as the Vietnam War in which the U.S. was involved. It seemed that holding the reserve country's currency, the dollar, by other countries was enabling the U.S. in engaging military conflicts. By the late 1960s, higher inflation rates and large dollar outflows made the dollar overvalued. At the same time, the German mark and the yen seemed undervalued. Despite these imbalances, countries were reluctant to make the necessary adjustments. The Germans and the Japanese didn't want to revalue their currencies because it would hurt their export performance. The U.S. avoided devaluation in order to maintain its international credibility. However, keeping everything the same was getting increasingly difficult because international currency markets were developing and large speculative capital was moving around in search of quick profits.

A political dimension of dissatisfaction with the U.S. as the reserve currency country also came into play. In 1971, détente (easing of strained relations) between the U.S. and the Soviet Union depreciated the role of the U.S. in protecting the Western world from the threat of communism. During the time of the Bretton Woods Conference in 1944 and throughout the 1950s, the protection the U.S. provided was valuable. However, when security fears lessened, the economic and military leadership of the U.S. became less acceptable.

Closing the gold window

On August 15, 1971, President Nixon issued an executive order that imposed a short-term wage and price ceiling as well as an import surcharge, in addition to ending the convertibility between U.S. dollars and gold by closing the gold window. The decision regarding the gold window was made to stabilize the economy by preventing a run on the dollar. While the U.S. made this decision unilaterally without consulting the international community, it was hardly a surprise. Earlier in 1971, West Germany and Switzerland left the Bretton Woods system, because they were not willing to devalue their currency to support the dollar.

By 1971, the U.S. had very few nongold reserves and only 22 percent gold coverage of foreign reserves. The dollar became significantly overvalued with respect to gold. Because of current account deficits, anti–free trade sentiments were rising in the U.S. Finally, President Nixon closed the gold window on August 15, 1971, ending the convertibility of the dollar into gold. The dollar was let to float according to its market price.

In December 1971, the Group of Ten met at the Smithsonian in an attempt to build a new international monetary system. The Smithsonian Agreement led to the devaluation of the dollar from $35 to $38 per ounce of gold. However, because U.S. expenditures and current account deficits were continuing, this devaluation did not stop the speculation against the dollar. In 1972, the devaluation of the dollar reached $44 per ounce of gold. Clearly, whatever remained of the Bretton Woods system couldn't be rescued. In February 1973, the U.S. and other industrialized countries let their currencies float.

Chapter 13

Exchange Rate Regimes in the Post–Bretton Woods Era

*T*his chapter is all about the exchange rate regimes observed during the post–Bretton Woods era. It uses some of the fundamental knowledge of the exchange rate regimes established in Chapter 11. In this chapter, you look at floating or flexible exchange rate regimes as well as pegged regimes which fall between the two extremes of fixed and flexible exchange rates. Because currency crises can occur under a pegged exchange rate regime, you learn both the reasons and consequences of a currency crisis. Additionally, following the end of the Bretton Woods era, the International Monetary Fund (IMF), a Bretton Woods institution, started providing funds to countries with pegged exchange rate regimes. Therefore, this chapter provides a discussion of the IMF's activities in the post-Bretton Woods era.

Using Floating Exchange Rates

Chapter 11 notes that a fiat currency doesn't imply a fixed exchange rate. In fact, fiat currencies are compatible with a floating exchange rate regime, in which the value of a currency is determined in foreign exchange markets.

This section focuses on two main subjects. First, I discuss the advantages and disadvantages of the floating exchange rate regime. Second, a floating exchange rate regime doesn't necessarily lack government or central bank interventions into exchange rates; therefore, I talk about the variety of exchange rate interventions under a floating exchange rate regime.

Advantages and disadvantages of floating exchange rates

Floating exchange rates have these main advantages:

- **No need for international management of exchange rates:** Unlike fixed exchange rates based on a metallic standard, floating exchange rates don't require an international manager such as the International Monetary Fund to look over current account imbalances. Under the floating system, if a country has large current account deficits, its currency depreciates.

- **No need for frequent central bank intervention:** Central banks frequently must intervene in foreign exchange markets under the fixed exchange rate regime to protect the gold parity, but such is not the case under the floating regime. Here there's no parity to uphold.

- **No need for elaborate capital flow restrictions:** Chapter 11 emphasizes the difficulty associated with trying to keep the parity intact in a fixed exchange rate regime while portfolio flows are moving in and out of the country. In a floating exchange rate regime, the macroeconomic fundamentals of countries affect the exchange rate in international markets, which, in turn, affect portfolio flows between countries. Therefore, floating exchange rate regimes enhance market efficiency.

- **Greater insulation from other countries' economic problems:** Chapter 11 shows that, under a fixed exchange rate regime, countries export their macroeconomic problems to other countries. Suppose that the inflation rate in the U.S. is rising relative to that of the Euro-zone. Under a fixed exchange rate regime, this scenario leads to an increased U.S. demand for European goods, which then increases the Euro-zone's price level. Under a floating exchange rate system, however, countries are more insulated from other countries' macroeconomic problems. A rising U.S. inflation instead depreciates the dollar, curbing the U.S. demand for European goods.

Floating exchange rates also have disadvantages:

- **Higher volatility:** Floating exchange rates are highly volatile. Additionally, macroeconomic fundamentals can't explain especially short-run volatility in floating exchange rates.

✔ **Use of scarce resources to predict exchange rates:** Higher volatility in exchange rates increases the exchange rate risk that financial market participants face. Therefore, they allocate substantial resources to predict the changes in the exchange rate, in an effort to manage their exposure to exchange rate risk.

✔ **Tendency to worsen existing problems:** Floating exchange rates may aggravate existing problems in the economy. If the country is already experiencing economic problems such as higher inflation or unemployment, floating exchange rates may make the situation worse. For example, if the country suffers from higher inflation, depreciation of its currency may drive the inflation rate higher because of increased demand for its goods; however, the country's current account may also worsen because of more expensive imports.

Intervention into floating exchange rates

A completely floating currency exists only in textbooks. Terms like *dirty float* or *managed float* refer to exchange rate regimes in which exchange rates are largely determined in foreign exchange markets, but certain interventions into exchange rates take place.

Interventions are divided into two categories:

✔ **Indirect interventions:** Chapters 6 and 7 show that monetary policy and the growth performance of countries affect exchange rates. Therefore, a change in monetary policy is considered an indirect intervention. Additionally, trade barriers are a form of indirect intervention into exchange rates. Chapter 5 shows that if a country imposes a tariff on imports from another country, the import-imposing country's currency appreciates, everything else constant.

✔ **Direct interventions:** These interventions imply that the central bank of a country uses its domestic currency or foreign currency reserves and engages in exchanging one currency for another. The aim may be to increase the country's competitiveness by avoiding further appreciation of the domestic currency. For example, on September 10, 2011, the *Economist* reported that the Swiss National Bank (SNB) was concerned about the Swiss franc's steady appreciation against the euro. Starting in early 2010, when the exchange rate was almost CHF1.5 per euro, the Swiss franc continued to appreciate toward CHF 1 per euro. Then the SNB stepped in and announced its determination to keep the exchange rate at CHF1.20 per euro. You can understand the SNB's concern about strengthening the Swiss franc when you realize that the export sector of this country is vital for the economy.

Direct interventions can be conducted in two ways: unsterilized and sterilized. In economics, the term *sterilization* is used as a countermeasure, where the countermeasure may be implemented through the changes in domestic money supply.

An unsterilized intervention implies that a central bank intervenes in the foreign exchange market by buying or selling its own currency without adjusting the domestic money supply. Continuing with the previous example of Switzerland, to prevent the Swiss franc from further appreciating, the SNB can engage in direct intervention by selling domestic currency in foreign exchange markets (Swiss francs), in exchange for foreign currency, such as the dollar or the euro. This particular intervention is called an unsterilized direct intervention if the SNB doesn't alter Switzerland's money supply. However, if the SNB wants to alter Switzerland's money supply following its direct intervention into foreign exchange markets, it's called a sterilized direct intervention.

The next example continues to be about Switzerland and provides a background analysis. It provides graphs for the previous definitions of unsterilized and sterilized direct interventions and explains how sterilization affects the domestic money market.

First, the demand–supply model introduced in Chapter 5 provides the necessary tools to see how the SNB can prevent the Swiss franc from further appreciating.

Figure 13-1 shows the market for euros. The price of the euro is measured as the number of Swiss francs necessary to buy one euro or the Swiss franc–euro exchange rate. The reason for using the euro market and the Swiss franc–euro exchange rate is that the previously mentioned *Economist* article reports on the Swiss franc–euro exchange rate.

Suppose that the equilibrium exchange rate of CHF 1.02 in Figure 13-1 indicates the exchange rate in late summer 2011, which made the SNB worry about Switzerland's exports. If the SNB wants to achieve its goal of bringing the Swiss currency to the level of CHF 1.20, it needs to sell Swiss francs in exchange for euros. Because the curves in Figure 13-1 indicate the demand for and supply of euros, the actions of the SNB are shown here as an increase demand for the euro. The SNB buys euros with Swiss francs, which essentially depreciates the Swiss franc from CHF 1.02 to CHF1.20 per euro.

So far, this example implies an unsterilized intervention, which means that the SNB intervened in the foreign exchange market without taking an independent action to change the country's money supply. Why does Switzerland's money supply matter? The SNB pays for euros with Swiss francs, which means an increase in the number of Swiss francs in foreign exchange markets. As the Swiss franc depreciates as a result of this action, these Swiss francs in the foreign exchange market likely will return to Switzerland as payments for Swiss exports, which may be inflationary.

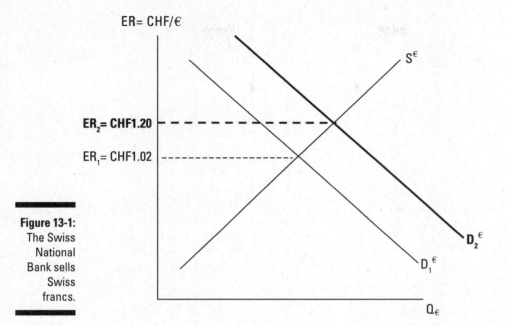

ER= CHF/€

S$^€$

ER$_2$= CHF1.20

ER$_1$= CHF1.02

D$_2$$^€$

D$_1$$^€$

Q$_€$

Figure 13-1:
The Swiss
National
Bank sells
Swiss
francs.

If the SNB is concerned about an eventual increase in inflation, it can steril-ize its actions in the foreign exchange market by doing the exact opposite in the domestic money market. Because the SNB increased the amount of Swiss francs in foreign exchange markets, it can decrease the country's money supply by selling Swiss government's bonds (also bills and notes) to financial markets in the same amount as the direct intervention.

WARNING!

Note that central banks cannot issue government bonds. In every country, the country's treasury or the fiscal authority can issue new government bonds. When referring to the central bank's sale or purchase of government bonds, you need to think in terms of secondary market bonds. All central banks hold the bonds of the relevant country's government in their portfolio, and they can change the money supply by buying or selling these bonds. The sale or purchase of secondary-market government bonds by a central bank is called open market operations.

The question is how successful direct interventions in foreign exchange mar-kets can be. Consider the size of the foreign exchange market: It's estimated to be up to 15 times larger than the bond market and about 50 times larger than the equity market. As of 2010, the average daily turnover was estimated to be about $4 trillion. Just compare this number to the nominal gross domestic product (GDP) of the U.S. in 2010, which was close to $15 trillion.

Therefore, direct interventions are likely to be overwhelmed by market forces. Because of the size of the foreign exchange market, a coordinated effort by a consortium of central banks may be more effective. Whether carried out by one central bank or a group of central banks, the argument for direct intervention in the foreign exchange market is that even interventions of short duration may be able to reduce the volatility in floating exchange rates.

Unilaterally Pegged Exchange Rates

Unilateral currency pegs appeared following the end of the Bretton Woods era. The difference between the pegged exchange rate regimes of pre- and post-1973 periods stems from the different types of money in these periods. As indicated in Chapter 12, the Bretton Woods system implied a variation of the metallic standard called the reserve currency standard. While the dollar as the reserve currency was pegged to gold, other currencies were pegged to the dollar, which implies a fixed exchange rate system. This kind of a system requires a multilateral agreement so that a country doesn't change the exchange rate unilaterally. If it does, the international monetary system may be weaken or broken, which would necessitate redefining the pegs.

In the post Bretton Woods era, however, unilateral pegs started to appear. In this case, a country pegs the value of its currency to a foreign currency or a basket of foreign currencies. In the early decades following the Bretton Woods era, especially developing countries were afraid of letting their currency float. Many were engaged in expansionary monetary policies that would have depreciated their currency at a faster rate if these currencies were floating. Therefore, many developing countries recognized that currency pegs can act as a nominal anchor and signal stability when economic and political stability is in short supply. Additionally, they thought that a pegged exchange rate, pegged in a certain way, can serve these countries' agenda regarding economic development.

There are different types of pegs among the unilateral currency pegs of the post Bretton Woods era. The most important difference between different types of pegs lies in their ability to restrict monetary policy in a country. As you will see in the discussion below, pegs can be divided between *hard* and *soft pegs*. Pegs that make it almost impossible for a country to have an autonomous or independent monetary policy are called hard pegs. Soft pegs indicate that monetary policy actions are taken at times and the peg is adjusted from time to time. Soft pegs are also called *crawling pegs*.

The central bank guarantees convertibility of domestic currency into the foreign currency to which it is pegged. Therefore, keeping reserves of foreign currencies or international reserves, especially of the foreign currency to which the domestic currency is pegged, becomes important.

Using hard pegs

Dollarization and currency boards are among the examples of hard pegs, which severely limit the possibility of an autonomous (independent) monetary policy in a country. Therefore, sometimes the exchange rate that stems from a hard peg is referred to as a fixed exchange rate, as in the case of a metallic standard.

In the case of dollarization, a country adopts a foreign currency to be circulated in its economy as the medium of exchange. A currency board backs the money supply or domestic currency liabilities with foreign currency or foreign currency–denominated assets to support the pegged rate. The following sections further examine these examples of hard pegs.

Dollarization

Dollarization is a general term that describes a country's act of giving up its domestic currency and adopting another country's currency to be used in all transactions. Despite the name, the replacing foreign currency doesn't have to be the dollar.

Consider some historical examples for dollarization. One of the smallest European countries, Monaco, adopted the French franc in the 19th century and currently uses the euro, after France adopted the euro in 1999. Also, the U.S. dollar is the legal tender in Panama since the early 20th century.

Clearly, eliminating a country's own money and, therefore, monetary policy is a radical step. After the domestic currency in circulation is replaced by a foreign currency, the country cannot have an autonomous monetary and exchange rate policy. Suppose that a country adopts the dollar. Because this country doesn't have its own money and its own central bank, it has to accept the monetary policy of the U.S., conducted by the Federal Reserve Bank (the Fed). Clearly, the monetary policy–making division of the Fed, the Federal Open Market Committee (FOMC), conducts its monetary policy in consideration of the economic outcomes in the U.S.; the dollarized country's economic situation doesn't matter to the Fed.

Therefore, the dollarized country loses its ability to address its domestic economic problems. In all countries, central banks have similar responsibilities: issuing currency, protecting the purchasing power of the currency or promoting price stability, implementing monetary policy to address business cycles (contractions and expansions), and regulating financial markets. The central bank of a dollarized country is able to regulate the country's financial markets and promote price stability by adopting a lower-inflation country's currency.

The dollarized country's central bank loses something else as well. In addition to the aforementioned responsibilities, all central banks act as a lender of last resort. In times of crisis, especially financial crisis, central banks inject liquidity into financial markets. In the most recent financial crisis, the Fed acted as a lender of last resort and provided liquidity to financial markets through loans and purchasing especially mortgage-backed securities from financial markets. The European Central Bank (ECB) did the same in early 2010 by buying Greek government bonds. In these examples, both the Fed and the ECB transferred toxic assets from the balance sheets of banks and other financial firms to their own balance sheets and provided financial markets with additional liquidity. Risk premium of these financial assets (mortgage-backed securities and Greek government bonds) increased so much that, if not for the Fed or the ECB, nobody would have bought them. This situation is how central banks fulfill their function as the lender of last resort. Dollarization, however, completely eliminates the possibility that the dollarized country's central bank can act as the lender of last resort.

You may ask what would inspire a country to dollarize. Usually countries dollarize because domestic institutions fail to keep inflation low. Following a severe banking crisis in 1999, Ecuador gave up its domestic currency, sucres, and replaced it with U.S. dollars in 2000. Ecuador was one of those countries that made too much use of the central bank's ability to derive revenues from printing its currency, which is seignorage. Inevitably, the central bank's ability and willingness to print money led to higher inflation rates. In the late 1990s, Ecuador's annual inflation rate reached 96 percent. After dollarization, Ecuador's inflation rate substantially decreased. The average inflation rate between 2003 and 2011 was about 4.4 percent. With lower inflation rates, interest rates declined as well. Whereas the average deposit rate was about 29 percent during the predollarization period, it was about 4.5 percent between 2003 and 2011.

Equating dollarization to common currency is a mistake. As the discussion in Chapter 14 indicates, when countries decide to have a common currency, they are essentially a part of a monetary union. In a monetary union, such as the Euro-zone, all participating countries are included in the decision making regarding the monetary policy of the monetary union. Dollarization, on the other hand, implies a unilateral decision by a country to replace its domestic currency with a foreign currency.

Currency board

Currency board is another example of a hard peg. Unlike dollarization, a currency board doesn't imply replacing the domestic currency with a foreign currency. Even though the country keeps its domestic currency in circulation, a currency board necessitates that the central bank conduct monetary policy with one objective in mind: to maintain the exchange rate with the foreign currency to which the domestic currency is pegged. What would impose discipline on the currency board's monetary policy decisions is the fact that foreign currency reserves back domestic currency.

As in the case of dollarization, a disadvantage of having a currency board is that the central bank cannot implement monetary policy to address the country's current economic problems. Additionally, the central bank loses its ability to act as the lender of last resort and may be able to provide temporary liquidity to the financial system during a financial crisis.

Also similar to dollarization, the main advantage of a currency board is its ability to control the inflation rate and promote price stability. Trying to keep the exchange rate at a certain level leads to discipline in monetary policies and prevents the central bank from conducting discretionary policies. Of course, if the central bank of a country can increase its reserves of the benchmark currency, it can increase the country's monetary base.

Hong Kong is one of the most successful examples of a currency board. The Hong Kong Monetary Authority (HKMA) has maintained a fixed exchange rate of HKD7.8 to one U.S. dollar.

A not-so-successful example of a currency board arose in Argentina. Argentina introduced a currency board and pegged the peso to the U.S. dollar. However, the Argentinean currency board collapsed in 2001. Following that currency crisis, the central bank let the peso float. The appreciation in the U.S. dollar in the late 1990s was one reason for the collapse of the Argentine currency board. As the dollar appreciated, so did the peso. Considering the relevance of exports for the Argentine economy, the appreciation in the peso made the country's exports more expensive, hurting its export performance. Still, the Argentine fiscal practices may have been more damaging to the currency board. Not only the central government, but also state governments (which have considerable autonomy in their budgets) substantially increased their spending based on loans from large U.S. banks. The central bank couldn't monetize the debt because of the currency board and both the central and state governments kept increasing their spending. However, at one point, the lenders became wary about the size of government spending in Argentina and weren't willing to extent more credit. The result was a severe financial and banking crisis in Argentina in 2001, which ended the currency board.

Trying soft pegs

The previous sections show that hard pegs tie the hands of the central banks. Soft pegs, on the other hand, aren't as restrictive. There are some reasons for a country to consider a soft peg: (1) The country wants to manage its exchange rate, to promote its policy of economic development. In such a case, the country can overvalue or undervalue the domestic currency to aid its development strategy. (2) The country wants to attract incoming portfolio flows. This section discusses soft pegs that relate to development objectives. The next section deals with the kind of soft pegs that aim to attract foreign investors.

If a soft peg is used to promote a certain development policy, it's done to either overvalue or undervalue the domestic currency. The objective itself has changed from overvaluing to undervaluing during the last decades.

I start here with overvaluing a country's currency. Until the early 1980s, the objective of most developing countries was to industrialize, whether or not these countries had a comparative advantage in industrialization. This policy was called import substitution because the objective was to produce previously imported goods domestically. But these countries faced formidable barriers to industrialization. They had limited resources, and industrialization was expensive. They also couldn't produce the entire final good (say, cars) domestically and were dependent on the imports of intermediate goods, energy, and so on. The import substitution strategy worked based on overvaluing domestic currencies.

As with other developing countries, Turkey followed the import substitution strategy until the early 1980s. Figure 13-2 shows the market for the Turkish lira, where the exchange rate is the dollar–Turkish lira exchange rate. The figure also indicates that if the lira were traded in international foreign exchange markets, the equilibrium exchange rate would be $0.60 per lira. Instead, the central bank announced that the exchange rate is $1.20 per lira. This example illustrates overvaluation of a currency. An overvalued currency makes imports cheaper. Considering the fact that the import substitution strategy required the import of intermediate goods, energy, and so on, many developing countries pegged their currencies to make their imports less expensive.

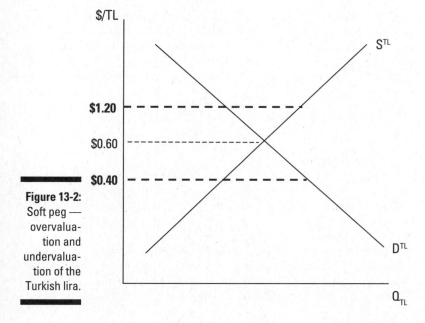

Figure 13-2:
Soft peg —
overvalua-
tion and
undervalua-
tion of the
Turkish lira.

In fact, countries such as Turkey maintained a variety of official exchange rates, depending on the goods they were importing. In terms of imports, overvaluation was exercised at a higher degree for goods that are strategically important for the country's industrialization efforts.

Starting in the early 1980s, the approach to economic development changed globally from import substitution to export promotion. An undervalued currency makes the foreign price of the domestic good cheaper, which promotes the country's export potential.

Even before the introduction of the export promotion strategy, developing countries were concerned about their exports. As in the case of imports, many developing countries applied different exchange rates applied to exports as well. Looking at the Turkish example in Figure 13-2, the exchange rate of $0.40 per dollar implies the undervaluation of the Turkish lira, which would make Turkish exports less expensive. Again, most countries applied undervaluation to their export goods at varying degrees, depending on whether they faced serious competition from other countries. Higher degrees of undervaluation applied to export goods that other countries also produced cheaply.

China is an obvious example of undervaluing a currency. Figure 13-3 shows that the current peg of $0.16 per yuan (as of November 12, 2012) is below the equilibrium exchange rate. Because some estimates put the current peg up to 40 percent below the equilibrium exchange rate, you see the equilibrium exchange rate as $0.22 per yuan.

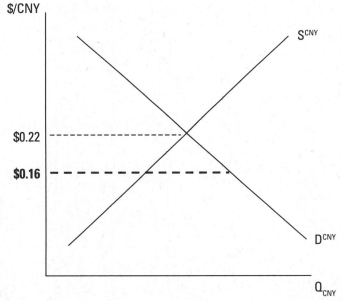

Figure 13-3: Soft peg — undervaluation of the yuan.

As in other developing countries, China followed the import substitution development strategy until the early 1980s. As Chapter 2 discusses, the dollar–yuan exchange rate was $0.58 in 1981. After changing to the export promotion strategy, the exchange rate went down to $0.12 in 1994, which was below the undervalued exchange rate of November 12, 2012, in Figure 13-3. Mainly due to criticism from developed countries, China implemented smaller revaluations in the early 2000s. This is called a *crawling peg*, when a country gradually devalues or revalues its currency.

The undervalued Chinese yuan, together with a lower labor cost, gave China stellar export performance, which led to large accumulations of foreign currencies (especially the dollar) by the Chinese central bank. Foreign exchange reserves of the central bank were $2 trillion in 2010.

You may have heard that China holds a large amount of U.S. government securities. When countries like China have large current account surplus, they become lenders to other countries. They buy bonds issued by other governments, which is just like providing a loan to these governments. As of 2009, China had more than $1 trillion of U.S. government bonds. As the Chinese government allows the yuan to approach the equilibrium exchange rate, China will start losing its foreign currency and asset holdings. Some fear that China will dump its dollar and dollar-denominated security holdings. But such a move would undermine the pegged exchange rate and significantly appreciate the yuan, worsening China's export performance.

If the objective of a soft peg is to create an advantage for a country in international trade, countries need to implement serious capital controls. In this case, if the currency isn't freely traded and the central bank of the country unilaterally determines the exchange rate, the country should control not only international capital flows, but also its citizens' access to foreign exchange. All developing countries that have implemented soft pegs for trade reasons have seen a lively black market arise for foreign currencies.

Attracting foreign investors with soft pegs

Unlike the examples in the previous section, the kind of soft pegs discussed in this section are implemented for other reasons than international trade. The aim here isn't to make exports or imports less expensive. Some soft pegs are introduced to attract foreign investors to the country. In this case, the idea isn't to attract long-term foreign direct investment (FDI), but to attract foreign portfolio investment in the country.

Portfolio investment implies investing in financial papers such as debt securities or equities. Especially developing or emerging countries are interested in attracting incoming foreign portfolio investment. These countries are in need of accumulating hard currency to finance their infrastructure investment. Among the usual sources of hard currency are export earnings and international borrowing. However, exports earnings are used to pay for imports. As to international lending, commercial bank lending to developing countries has significantly declined since the debt crisis of 1982. Therefore, some developing countries liberalized capital movements into and out of the country (capital account convertibility) in an attempt to attract foreign portfolio investment.

Although intentions were good, allowing foreign capital inflows into a developing country turned out to be risky business. During the 1990s and early 2000s, a number of currency crises arose because of the soft pegs implemented to attract foreign portfolio investment.

Currency crises may take place in different countries, but their anatomy and timeline are very similar. Following are the steps toward a currency crisis:

- ✔ **Attempt to attract foreign portfolio investment:** The government is in need of external financing and wants to make the country attractive for foreign portfolio investment.

- ✔ **Identify the reasons for foreign investors' reservations:** The government realizes that the country will not attract portfolio investment because of the exchange rate risk. Even though this country's (nominal) returns may be higher, investors are aware of the risk that this country's currency will depreciate over and above the returns and the risk that they will lose money.

- ✔ **Understand that the government is fiscally undisciplined and influences the central bank:** One of the reasons investors expect depreciation of this currency in the future is that the government hasn't shown any monetary and fiscal discipline in the past. Investors are concerned that the country will continue its path of expansionary macroeconomic policies. They also know that the central bank of the country isn't independent from the fiscal authority and surrenders to the wishes of the government.

- ✔ **Peg the domestic currency to a hard currency:** The government realizes the possibility of changing investors' expectations without changing the country's institutions. Why not peg the domestic currency to a hard currency such as the dollar? Suppose that this country's currency is the krank (KR). The government announces that the pegged exchange rate is KR2 per dollar. In this case, the country uses the peg as a nominal anchor to signal stability.

✔ **Eliminate exchange rate risk:** Announcing the pegged rate isn't enough. The government needs to make the exchange rate risk disappear for foreign investors. Therefore, the government announces that if foreign investors invest in krank-denominated assets, then when they feel like it, they can convert their kranks into dollars at the pegged rate and leave the country. Now foreign investors have virtually no exchange rate risk and can enjoy the higher returns on krank-denominated assets.

✔ **Watch to see if the peg will break:** While the peg is credible, foreign investors have the best of both worlds: no exchange rate risk and higher returns on krank-denominated assets. But they are watching the country. Specifically, they are watching the country to figure out whether the current peg is credible. Note that they won't wait until something happens to cash in their krank-denominated portfolio and get out of this country. If the peg is broken, the krank will depreciate so much that foreign investors will incur large losses, despite higher returns in this country. Therefore, foreign investors observe the country to understand whether conditions exist that will break the peg.

✔ **Causes for the peg to break:** Over the years, views on what would break the peg have changed.

- When the portfolio inflows to emerging markets were increasing starting in the late 1980s, investors were watching the fiscal and monetary policies of these countries. A credible peg indicates no expected changes in fiscal or monetary policy that will break the peg. Suppose that, while pegging the krank, the government increases its spending without raising taxes, which pressures the monetary authority to decrease its key interest rate; this situation is called *monetizing the deficit*. In this case, both monetary and fiscal authorities follow expansionary policies. Investors understand that the peg (KR2 per dollar) will not remain credible for long. They then expect that the peg will be broken and that the krank will substantially depreciate. When foreign investors see this, they cash in their krank-denominated assets and get dollars or other hard currencies in return. Many of the currency crises of the 1980s and early 1990s had inconsistency between the peg and the countries' macroeconomic policies as the root cause. These kinds of crises are called first-generation currency crises.

- Some of the currency crises of the late 1990s, such as the Asian crisis of 1997–1998, belong to the group of second-generation currency crises. One after another, Thailand, Indonesia, and South Korea entered a currency crisis between August and November 1997. It wasn't obvious that these countries were engaged in expansionary fiscal and monetary policies. The second-generation currency crises implied that foreign investors learned about emerging markets and started looking at obvious but also not-so-obvious circumstances that would break the peg. One common characteristic of the previously mentioned Asian economies was a weak financial structure that wasn't equipped to distribute the incoming portfolio investment efficiently. For example, banks' assets in these countries were viewed as inflated because of real estate bubbles in these countries. Investors thought that if anything went wrong in the financial systems of these countries, governments would provide large bailouts, which would break the peg. Therefore, the questionable strength of the financial system played a role in the second-generation currency crises.

✔ **Pay out with hard currency:** When investors sell their portfolios for hard currency, the central bank must do what it promised foreign investors when the country introduced the peg: The central bank must exchange the domestic currency for hard currency at the pegged exchange rate. Because foreign investors are now leaving the country, soon the central bank will run out of its foreign currency reserves. This event, with foreign investors cashing in their portfolios and depleting the foreign currency reserves of the central bank, is called a *speculative attack* on the currency.

✔ **Allow currency to float:** Now the peg is broken. The government lets the domestic currency float, which generally leads to a large depreciation. Additionally, because the country is out of foreign currency reserves, it must restore its short-run liquidity. The country goes to the IMF and receives a loan.

Often currency crises are called by the name of the country, such as the Mexican, Argentine, or Indonesian crises. But the previous discussion about the anatomy and timeline in a currency crisis implies that although currency crises occur in different countries, why and how they happen is very similar.

Dealing with Currency Crises and the IMF

The previous section on soft pegs mentions the role of the IMF in currency crises. The timeline in a currency crisis indicates that when a country's currency is attacked and its central bank starts losing its foreign currency reserves, the country is likely to receive financial support from the IMF. In fact, in the post–Bretton Woods era, the IMF started providing financial support to developing countries with pegged exchange rates and balance of payments problems. The IMF's involvement in developing countries, especially between the 1970s and the late 1990s, made the institution almost a permanent fixture in many developing countries' affairs. Therefore, this section focuses on the IMF and has two objectives: to explain the role of the IMF in the post–Bretton Woods era and to examine the role of the IMF in currency crises of the post–Bretton Woods era.

Decoding the IMF's role in the post–Bretton Woods era

The IMF was originally a Bretton Woods organization (see Chapter 12). At the Bretton Woods Conference of 1944, it was clear that the post–World War II international monetary system was going to depend on a multilateral arrangement. The earlier periods of metallic standard didn't have the multilateral nature of the Bretton Woods era, which was thought to have led to unilateral changes in exchange rates, undermining the fixed exchange rate regime. Additionally, the international monetary system chosen for the post–World War II period was a variation of the gold standard — namely, the reserve currency standard. This system envisioned establishing the gold parity with the reserve currency, the dollar, and pegging all other currencies to the dollar.

The role of the IMF

The Bretton Woods Conference created the IMF as a multilateral organization to oversee the pressures of current account imbalances in countries whose currencies were pegged to the dollar. As discussed in Chapter 12, the IMF tried to uphold the Bretton Woods system by providing funds to current account-deficit countries. However, as early as the late 1940s, the IMF didn't have enough funds to manage the Bretton Woods system.

Despite this fact, the IMF wasn't abolished with the Bretton Woods system in 1971. Developed countries were adopting flexible exchange rates, and developing countries were unwilling to let their currency float. Given their mostly expansionary fiscal and monetary policies and political uncertainty, these countries expected large depreciations in their currency if they let them float. Developing countries wanted to have a nominal anchor — something stable in their sometimes highly unstable economies. Additionally, as mentioned previously, these countries wanted to manage their exchange rates to support their development strategy of import substitution. The IMF had another important reason to stick around, too. As the Bretton Woods system ended, the first oil price increase of 1973 hit all countries, especially developing countries. The IMF fit naturally in the role of the provider of additional liquidity to developing countries. Consequently, as developed countries were adopting flexible exchange rates, the age of unilateral pegs started for developing countries.

The IMF and unilateral pegs

With many developing countries deciding on unilaterally pegged exchange rates, the IMF was on familiar ground. Although using unilateral pegs is different than pegging currencies to the dollar under the reserve currency system, currency pegs need outside financing (albeit for different reasons). In the

Bretton Woods system, persistent and large current account deficits initiated a loan from the IMF. In the post–Bretton Woods era, unilateral pegs periodically led to reserve depletion in countries, which necessitated a loan from the IMF.

In a unilateral peg, the country pegs its currency to a hard currency such as the dollar. For the peg to be credible, the country cannot make extensive use of monetary policy, especially expansionary monetary policy involving increases in the money supply. In many developing countries, this scenario was (and, to some extent, still is) difficult to accomplish. Most of their central banks aren't independent from the fiscal authority, and the fiscal authority can exercise strong control over the monetary authority. Therefore, when- ever the fiscal authority wants to increase its spending without increasing taxes, monetary policy is the easiest way to get these funds. Of course, an expansionary monetary policy leads to higher inflation and, at times, hyper- inflation, which reduces the credibility of the peg. As previously discussed in this chapter, when the peg loses its credibility, investors expect that the peg will be broken and the currency will depreciate. To avoid future losses, hold- ers of the domestic currency exchange the domestic currency at the pegged rate for the hard currency, such as the dollar, which leads to the depletion of the central bank's reserves. At this point, the country can't make payments on its debt or for its imports. Then it's time to go to the IMF and get a loan.

Unlike the IMF's financial assistance during the Bretton Woods era, IMF loans during the post–Bretton Woods era are associated with conditional- ity. The reason for attaching conditionality to the IMF support during the post–Bretton Woods era is that a unilateral peg loses its credibility for only one reason: The country was following incompatible fiscal and monetary poli- cies under the peg. In other words, rapidly increasing public-sector spending pressures monetary policy to be expansionary, creating expectations that the peg will be broken and the currency will depreciate.

In 2009, the IMF introduced a major overhaul in its programs and conditional- ity. Since then, the IMF also provides financial support to countries that are experiencing a financial crisis that didn't stem from pegged exchange rates. Consider the example of Greece, a member of the European Union and the Euro-zone. In 2010, the IMF approved a €30 billion three-year loan for Greece to help the country get out of its debt crisis. This example is one of the largest financial supports the IMF has provided to any country. Because Greece is in the Euro-zone, there is no pegged exchange rate situation here. (This is more a problem of implementing independent and expansionary fiscal policies as a member of a common currency area.) As discussed in Chapter 14, the recent cases involving Greece, Italy, Spain, Ireland, and others in the Euro-zone don't imply exogenous crises. These countries' financial problems didn't come out of nowhere. The Euro-zone countries in crisis have varying degrees of expansionary fiscal policies, uncoordinated public finance schemes, and proneness to banking crises.

In a way, the IMF has remained the same since its inception: an institution that provides financial support to countries with home-brewed economic problems.

Providing stability or creating moral hazard?

Because the IMF support to countries without pegged exchange rates is still new, not much evidence indicates what this kind of support achieves. However, the IMF's support to developing countries and the effects of its support have been widely examined. The most important effect of the IMF's support is the provision of much-needed liquidity to a country following a currency crisis. Private international lenders would be unwilling to step in and provide funds to a country in crisis. With the help of the IMF, the crisis country with depleted foreign currency reserves can pay for its imports and make payments on its debt. Additionally, evidence indicates that IMF support decreases the spread on a country's sovereign bonds and other debt instruments, which implies a decline in the default risk of a country.

Countries receiving financial support have widely criticized the IMF's conditionality. In terms of its traditional lending to developing countries with pegged exchange rates, the IMF's conditionality prescribes a reduction in public spending (reducing subsidies, freezing civil servants' wages, and so on) and discipline in monetary policy. Even the conditionality associated with the IMF's recent lending to European countries such as Greece has been criticized for being too intrusive. Three facts can help put this view of intrusive IMF conditionality in perspective:

- First, the IMF sometimes provides very large funds to troubled countries, so large that crisis countries can't get these amounts from any other lender.
- Second, interest rates associated with these funds are much lower than the market rate, meaning that they are much lower than the interest rate that a commercial bank would charge.
- Third, most of the time, the problems forcing a country to go to the IMF are home-brewed or preventable problems.

Therefore, when putting these three facts together, conditionality serves as the shadow price of IMF programs because their nominal price (the interest rate on IMF loans) is so low.

Even though the IMF's conditionality made sense, the institution introduced a new approach to its programs and conditionality in 2009, possibly because it grew tired of criticism. In its own words, the IMF modernized its conditionality to reduce the stigma associated with its lending. Here's what it did:

- First, the IMF wants conditions attached to IMF loans to reflect program countries' strength in policies and fundamentals. This point reflects a change from ex-post to ex-ante conditionality. Before 2009, the IMF considered the crisis situation of a country and formulated its conditionality after the fact (ex-post). Now, especially when providing the short-term liquidity facility (SLF) to countries currently in a temporary crisis but otherwise with strong fundamentals, the Fund doesn't engage in ex-post monitoring of these countries.

- Second, the IMF wants stronger ownership of IMF programs by program countries. Program countries' government should be able to defend the conditions attached to IMF loans to their constituents and work diligently to fulfill them.

- Third, the IMF wants to be mindful of the effects of its conditions on the most vulnerable segments of the population in program countries.

Additionally, the IMF increased member countries' access to quotas. As discussed in Chapter 12, the Bretton Woods system provided the IMF with its own funds through a quota system. It worked just like a membership subscription. The same setup continued after the end of the Bretton Woods era. Of course, now the IMF has 188 member countries, and each member country is assigned a quota based on the country's relative size in the world economy. In addition to the member country's voting power, quota affects its access to the IMF's financial support. The overhaul in 2009 doubled the access limits to 200 percent of quota on an annual basis and to a 600 percent of quota cumulative limit. Exceptions include Greece, where the IMF's support amounted to more than 3,200 percent of this country's quota.

Reducing the nominal vigor of conditionality and substantially increasing member countries' access to financial support may increase the criticism of the IMF, which focuses on moral hazard. The term *moral hazard* means creating an environment in which people or countries can make wrong decisions without paying the price for these decisions (or paying a much smaller price than they otherwise would).

One of the signs of moral hazard associated with IMF programs is the recidivism observed in these programs. In this context, *recidivism* means the recurrence of the economic problem that requires the country to seek the IMF's assistance. In the post–Bretton Woods era, most developing countries with pegged exchange rates have received multiple IMF programs. This fact has been interpreted as a sign of the ineffective nature of the IMF programs. The view implies that, despite conditionality, IMF programs cannot prevent future domestic macroeconomic policies that lead to a reserve loss. It means that the total cost of IMF support (conditionality plus interest rate) may not be higher than the benefit of what countries think they are receiving by implementing policies that are incompatible with their peg. Now that, since 2009, the IMF has enlarged its support to developed countries without a peg but with a financial crisis, it can create a different kind of recidivism.

The counterfactual argument is used against the criticism of the IMF. In this context, the counterfactual indicates the outcome in the absence of the IMF's support. The IMF and its supporters maintain that the economic outcome would have been much worse without the IMF's support. It means that, despite possible moral hazard, funds provided by the IMF prevent currency or financial crises from getting larger and more harmful. However, measuring the counterfactual and proving that the IMF's support actually averts a much larger crisis is difficult, if not impossible.

Additionally, whether it's a problem with pegged exchange rates in a developing country or a financial crisis in a developed country, the policy combinations leading to these crises are well known. If these policy combinations are avoided, to a large extent, receiving financial support from the IMF can be avoided as well.

Mirror, Mirror: Deciding Which International Monetary System Is Better

Until now, this chapter and the previous two chapters have examined various types of exchange rate regimes. Professional and laymen alike have an opinion about what kind of an international monetary system the world should have. Therefore, this section compares alternative international monetary systems by highlighting their advantages and disadvantages.

Nostalgic about the Bretton Woods system? The case for fixed exchange rates

A metallic standard system such as the gold standard or the reserve currency standard has the following advantages:

✔ **Price stability:** This advantage has been viewed as one of the virtues of the metallic standard. Price stability implies that changes in prices are small, gradual, and expected. One of the most important factors that can affect price stability is monetary policy. As discussed in Chapters 11 and 12, conducting monetary policy under a metallic standard isn't possible. Most of the time, the concern is that the central bank inflates the economy through expansionary monetary policies or, in extreme cases, by printing money. In a metallic standard, no such fear exists because, if a country implements especially expansionary monetary policies, the metallic standard is no longer viable and must be abandoned. Therefore, price stability is embedded in the metallic standard. This system avoids hyperinflation as well. In contrast, a central bank can print fiat currency at a high rate and generate hyperinflation. There are examples of high inflation rates where central banks had to introduce incredibly large banknotes. For example, in 1923, Germany introduced a banknote for 20 billion German marks, which could buy 20 pounds of bread, 20 glasses of beer, or a little more than half a pound of meat. Similarly, in 1993, Yugoslavia introduced a banknote for 500 billion dinars.

✔ **Economic stability and prosperity:** A metallic standard can diminish the short-run fluctuations in a country's output, which are also called business cycles. The reason for decreasing volatility in output may lie in price stability. Price stability, or the absence of large and unexpected changes in the average price level, may work as a signal to producers for how much to produce. Therefore, when price stability exists, fewer busts and booms and more economic prosperity may result.

✔ **Fixed exchange rates:** A metallic standard leads to fixed exchange rates (see Chapters 11 and 12). In a gold standard, each country determines the gold parity of its currency, which fixes the exchange rates between countries. In a reserve currency system, the reserve currency has a gold parity, and all other currencies are pegged to the reserve currency, which also leads to fixed exchange rates. Fixed exchange rates enable the following:

- **The reduction of uncertainty in international trade and portfolio flows:** Exchange rate risk is a barrier to international business. Under the fixed exchange rate regime, nobody has to use scarce resources to guess the next period's exchange rate.

- **An automatic balance of payment adjustment mechanism to maintain internal and external balance:** This mechanism, also called the price–specie–flow mechanism, takes care of imbalances between countries' current account and price levels. If a country runs a current account surplus and accumulates specie, prices increase, making this country's goods more expensive to foreign-ers. This situation reduces the current account surplus in the home country and the current account deficit in the foreign country. In the case of a current account deficit, the country is losing specie. Prices decline, making this country's goods less expensive to foreigners and reducing the current account deficit.

- **A symmetrical adjustment of monetary policies under a gold standard:** If the home country's central bank increases the money supply, it puts downward pressure on the home country's interest rates. This situation makes other countries' assets more attractive to investors. Because central banks are obligated to trade their currencies for gold at fixed rates, investors sell the home country's currency, buy gold, and sell gold to other central banks so that they can get other currencies to make use of countries' higher interest rates. The home country lost gold reserves, and the other countries now have larger gold reserves. Because gold reserves are part of the money supply, the money supply is declining in the home country and increasing in other countries. This situation increases interest rates in the home country and decreases them in foreign countries.

However, fixed exchange rates have disadvantages as well. Before presenting these disadvantages, we can question some of the advantages of fixed exchange rates:

- **Questionable price stability:** A metallic standard is considered to promote price stability. However, some studies indicate that the gold standard era experienced large fluctuations in the average price level. These fluctuations appear to have been caused by the changes in the relative price of gold with respect to the price of goods and services. For example, suppose that the gold parity indicates $35 for an ounce of gold, and the price of a typical basket is twice as much ($70). This situation implies a price level of $70 per output basket. If a major gold discovery occurs, the price of the output basket would increase, say, to $85. At the same time, the relative price of gold in terms of output would decline. It was 0.5 ($35 ÷ $70) before the discovery of new gold; it would be 0.41 ($35 ÷ $85) now. If no change takes place in the gold parity of $35 for an ounce of gold, the price level increases from $70 to $85, creating an inflation rate of 21 percent.

- **Questionable economic stability and prosperity:** As mentioned previously, because price stability leads to economic stability and, therefore, prosperity, the usual assumption is that the metallic standard years are associated with higher growth and lower volatility in growth. One of the disastrous economic slowdowns in recent history, the Great Depression, happened under the gold standard. Additionally, as discussed in

Chapter 11, competitively contractionary monetary policies were implemented during the gold standard starting in the 18th century, which led to lower output growth and higher unemployment.

✓ **Questionable price–specie–flow mechanism:** The price–specie–flow mechanism didn't work as well in theory under a gold standard. But it really doesn't work in a reserve currency standard. If the price–specie–flow mechanism had functioned, all countries' current accounts would be balanced. However, as discussed in Chapter 12, during the Bretton Woods era, some countries had persistent current account surpluses, and others had current account deficits. Theoretically, surplus countries were to lend to deficit countries. This scheme doesn't work when countries with persistently large current account deficits also have problems repaying their loans.

Additional disadvantages of the metallic standard follow:

✓ **Imports of other countries' unemployment and inflation rates:** Because countries can't implement autonomous monetary policies under a metallic standard, they many import their trade partner's inflation and unemployment rates. For example, if the inflation rate is increasing in a country, at the given exchange rate, its consumers may increase their demand for foreign goods, thus increasing the prices in other countries. Similarly, if a country experiences lower output growth and higher unemployment, at the given exchange rate, it buys less from other countries, which may have an adverse effect on other countries' output and employment.

✓ **Increase in precious metal reserves:** Under a metallic standard, such as the gold standard, central banks need to hold an adequate amount of gold reserves to maintain their currency's gold parity and have some additional gold to intervene in their exchange rates. However, central banks cannot increase their gold reserves as their economies grow. One possibility for increasing gold reserves is discovering new gold mines. If gold production isn't increasing, central banks compete for gold. They sell their domestic assets to buy gold, decreasing their money supply and possibly adversely affecting output and employment.

✓ **Potential influence of precious metal producers:** Whatever precious metal is in the metallic standard, producers of this metal may have an influence on the macroeconomic conditions in countries with the metallic standard. In terms of gold production, South Africa, China, and the Russian Federation occupy first, third, and seventh places. In terms of gold reserves, South Africa, the Russian Federation, and Australia take the first three places.

Don't like fixed things? The case for flexible exchange rates

As mentioned in Chapters 11 and 12, during wars and other military conflicts, the gold standard was abandoned. During these times, fiat currency and, consequently, flexible exchange rates ruled. Therefore, the post–Bretton Woods era starting in 1973 with its fiat currency and flexible exchange rates is no stranger to the international monetary system. The only difference is that, although the fiat currency/flexible exchange rate combination was implemented as a transition policy during wars under a metallic standard, this combination became the norm after 1973.

A perception problem crops up with the gold standard. Because the gold standard is associated with fixed exchange rates and renders monetary policy ineffective, the gold standard means stability. However, as indicated in Chapters 11 and 12, history has seen no continuous gold standard period. The impossibility of conducting independent monetary policy under a metallic standard prompted countries to go off the standard during wars, independence wars, revolutions, and similar events.

In terms of how the Bretton Woods period went, the problem of selective memory is at work. Especially in the U.S., some people prefer to remember the mid-1940s portion of the Bretton Woods era, when the U.S. and the U.S. dollar seemed strong. This memory is reflected over the entire Bretton Woods era, describing it as a stable period. As discussed in Chapter 12, in reality, only the first five or six years of the era were good for the U.S., with a strong U.S. economy and dollar. Starting in the 1950s, the conditions worsened steadily for the U.S. until 1971, when the Bretton Woods system broke down. When the Bretton Woods system ended in 1971, the U.S. was a country with a higher inflation rate, a large current account deficit, and a weaker currency, none of which happened overnight.

The flexible exchange rate system has these advantages:

- **Flexible exchange rates as automatic stabilizers:** The necessity of maintaining internal and external balance under a metallic standard is based on the fact that a metallic standard leads to a fixed exchange rate regime. If the relative price of currencies is fixed and a country's output, employment, and current account performance and other relevant economic variables change, the exchange rate cannot change. This fact causes friction in the entire economic system. However, if exchange rates are allowed to change, they change in the appropriate direction, given the nature of changes in the variables affecting the exchange rates. As mentioned in Chapters 5–7, the monetary policy and growth performance of a country affect exchange rates. For example, when foreigners' demand for a country's exports declines, output also decline and the country's currency depreciates. This situation helps improve the country's export performance because depreciation makes the country's goods cheaper to foreigners. If the same initial shock happened under the fixed exchange rate regime (decline in the demand for the country's exports), then because the exchange rate can't change, the country must reduce the money supply, which further decreases the output.

✓ **Monetary policy autonomy:** Under the flexible exchange rate regime, countries can implement autonomous monetary policies to address problems with inflation and output. Because monetary policies affect inflation rates, countries can decide on their long-run inflation rate and don't have to import their trade partners' inflation rate, as is the case under a fixed exchange rate. A larger divergence among inflation rates has occurred during the post–Bretton Woods era. Clearly, the extent of monetary policy in either direction (expansionary or contractionary) affects the exchange rate under the flexible exchange rate system. An increase (decrease) in the money supply leads to the depreciation (appreciation) of a currency.

The main disadvantages of the flexible exchange rate system follow:

✓ **Exchange rate risk:** The main disadvantage of flexible exchange rates is their volatility. In the post–Bretton Woods era, one of the characteristics of flexible exchange rate is their excess volatility. The changes in exchange rates are more frequent and larger than the underlying fundamentals imply.

✓ **Potential for too much use of expansionary monetary policy:** The downside of being able to conduct autonomous monetary policies is the ability to create higher inflation rates. Under a flexible exchange rate regime, expansionary or contractionary monetary policies can address recessionary or inflationary pressures, respectively. Especially when expansionary monetary policies are frequently used, higher rates of inflation follow.

✓ **Questionable stabilizing effects:** Previously, automatic stabilizing was mentioned as an advantage of the flexible exchange rate system. Exchange rates change in the appropriate direction when the country's inflation rate, output, and current account balance change. Especially in terms of current account imbalances, exchange rates determined in the foreign exchange markets are supposed to change to prevent the occurrence of persistent and large current account deficits and surpluses. However, some countries have deficits (such as the U.S., Spain, Portugal, and Greece), and some countries have a surplus (such as Germany and China). Moreover, the data indicate long swings in major exchange rates, which are called misalignments. Therefore, it seems that flexible exchange rates do not change frequently enough to eliminate current account imbalances. An adverse effect of these misalignments is that they give deficit countries the motivation to impose trade restrictions.

Intermediate regimes and overview of alternative exchange rate regimes

As discussed in this chapter under the title "Unilaterally pegged exchange rates," in addition to the fixed and flexible exchange rate regimes, intermediate foreign exchange regimes also have appeared in the post–Bretton Woods era. Pegged exchange rates, especially the soft or crawling pegs, have the characteristics of the fixed and flexible exchange rate regimes without the metallic standard. After 1971, unlike the Bretton Woods system, many developing countries adopted a unilateral peg.

These pegs have been implemented to improve the trade position of countries (making either exports or imports cheaper). Starting in the mid-1980s, emerging markets pegged their exchange rates to attract foreign portfolio flows into their countries and improve their hard currency receipts. These pegs fulfilled their objectives for awhile. When developing countries wanted to affect the prices of their exports and imports, they certainly could do that. When pegs were introduced to attract foreign investors, this happened as well.

However, substantial costs were associated with these soft pegs. The sort of pegs aiming to favorably affect developing countries' exports and imports distorted relative prices in these countries, which led to inefficient use of scarce resources. The kind of pegs implemented to attract foreign investors proved to be extremely harmful when investors became suspicious that the pegs couldn't be maintained for long. Countries with these kinds of pegs either weren't careful with their fiscal and monetary policy, which put the credibility of the peg in danger, or didn't have the necessary stability and strength in their political environment and financial structure. In either case, speculative attacks on pegged currencies had extremely harmful effects on some emerging countries.

This section has been all about comparing alternative exchange rate regimes. Table 13-1 summarizes this section's discussion on the subject.

One point Table 13-1 illustrates is the undeniable presence of tradeoffs. Especially during times of uncertainty, policymakers and people alike desire stability. If the understanding of stability is that an international monetary system has inherent mechanisms that ensure stability, then the discussion provided since Chapter 11 indicates that no such system exists. Reality has shown that stabilizing mechanisms inherent in any system work a lot better on paper than in reality. Therefore, selecting an international monetary system among the alternative systems doesn't entail selecting one without a price — it involves selecting one whose price countries are willing to pay.

Table 13-1   Advantages and Disadvantages of Alternative Exchange Rate Regimes

Exchange Rate Regimes	Pro	Con
Fixed	No sudden changes in ER; no need to forecast future exchange rates	Import of other countries' domestic economic problems, such as inflation and unemployment
Flexible	Insulation of countries from other countries' economic problems, such as inflation and unemployment	Excessive volatility in exchange rates
Pegged	Stability provided by a nominal anchor	Prone to speculative attack
	Financing economic development through incoming portfolio flows	Hot money leaving the country fast if investors doubt the credibility of the peg

Chapter 14

The Euro: A Study in Common Currency

Most of this book focuses on exchange rates between countries, implicitly assuming that these countries have their national currencies. What if a number of countries that have had their national currencies for a long time decide to abolish their currencies and adopt a common currency? Once the common currency is in place, then, in accordance with exchange rate determination, you start asking questions about the monetary authority of the common-currency area. Who is conducting monetary policy? What kind of monetary policy will they conduct? Is it likely that governments of the common-currency area affect monetary policy? Establishing a common currency area among sovereign nations is no doubt an important undertaking. Therefore, this chapter starts with the preparation period during which European countries worked toward a common currency. I also discuss the theory of the optimum currency area (OCA), to explore the requirements of a common currency. This chapter then examines the accomplishments and challenges of the euro.

Introducing the Euro

The euro was introduced as an accounting unit in 1999 and as currency in circulation in 2002. But the emergence of the common currency was based on almost half a century of discussions and preparations. In this section, I highlight the historical and theoretical origins of the common currency.

A very brief history of the European Union

In 1946, following the end of World War II, British Prime Minister Sir Winston Churchill gave a famous and momentous speech at the University of Zurich. He talked about Europe as a continent of great wealth and distinct cultural heritage. But he called the devastating conflicts and wars on this continent as the tragedy of Europe. Churchill's proposal recognized the common historical and cultural inheritance among the European people and called for the creation of a European family. This famous speech introduced the phrase "the United States of Europe."

The first attempt at European integration started with the European Coal and Steel Community (ECSC), introduced by the Paris Treaty (1951). Because coal and steel had been crucial for European countries' war industry, the aim was to introduce a supranational authority that would oversee the peaceful use of these strategic resources. Six countries (France, West Germany, Italy, Belgium, the Netherlands, and Luxembourg) signed the Paris Treaty.

In 1957, the same six countries signed the Rome Treaty, which introduced the European Economic Community (EEC). Even though the EEC started as a customs union among these countries, it became instrumental for the subsequent economic and monetary unification of Europe. Between the establishment of the EEC and the Maastricht Treaty in 1992, the economic and political integration of Europe continued in the areas of defense, the judicial system, and foreign policy. By the time the Maastricht Treaty was signed in 1992, European integration was much more than just an economic cooperation. This treaty thus renamed the EEC as the European Union (EU). Most important, the Maastricht Treaty formally introduced the idea of a single European currency, which became the euro. The first step toward a common currency was the European Currency Unit (ECU), an accounting unit consisting of a basket of a specified amount of member countries' currencies.

Optimum currency area (OCA)

An important question for the euro was whether there was a good economic reason to have a single money for the EU. In economics, this question is answered in terms of whether an area is an "optimal currency area." An optimum currency area (OCA) refers to a geographical region consisting of a number of countries in which the use of a single currency increases economic efficiency. The theory of the OCA became important in the 1950 and 1960s when the fixed exchange rate regime of the Bretton Woods system (see Chapter 12) was thought to create balance of payments crises. At that time, as some economists were calling for flexible exchange rates, others were searching for other exchange rate systems. The OCA was an example of the latter. Additionally, as discussed previously, the EEC was introduced in the late 1950s as a custom union to encourage free trade among the member countries. Whether member countries should have flexible or fixed exchange rates within the EEC and whether they should share a single currency were important questions at that time.

The OCA argument doesn't deny the efficiency of using a common currency in an area (region) previously consisting of nations with their distinct currencies. However, the term *optimum* in *optimum currency area* suggests that a common currency isn't suitable for every region. An OCA should have the following characteristics:

- ✔ Countries in the region should have a similar economic structure and, therefore, be affected by similar economic shocks. For example, if all countries in the region produce textiles and wheat, a productivity shock to the textile industry would affect all countries in the region. The region then is a good candidate for an OCA.

- ✔ The region should have labor mobility. If free movement of labor is restricted, unemployment rates would persist in some countries. Additionally, national stabilization policies cannot address economic shocks to all sectors. In this case, labor mobility may help decrease the unemployment rate.

With these characteristics present, a common currency requires coordinating monetary policy among the countries in the region and, therefore, establishing a common central bank. In an OCA, nation-based monetary policies weaken the credibility of a common currency. In addition, symmetric economic shocks are helpful so that the common currency's central bank can implement stabilization policies that affect the entire area or region.

After fulfilling the requirements of symmetric shocks and labor mobility, the efficiency-enhancing effects of a common currency take place in the flows of goods, services, and capital within the area. For example, as the use of a common currency increases trade among the common-currency countries, increased trade lead to price convergence within the common currency area.

Ease of use

Nineteenth-century philosopher and economist John Stuart Mill called the situation in which every nation has its distinct currency a barbarism and an inconvenience. But note that this view of a common currency considers only the medium of exchange function of money. Clearly, it's more efficient to use the same currency, the dollar, every time I cross the bridge over the Mississippi River from Illinois to Missouri so that I can have dinner in St. Louis. You can make the same argument when going from Offenburg (Germany) to Strasburg (France). In fact, the distance between these two cities may be less than that between my town in Illinois and St. Louis.

Walking the Stages of European Monetary Integration

The EU took about two decades to introduce the Euro. The road to the common currency was paved by various monetary arrangements among the EU members. This section discusses the progression in Europe, from having a number of national currencies to introducing the euro.

European Monetary System (EMS) and the European Monetary Union (EMU)

Introducing a common currency in countries that have their national currencies for a long time is a challenging proposition. There needs to be a preparation period during which countries in the common currency area are ready to use the common currency. In the case of euro, the European Monetary System (EMS) and the Economic and Monetary Union (EMU) reflect these preparation periods.

The EMS (1979–1998) originally included eight members: Belgium, Denmark, France, Germany, Ireland, Italy, Luxembourg, and the Netherlands. Among other things, the EMS introduced the European Exchange Rate Mechanism I (ERM I) to reduce exchange rate variability among the EMS countries, which was a step toward the introduction of the common currency. While the EMS countries' currencies were floating against other currencies, the ERM I introduced a pegged exchange rate system for the EMS countries' currencies. The changes in EMS currencies were forced to be within an interval of ±2.25 percent, in other words, with a maximum increase of 2.25 percent and a maximum decline of 2.25 percent.

As with any other pegged exchange rate regime (see Chapter 12), the EMS had problems. When the previously mentioned interval was reached in an exchange rate between two EMS countries, both countries' central banks had to intervene so that the exchange rate remained in the interval. The central bank intervention can also be unilateral to defend its currency. When defense wasn't possible, countries such as France and Italy introduced capital controls to limit the possibility of speculative attack and the outflow of funds. Additionally, central banks of stronger currencies provided credit to countries with weaker currencies, to prevent the EMS from disintegrating. Toward the early 1990s, some currencies were finding it increasingly difficult to remain within the EMS interval, even with interventions in the foreign exchange markets. In these cases, some countries in the EMS realigned their exchange rates by revaluing and devaluing their currencies.

Additionally, the German unification in 1990 put pressure on the EMS. The unification of East and West Germany required an expansionary fiscal policy that resulted in higher inflation in Germany. The Bundesbank had no choice but to follow a contractionary monetary policy and raise its key interest rates. For EMS pegs to remain within the band, other countries in the system should have followed similar monetary policies. However, countries such as France, Italy, and the U.K. weren't willing to adhere to the EMS rules at the expense of a recession in their countries.

Despite the many pressures on the EMS, the system helped inflation rates converge among the member countries. Although most EMS countries started out with higher inflation rates (in some cases, double-digit, inflation rates) in the late 1970s (except for Germany), by the mid-1990s, inflation rates in the EMS countries converged with rates in Germany.

As the EMS was making progress in aligning the exchange rates of the participating countries, a big push for a single currency came from the Maastricht Treaty of 1992. This treaty introduced the Economic and Monetary Union (EMU) part of EU law that a single currency will be established by 1999, and countries in the EU are expected to eventually join the common currency area.

Following the introduction of the euro as an accounting unit in 1999, the Exchange Rate Mechanism II (ERM II) was introduced. The reason for the ERM II was that the original eight members of the ERM I closely worked together up to the introduction of the euro. But as of 1999, there were other EU countries such as Estonia, Lithuania, and Cyprus, which were not in the ERM I and therefore not in the euro-zone. The objective of the ERM II was to acclimatize the more recent member countries of the EU toward becoming members of the Euro-zone. The ERM II provided non-euro countries with a larger leeway of 15 percent to have their currency fluctuate above or below the determined exchange rate. Entry into ERM II required agreement among the ministers and central bank governors of the candidate country, the Euro-zone countries, and the European Central Bank (ECB). The conditions of ERM II reflect how the Euro-zone works, to ensure a smooth transition of the countries from ERM II into the Euro-zone. Countries must successfully participate in ERM II for at least two years before becoming a member of the Euro-zone.

To maintain price stability in the then-planned Euro-zone, the Maastricht Treaty of 1992 introduced convergence criteria related to controlling inflation, public deficit, and public debt, as well as to exchange rate stability and the convergence of interest rates. These conditions imply the benchmarks for joining the EMU as well the Euro-zone:

- ✔ The inflation rate must be no more than 1.5 percentage points higher than the average of the three lowest-inflation member states of the EU.

- ✔ The ratio of the budget deficit to the GDP (gross domestic product) must not exceed 3 percent at the end of the preceding fiscal year.

✔ The ratio of gross government debt to GDP ratio must not exceed 60 percent at the end of the preceding fiscal year.

✔ Applicant countries must join ERM II under the EMS for two consecutive years and must not devalue their currency during the period.

✔ The nominal long-term interest rate must not be more than 2 percentage points higher than those in the three lowest-inflation member states.

Additionally, in 1997, based on Germany's initiative, the Stability and Growth Pact (SGP) was introduced. This pact aimed to avoid large budget deficits among the EMS countries and suggested a budget close to balance or in surplus. Germany's concern was that fiscal imbalances such as large budget deficits in some countries may pressure monetary policy to be expansionary. In retrospect, Germany may have been correct in its suspicion of fiscal policies: The last section in this chapter discusses the fiscal follies of some of the EU members in the late 2000s and early 2010s.

European System of Central Banks (ESCB) and European Central Bank (ECB)

In 1998, the European Central Bank (ECB) was established under the European System of Central Banks (ESCB). The ESCB includes the ECB and the national central banks (NCB) of all EU member states, independent of their adoption of the euro. The Eurosystem, on the other hand, consists of the ECB and the NCBs of the EU member states whose currency is the euro. Because some EU member states still have their national currency, making a distinction between the Eurosystem and the ESCB is important.

All for one, and one for all

When the euro was introduced as an accounting unit in January 1999, the Frankfurt-based ECB took over the responsibility of monetary policy for the Euro-zone from the central banks of 11 member states. As discussed previously, introducing the common European currency requires putting a central bank in charge of conducting monetary policy in the Euro-zone. Therefore, a country in the Euro-zone has no autonomy to respond to economic shocks using its own monetary policy. Individual central banks cannot take steps to stabilize their economies. The idea is that countries in the Euro-zone use fiscal policies and structural changes to manage their economy.

The aims of the ECB are similar to the aims of any modern central bank. The ECB's primary objective is to maintain price stability. Quantitatively, it aims to maintain a medium-term inflation rate below but close to 2 percent. The ECB's primary goal is also consistent with the EU's goals. The Treaty on European Union lists price stability, economic growth, a highly competitive social market economy, full employment, and social progress among its goals. Therefore, the ECB's primary objective of price stability is helpful in achieving economic growth and full employment.

When conducting monetary policy, as in the case of other central banks, the ECB adjusts its key interest rate instead of exchange rates. Modern central banks are aware of the impossibility of maintaining interest rate and exchange rate targets simultaneously, unless they implement capital controls. Therefore, the ECB has chosen the monetary autonomy, and the euro floats against other currencies.

Additionally, as any other modern central bank, the ECB issues currency within the Euro-zone, collects data about the ESCB and the Eurosystem, and provides supervision (whether rules are followed), regulation (which rules to follow to reduce risk), and monitoring (identifying weaknesses and vulnerabilities) of the financial system.

The makeup of the ECB

The Governing Council is the main decision-making body of the ECB. It consists of the six members of the Executive Board, plus the governors of the national central banks of the 17 Euro-zone countries. The Governing Council usually meets twice a month in Frankfurt. At its first meeting each month, the Governing Council assesses economic and monetary developments and makes its monthly monetary policy decision. At its second meeting, the Council discusses issues related to other tasks and responsibilities of the ECB and the Eurosystem. The minutes of the meetings aren't published, but to promote transparency, the monetary policy decision is explained in detail at a press conference by the president of the Governing Council held shortly after the first meeting each month.

Characteristics of the ECB

An important characteristic of a modern central bank is its *independence* from the fiscal authority, which is important for a central bank to maintain price stability. In the case of the Euro-zone, although there's only one monetary authority (the ECB), there are many fiscal authorities in the Euro-zone, matching the number of Euro-zone countries. However, neither the ECB nor any NCB is allowed to seek or take instructions from any EU institution or any government. The ECB is also financially independent from the EU and has its own budget. Its capital is subscribed and paid up by the central banks of the Eurosystem.

The ECB is aware that it functions independently in a democratic society and, therefore, values *accountability*. Here are the ways accountability is maintained:

- ✔ The ECB is committed to regular and accurate reporting of its activities and decisions to the public. The ECB publishes a Monthly Bulletin, and the members of the Governing Council deliver speeches to share with the public the ECB's ideas on relevant topics.

- ✔ Immediately following the first Governing Council meeting of each month, the ECB president and vice president hold a press conference to provide in-depth explanations of the ECB's monetary policy decision and its rationale.

- ✔ Because the European Parliament derives its legitimacy directly from the citizens of the EU, the ECB has dialogue with the European Parliament.

  - • The president of the ECB informs the European Parliament's Committee on Economic and Monetary Affairs (ECON) about its monetary policy on a quarterly basis.

  - • The president of the ECB presents the ECB's annual report before the plenary session of the European Parliament.

  - • Other members of the ECB's Executive Board appear before the European Parliament to address specific issues.

  - • The ECB provides replies to written questions of the members of the European Parliament.

  - • The ECB is also involved in informal discussions with the members of the European Parliament about the ECB's monetary policies, as well as subjects related to the ECB's expertise.

For a discretionary monetary authority that identifies its policies as events unfold, *transparency* is also important. A transparent central bank makes its objectives and decision process clear so that markets aren't surprised when the central bank announces its monetary policy decision. Transparency in monetary policy promotes efficient and accurate market expectations, which helps rapidly transmit any monetary policy decision into relevant economic variables such as consumption and investment. The ECB considers three aspects of transparency:

- ✔ The ECB wants to be clear that its primary objective is price stability.

- ✔ The ECB wants to be realistic about monetary policy and communicate with the public on what monetary policy can and cannot do.

- ✔ The ECB considers the timely provision of its assessment of the current economic situation and policy decisions as crucial aspects of its transparency.

Getting the Lowdown: Euro's Report Card

The previous sections discuss the origins of the European economic cooperation, the preparations for the euro, and the characteristics of the European Central Bank that issues euro. This section provides a quick review of which countries are in the EU and which ones are included in the Euro-zone. It also discusses how the euro has been doing compared to the other currencies. Finally, some of the recent challenges of the euro are examined.

Euro-zone countries

The Greek epsilon (ε) supposedly inspired the symbol for the euro, €. The additional two parallel lines in the middle were supposed to imply stability. As mentioned previously, the euro was introduced as an accounting currency on January 1, 1999. Euro notes and coins started circulating on January 1, 2002, and in about two months, the euro replaced the national currencies at fixed conversion rates.

The ECB and the NCB in the Euro-zone jointly issue euro banknotes without distinguishing which central bank issued them. The NCB puts into circulation more than 90 percent of euro banknotes reflecting the corresponding country's share in the ECB capital, which reflects the country's share in the EU population and the GDP.

As of 2012, 17 of the 27 member states of the European Union use the euro: Austria, Belgium, Cyprus, Estonia, Finland, France, Germany, Greece, Ireland, Italy, Luxembourg, Malta, the Netherlands, Portugal, Slovakia, Slovenia, and Spain. The remaining 10 EU members (Bulgaria, Czech Republic, Denmark, Latvia, Lithuania, Hungary, Poland, Romania, Sweden, and the U.K.) don't currently use the euro. Although adopting the euro is a requirement for the EU countries upon meeting the convergence criteria, exceptions do exist. The U.K. and Denmark negotiated exemptions, and Sweden (which joined the EU in 1995, after the Maastricht Treaty was signed) rejected the adoption of the euro in a 2003 referendum.

Prior to the introduction of the euro, the European micro-states, including Monaco, San Marino, Vatican City, and Andorra were using the currency of the closest country (Italian lira in San Marino and Vatican City, French franc in Monaco, and French franc and Spanish peseta in Andorra). With France, Italy, and Spain adopting the Euro, the micro-states adopted the euro as well. Some European countries adopted the euro without becoming an EU member, among them Montenegro (a candidate country for the EU) and Kosovo. Additionally, more than 175 million people in the world use currencies pegged to the euro; these include Cuba, North Korea, and Syria, as well as the former colonies and territories of the Euro-zone countries. Therefore, more than 300 million people in the world use the euro in various forms. All this makes the Euro-zone the second-largest economy, the second-largest reserve currency, and the second-most-traded currency in the world.

How the euro stands up to other currencies

Since its introduction in 1999, the euro has become one of the major reserve currencies, along with the dollar, the Japanese yen, the pound sterling, and the Swiss franc. Figures 14-1 and 14-2 indicate the annual changes in major currencies with respect to the euro. These figures show that, between 1999 and late 2000, the euro depreciated against most major currencies. But this trend was reversed afterward, and the euro appreciated until 2008 against most major currencies. The appreciation of the euro during this period was especially strong against the U.S. dollar and the yen.

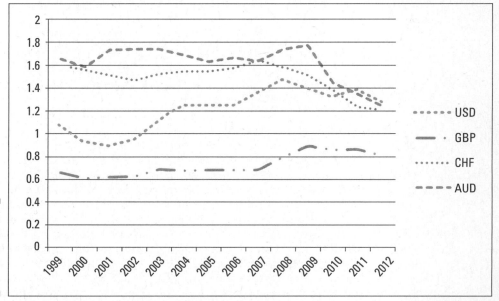

Figure 14-1: Selected euro exchange rates.

Data available at www.ecb.int/stats/exchange/eurofxref/html/index.en.html. Annual averages are calculated from daily data. USD, GBP, CHF, and AUD represent the U.S. dollar, British pound sterling, Swiss franc, and Australian dollar, respectively.

The depreciation of the euro started in 2008 with the global financial crisis and, most important, with the European sovereign debt crisis that seemed to be worsened by the global financial crisis. The Australian dollar, the Swiss franc, and the yen appreciated substantially against the euro. This trend continued as the Greek debt and the problems of the Spanish banking sector made headlines in summer 2012.

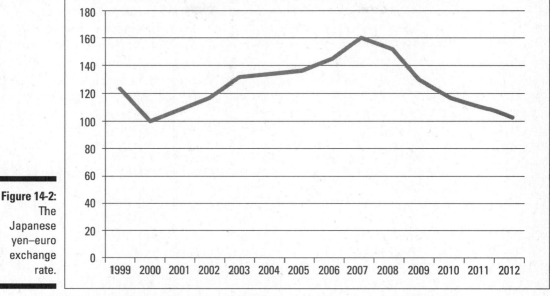

Figure 14-2:
The
Japanese
yen–euro
exchange
rate.

Data available at www.ecb.int/stats/exchange/eurofxref/html/index.en.html. Annual averages are calculated from daily data.

Accomplishments of the Euro-zone

Since its introduction in 1999, the euro has accomplished many positive milestones:

- ✔ The most obvious benefit of adopting a single currency is to remove the transaction cost of exchanging currency. Consumers and firms pay no fees for cross-border transactions. Inside the Euro-zone, all monetary transactions use the same currency even if a transaction is across national borders.

The risk of unanticipated exchange rate movements always adds uncertainty for individuals or firms when investing or trading outside their own currency. But the common European currency removes all exchange rate risk within the common currency area. All transfers within the Euro-zone are treated as domestic transactions and there is no exchange rate risk. Companies that hedged against exchange rate risk no longer need to consider this additional cost. This factor is particularly important for countries whose currencies fluctuated a great deal, such as some of the Southern European countries.

- ✔ Studies suggest that the introduction of the euro increased trade within the Euro-zone by 5 to 10 percent.
- ✔ The absence of exchange rate risk and restrictions to capital transfers within the Euro-zone seems to have increased investment in physical

capital within the Euro-zone by 5 percent since the introduction of the euro. Studies also suggest a large increase of 20 percent in foreign direct investment within the Euro-zone. Additionally, the euro increased investment in countries with previously weaker currencies by an average 22 percent.

✔ A common currency promotes the integration of financial markets in the common currency area, which increases the liquidity of financial markets. Increased liquidity and lower transaction costs may help financial firms in the common currency area compete better within and outside the common currency area. In fact, strong evidence indicates that the introduction of the euro has greatly contributed to European financial integration. The euro has decreased the cost of trading in bonds, equity, and bank assets within the Euro-zone.

✔ Differences in prices motivate arbitrage; therefore, commodities are traded just to exploit price differentials. But a common currency is expected to decrease differences in prices. The evidence on the convergence of prices in the Euro-zone is mixed. Some studies cannot find any evidence of price convergence since the introduction of the euro, but they find evidence that ERM I had largely achieved convergence by the early 1990s. Other studies find evidence of price convergence following the introduction of the euro in a sector-specific way. The evidence points to the automobile sector as an area of strong price convergence.

Challenges of the Euro-zone

Some economists argue that the euro-zone isn't an OCA and provide the following explanations:

✔ By the time the euro was introduced in 1999, the intra-EU trade made up 10 to 20 percent of the EU members' output. Since the euro, the intra-EU trade makes up about 16 percent of the Euro-zone's GDP. The euro's contribution to the increase in intra-EU trade is suggested to be about 9 percent, which isn't a substantial reason to have a single currency.

✔ Despite the laws regarding the free movement of labor within the EU, labor mobility has remained at a minimum, possibly due to cultural, linguistic, and other legal barriers. Although labor is allowed to move freely within the EU, because a high percentage of the European labor is unionized, labor laws and regulations related to benefits still discourage mobility within the EU Strong union presence, as well as generous and longer unemployment benefits in Europe, have contributed to persistently high unemployment rates. Some economists recommend introducing supranational employment policies to make labor more mobile in the Euro-zone.

✔ European economies are diverse and experience asymmetric economic shocks. The economies of Germany and France have not much in common with the economies of the smaller Baltic or Balkan countries, or some of the Mediterranean countries. For example, whereas Greece runs large current account deficits, Germany usually has current account surpluses. Greece and Spain have larger public debt than other countries in the Euro-zone.

✔ Diverging economies may be more problematic than dissimilar economies for a common currency area. The ECB is committed to lower inflation rates and a strong euro. However, lower inflation and a strong euro may be costly for the export sectors of some of the weaker Euro-zone countries. Therefore, current differences may lead to divergence among economic performance in Euro-zone countries.

✔ The ECB's commitment to price stability takes monetary policy out of the list of possible remedies for countries with weaker economies and higher unemployment rates. Additionally, fiscal policy is a problematic issue in the EU in general and the Euro-zone, in particular. In terms of fiscal policy, most EU countries have been skeptical toward a supranational fiscal authority. Therefore, fiscal policy remains as the individual Euro-zone country's affair. The EU budget is too small to transfer resources into slow-growth areas.

✔ One predictable consequence of adopting the euro is the decline in interest rates. This factor increases the market value of firms, especially in countries with weaker economies and currencies. Before the sovereign debt crisis in the Euro-zone, the cost of borrowing fell significantly in Greece, Ireland, Portugal, and Spain. Although the convergence criteria could prevent a prospective EU member with large government deficits from entering the ERM II or the Euro-zone, after a country is in the Euro-zone, the EU's control over the country's fiscal affairs may weaken. Consequently, countries may be in the position of accumulating substantial public debt.

Finding What the Future Holds for the Euro

Considering the sovereign debt crisis of the early 2010s, the EU and the Euro-zone are facing formidable challenges. This crisis has sparked questions regarding the long-term viability of the euro. Therefore, this section starts with reviewing what the euro-zone's sovereign crisis is all about. But the crisis has sparked questions regarding some of the fundamental challenges of the euro-zone in particular and the EU in general. These questions are related to the direction of political integration and the possibility of fiscal policy coordination, which is also addressed in this section.

Sovereign debt crisis taking a toll

In terms of the timeline, following the U.S. financial crisis in 2008, the European sovereign debt crisis started in 2009. It included the Euro-zone member countries Greece, Ireland, Italy, Spain, and Portugal. In some of these countries, bank bailouts or nationalization of some of the private banks and related recessions led to a significant increase in sovereign debt. Although these decisions were costly, they prevented a systemic failure of the banking system in these countries.

The previous section states that nominal interest rates decline after countries enter the ERM and the Euro-zone. But recently, increasing sovereign debt led to increasing interest rates and spreads on these countries' sovereign bonds. The crisis was visible in 2012, when nominal interest rates in Greece, Ireland, and Portugal diverged significantly from rates in the rest of the Euro-zone. In Greece, long-term interest rates reached almost 30 percent in 2012, while they remained around 12–13 percent in Ireland and Portugal. *Spread* is defined as the difference between the interest rate on a debt security and the interest rate on a riskless debt security with comparable maturity. If Germany's bond rate is considered the riskless rate of borrowing, in late 2010, the spread over Germany's interest rates started increasing to 9 percent in Greece and 3 percent in Ireland and Portugal.

Creating the EFSF

Some people argue that the EU acted indecisively at first, which led to the depreciation of the euro in early 2010. Then, realizing that the crisis couldn't end on its own, the EU introduced the European Financial Stability Facility (EFSF), which implied borrowing €750 billion from world financial markets and the IMF. In addition to the commitment from the IMF, all Euro-zone countries contributed to the EFSF, where their contributions to the EFSF reflected the size of their economy (as measured by their GDP or Gross Domestic Product). Therefore, Germany, France, and Italy have been the top three contributors to the EFSF, in that order.

The alternative to the EFSF would have been troubled countries raising funds through issuing debt at higher interest rates, which were deemed to be unacceptable. The decision was to have the EFSF raise funds by issuing bonds and other debt instruments. The funds raised have been used to recapitalize banks and buy sovereign debt of troubled Euro-zone countries. The ECB also reversed its "no bailout" policy and started buying government papers of the crisis countries, to avoid panic and illiquidity (lack of cash) in financial markets.

Utilizing the EFSF

A Euro-zone member can apply for the EFSF if it can show the difficulty of borrowing at reasonable interest rates in financial markets. Additionally, the country must work out an austerity program and present it to the European Commission (the 27-member executive body of the EU) and the IMF. Then the Euro-zone's finance ministers must unanimously accept the program.

Between 2008 and 2012, more than €490 billion was distributed to Greece, Hungary, Ireland, Latvia, Romania, and Spain. Greece received almost half of these funds. The €110 billion of the bailout to Greece in 2010 wasn't part of the EFSF; it came partly from the IMF and partly from bilateral lending by some of the Euro-zone countries. The situation of Greece was particularly severe, with higher unemployment rates, a ratio of budget deficit to GDP of 10 percent, and a ratio of debt to GDP of more than 100 percent. Ireland also received a sizeable package of more than €65 billion in late 2010.

Although downgrading Greek bonds was severe (down to a position reflecting default of the issuer), Greece wasn't the only country whose bonds major rating agencies have downgraded. Rating agencies initially assigned an AAA rating to EFSF bonds, but in 2012, Standard & Poor's downgraded the sovereign bonds of eight Euro-zone countries, as well as the EFSF bonds.

Pain of political (and fiscal) integration

The sovereign debt crisis in the Euro-zone hasn't been kind to intra-Euro-zone political relationships. By 2012, the financial stress caused frictions between Germany and France, much like during the 1992–1993 period, when the EMS was in trouble. Such difficult times have always fueled skepticism regarding the European integration (called *Euroskepticism*).

One function of a common currency is to promote international risk sharing within the common currency area. With risk sharing, one usually means fighting against the same shocks. In the case of the European sovereign debt crisis, the shock originated in a handful of countries as home-made problems. Therefore, instead of bringing the Euro-zone members together, the national nature of the underlying problems caused frictions among the EU and Euro-zone members.

It seems that certain structures aren't yet in place in the Euro-zone, in particular, and in the EU, in general. The EU has made great progress in such areas as environmental and judicial cooperation and competition policies, but fiscal issues have remained untouchable. This fact may be surprising because two of the Maastricht convergence criteria are related to the budget deficit and public debt. Although countries are expected to implement these criteria to be included in the Euro-zone, not much oversight on fiscal policies may occur after countries enter the Euro-zone.

Another sign of missing guidelines is the fact that the ECB changed its mind about bailing out countries in the Euro-zone. The Eurosystem (the ECB plus the NBC in the Euro-zone) was prohibited from granting loans to other EU bodies or member countries' public sectors, to protect monetary authority from the influence of fiscal authority. To be fair, the Maastricht Treaty of 1992 and the Stability and the Growth Pact (SGP) of 1997 were against bail-outs as well. At the end, the Euro-zone backed down from this rule and provided one of the largest bailouts in financial history.

An important reason for this making-rules-as-events-unfold attitude is Europe's fundamental quarrel regarding the nature of fiscal policy coordination. The European sovereign debt crisis revealed the lack of fiscal policy coordination, which, in turn, reflects the EU's struggle with political unification. Some countries and some groups in almost all European countries strongly oppose fiscal federalism. It seems that no country is ready to limit its control over fiscal policy or partially hand it over to a supranational or federal fiscal authority. In a way, having a supranational central bank such as the ECB as the monetary authority and a number of national fiscal authorities may put continuing political pressure on the ECB, despite its dedication to price stability and independence.

Part V
The Part of Tens

Enjoy an additional International Finance Part of Tens chapter online at www.dummies.com/extras/internationalfinance.

In This Part . . .

✔ I share great tips on important factors to remember in international finance.

✔ You'll find out that knowing what not to think is just as important as what to remember in international finance.

Chapter 15

Ten Important Points to Remember about International Finance

*T*his chapter reminds you of some important points in international finance. Many chapters in this book explain these points in detail; here you find short reminders.

Catching Up on What a Relative Price Is

As Chapter 2 indicates, an exchange rate (at least, the nominal exchange rate) is nothing but a relative price of one currency in terms of another one. In terms of apples and oranges, the relative price of oranges in terms of apples implies the number of apples that you have to give up to buy one orange. Similarly, the dollar–euro exchange rate indicates the number of dollars necessary to buy one euro. If the dollar–euro exchange rate is $0.95, this is the price of the euro in dollars. You give up $0.95 to buy one euro.

Finding Out What Makes a Currency Depreciate

Theories of exchange rate determination (Chapter 5, 6, and 7) provide a set of nominal and real variables that affect the exchange rate. In terms of nominal variables, higher growth in the money supply, higher inflation rates, and higher nominal interest rates lead to the depreciation of a currency. In terms of real variables, most models predict depreciation in a currency when a country's output growth rates and real interest rates are lower.

Keeping in Mind That Higher Nominal Interest Rates Imply Higher Inflation Rates

A positive relationship exists between nominal interest rates and inflation rates (Chapter 7). Higher inflation rates lead to higher nominal interest rates. Therefore, be careful when you compare nominal returns on comparable debt securities in different countries. When you observe a nominal return of 15 percent on a country's security and 5 percent in another, you find that inflation rates are higher in the former than those in the latter.

Paying Attention to Interest Rate Differentials When Investing in Foreign Debt Securities

Related to the previous point, as an international investor, you need to keep track of nominal returns and inflation rates in the countries you're considering investing in. Using the Fisher equation (Chapter 8), you can figure out your real returns in these countries. The real interest rate equals the difference between the nominal interest rates and the inflation rate. One problem crops up: People make financial decisions today without knowing the next period's inflation rate (for example, next year's rate). Therefore, when considering two countries for investment purposes, you need to have an expectation regarding these countries' future inflation rates.

Uncovering the Two Parts of Returns When Investing in Foreign Debt Securities

International investment is different than domestic investment. In domestic investment, you compare interest rates for similar risk and maturity. In international investment, in addition to considering interest rates or returns, you need to think about exchange rates. Therefore, you have two sources of possible income or profit (or loss) as an international investor. One source is your return on the financial instrument that you will hold for a certain period. The other is the possible change in the exchange rate while you are holding this instrument. The speculation examples in Chapter 3 show that you must keep an eye on both returns and the change in the exchange rate. The best-case scenario is that you earn a higher return on the foreign security, and the foreign currency appreciates while you're holding it.

Adjusting Your Expectations As Information Changes

International investment requires that investors keep track of the relevant countries' economic and political conditions. In the case of debt securities, you know the nominal return that you will receive in all countries. What you don't know at the time of the investment, and what can change during the period when you are holding another country's financial instrument, is the inflation rate and the change in the exchange rate. A change in government can introduce a more expansionary monetary policy, higher inflation rates, and depreciation of the currency down the line. All this can decrease your real return and possibly lead to a loss.

Appreciating the Size of Foreign Exchange Markets

The foreign exchange market is highly liquid and very large. In 2010, the average daily turnover was estimated at almost $4 trillion. Central banks intervene in the foreign exchange market to prevent unwanted upward or downward pressure on their currency (Chapter 13). You may ask what central banks can achieve through intervention.

It's true that the foreign exchange market is large, and this fact is probably why a number of developed countries' central banks come together at times and intervene (a concerted intervention). The number of central banks and the amount of intervention is important for the effectiveness and success of this kind of intervention. Even in a concerted effort, central banks try not to intervene against the market trend because, however large their intervention fund is, the market is much larger. Therefore, the preferred time for intervention is when the market is moving toward the desired direction on its own.

Using Foreign Exchange Derivatives for the Right Reason

Remember that spot foreign exchange markets are volatile, which is risky for a multinational company. If a company has future receivables or payables in foreign currency and if spot exchange rates are volatile, it faces considerable exchange rate risk. Instead of relying on spot markets, this company can use foreign exchange derivatives (Chapter 10) to hedge against the exchange rate risk. While volatility in spot foreign exchange markets is a problem for multinational companies, it presents an opportunity to speculators. Based on their expectations regarding the future spot rate, speculators can also use foreign exchange derivatives such as futures and options to make a buck.

Noting That Going Back to the Gold Standard Means Dealing with Fixed Exchange Rates

Especially in times of economic instability and pessimistic expectations, people tend to have nostalgic ideas about the gold standard era. The most remembered gold-standard episode is the Bretton Woods era (1944–1971) (Chapter 12). But what may be most remembered is the start of the Bretton Woods conference, when the U.S. emerged as the world's new economic and military superpower. With its new status, the U.S. successfully imposed its wishes at the conference. Among these wishes was the reserve currency setup, in which the dollar was pegged to gold and other currencies were pegged to the dollar. At the beginning, the dollar was perceived as good as or maybe better than gold because the dollar earned interest.

Problems started appearing as early as the late 1940s. Some of the problems were similar to those experienced in the earlier gold standard episodes. Despite the International Monetary Fund, current account imbalances couldn't be eliminated. More important, the reserve currency country, the U.S., started running large current account deficits in the 1950s. Not just the dollar, but also other currencies such as the British pound, seemed to be overvalued. Additionally, the disparity between the gold parity and the market price of gold was growing. Buying gold at the Bretton Woods price and selling it at the market price became a profitable business for speculators toward the 1960s. By 1971, the U.S. was a different superpower than in 1944, with a large current account and a budget deficit, higher inflation, and a loss in the value of its currency.

The Cold War and potentially dangerous crises such as the Cuban Missile Crisis in 1962 fueled increases in the market price of gold and make the policy adjustments difficult. However, in terms of the difficulty of keeping the exchange rate fixed and maintaining the internal and external balance, the Bretton Woods era was as unsuccessful as previous periods of metallic standard–based fixed exchange rate system.

Realizing the Value of Policy Coordination in a Common Currency

As discussed in Chapter 14, a common currency such as the euro offers important benefits to its member countries. The elimination of transaction costs in trade due to the existence of different currencies increases trade and financial integration, which in turn promotes price convergence and interest-rate convergence among countries.

But a common currency necessitates coordinating monetary and fiscal policies among the countries in the common currency area. In a monetary union, the most obvious and necessary coordination area is monetary policy. The European Central Bank (ECB) was established right before the introduction of the euro as an accounting currency in 1999.

In the Euro-zone, fiscal policy has been coordinated on an ad hoc basis. Although the Maastricht Treaty (1992) laid out the convergence criteria to join the Euro-zone, these criteria were applied to the applicants of the Euro-zone. Two of the four convergence criteria were related to the size of the budget deficit and debt. However, no supranational fiscal authority in the European Union (EU) monitors fiscal policy–related criteria after a country enters the Euro-zone. Given the recent problems with Greece, Spain, and Ireland, the lack of fiscal policy coordination may adversely affect the credibility of the euro.

Chapter 16

Ten Common Myths in International Finance

. . . .

In This Chapter

▶ Looking at thoughts you may want to steer clear of

▶ Keeping international finance ideas in check

. . . .

This chapter reminds you of some important points about international finance. These points imply ideas that you may be inclined to have, but that may be incorrect. Here you find ten short reminders of what not to think.

Expecting to Make Big Bucks Every Time You Speculate in Foreign Exchange Markets

You can lose big money in foreign exchange markets. Most speculative activity in foreign exchange markets is short term, with a time horizon of less than a year. There is *high* short-term volatility exists in exchange rates in spot foreign exchange markets. The term *high* emphasizes that the changes in exchange rates are greater than the changes in well-known fundamentals of exchange rates, such as inflation rates, interest rates, and growth rates. If you speculate using foreign exchange derivatives (Chapter 10), derivatives are not a guarantee for making profits; they only help you hedge against exchange rate risk.

Thinking You Can Buy a Big Mac in Paris at the Same Price as in Your Hometown

The Law of One Price doesn't work in reality (See Chapter 9). You can't buy a similar good, even one as standardized as a Big Mac, at the same price everywhere in the world after converting local prices into a common currency. Local production costs and market conditions vary among countries. A Big Mac is more expensive in many European countries than in the U.S. after its local price is converted into the dollar. Labor regulations make the cost of even unskilled labor more expensive in Europe. Additionally, reflecting different tastes, in some developing countries, McDonald's is considered a relatively upscale restaurant, compared to local restaurants. Therefore, the price of even similar goods differs between countries.

Ignoring Policymakers When It Comes to Exchange Rates

The monetary authority of a country is influential on long-term exchange rates because, through monetary policy (indirect intervention), central banks have an influence on nominal interest rates, inflation rates, and, consequently, real interest rates (as Chapters 6 and 7 show). Through direct interventions into foreign exchange markets by buying and selling currencies, central banks can have short-term influence on exchange rates or can help steer exchange rates into the desired direction. To the extent fiscal authority exercises influence on monetary authority, most of the time, this influence leads to expansionary monetary policy and eventual depreciation of the currency. Understand your home country's central bank in terms of its objectives, its attitude toward transparency, and the degree of its independency from fiscal authority. If you have foreign currency–denominated assets in your portfolio, do the same for the corresponding foreign central banks as well.

Giving Up on Theory Too Easily

Macroeconomic fundamentals don't explain short-term changes in exchange rates, but they're not necessarily wrong or meaningless. Differences in nominal interest rates, inflation rates, and output growth rates are important predictors of exchange rates in the long run. If you're interested in exchange rates and understand where they're headed in the long run, keep track of these variables.

Forgetting about High Short-Term Volatility in Exchange Rates

In terms of their characteristics, foreign exchange markets are closer to asset markets than to commodity markets. Therefore, fundamentals cannot explain their short-term volatility. Even though the macroeconomic fundamentals of exchange rates, such as money supply growth, inflation rates, nominal interest rates, and output growth rates, are helpful in predicting long-term exchange rates, they don't have much explanatory power in the short term. Therefore, if you have to involve foreign exchange markets for a couple days, weeks, or months, do make use of derivatives to hedge against foreign exchange risk (See Chapter 10).

Thinking that All Changes in the Exchange Rate Are Traceable to Changes in Fundamentals

Not every change in the exchange rate has an explanation based on a change in monetary policy. Models of exchange rate determination (as in Chapters 6 and 7) that include short-run nominal rigidities and overshooting demonstrate the relevance of adjustments when examining the changes in exchange rates. These adjustments are due to short-run rigidities (sticky prices) and the timing of the change in expectations. For example, in the overshooting example in Chapter 7, investors adjust their expectations regarding the future spot exchange rate as soon as they know about the change in monetary policy. As the name overshooting suggests, this leads to a large change in the exchange rate (appreciation or depreciation, depending upon the nature of the change in monetary policy). But the exchange rate doesn't stay there, because the rigid variable (in this case, sticky prices) haven't adjusted yet. When prices adjust in the appropriate direction, the exchange rate will change as well. But, as Chapter 7 indicates, this particular change in the exchange rate is in the opposite direction of the initial change and has nothing to do with the change in monetary policy. In this case, the change in the exchange rate is an adjustment and these adjustments may contribute to short-term volatility in exchange rates.

Thinking about Foreign Exchange Markets as Just Another Market

Chapter 5 introduces the demand–supply model of exchange rate determination and argues that no difference exists between the orange market and the market for dollars. For the purpose of exchange rate determination, the demand–supply model is a good approximation and provides predictions about the changes in exchange rates, which empirical studies confirm. You know by now that these predictions are long-term predictions. In light of high short-term volatility in exchange rates, thinking about foreign exchange markets (at least in the short term) as asset markets is helpful. The rules of the game are quite different in asset markets where expectations have positive and, therefore, self-fulfilling feedback, and where the characteristics of market participants (rational or irrational) may matter. (See Appendix for this discussion).

Assuming that Central Bank Interventions Are Meaningless

You may think about the usefulness of a central bank's direct intervention in foreign exchange markets (See Chapter 13). Thinking that these markets are so large that even a concerted effort by a number of central banks may not change the exchange rate is plausible. And you may be more puzzled if the direct intervention is sterilized. If the Fed wants to support the dollar against the euro, it purchases dollars in foreign exchange markets in exchange for its euro reserves. If the Fed doesn't do anything afterward, the U.S. high-powered money supply declines by the amount of dollars purchased. If the Fed doesn't want to have this change in the domestic money market, it can offset the decline in the money supply by buying government papers such as T-bills from financial markets, increasing the high-powered money supply to its original level. So what has changed? The portfolio balance has changed. This effect implies that even though money supply didn't change, the relative supply of government papers did. Sterilization decreased the quantity of U.S. government papers held by the public and probably increased that of the euro-denominated government papers.

Thinking that Pegged Exchange Rates Are a Great Idea

Sure, pegged exchange rates can act as a nominal anchor and signal stability in a country that hasn't had much stability. But pegged exchange rates don't automatically provide stability. They don't signal stability for long if macroeconomic stability doesn't exist. Especially when a country wants to attract foreign portfolio investment and pegs its currency to eliminate exchange rate risk for foreign investors, the country must be very careful. Foreign investors will bring in hot money: It will come fast and leave the country even faster (See Chapter 13). Investors will always look for reasons that may force the country to break the peg because this scenario is disastrous for them. Investors seemingly have learned from their experience in emerging markets with pegged exchange rates, and they pay attention to various characteristics of the country. In addition to the obvious sources of trouble, such as expansionary fiscal and monetary policies, weaknesses of the financial sector attract investors' attention. If a financial crisis occurs, the fiscal and monetary authority will provide bailout funds to prevent the crisis from getting larger, which will again break the peg.

Being Nostalgic about the Good Old Gold Standard Days

A metallic standard doesn't automatically mean stability. (See Chapters 11 and 12 for episodes of metallic standard). If anything, the experiences of the 19th century until the end of the Bretton Woods era in 1971 have demonstrated the appearance of the same problems in all major eras of the metallic standard. A metallic standard is one of fixed exchange rates. Persistent and large current account deficits or surpluses occur under fixed exchange rates and these are not desirable. Current account deficit countries try to stop the outflow of funds by implementing contractionary monetary policies to keep interest rates high, which can create a deflationary vortex. This interferes with the objectives of the internal balance of growth and full employment. Growth declines, and unemployment increases. The current gold parity and the resulting fixed exchange rates are no longer realistic. Without exception, recessions due to fixed exchange rates happened in all major eras of the metallic standard.

Appendix

Famous Puzzles in International Finance

⚫ ⚫

As if international finance is not puzzling enough, there are famous puzzles in international finance as well. Lucky for you! What I mean with puzzle is that empirical observations of the real world aren't always compatible with the predictions of some theories.

This appendix discusses six well-known puzzles:

- ✔ **The home bias in trade puzzle:** People have a strong preference for consumption of their home goods.
- ✔ **The home bias in portfolio puzzle:** Home investors prefer to hold home equities.
- ✔ **The Feldstein–Horioka puzzle:** Savings and investment are highly correlated at the country level.
- ✔ **The consumption correlation puzzle:** Consumption is much less correlated across countries than output.
- ✔ **The exchange rate disconnect puzzle:** Short-term volatility in exchange rates doesn't reflect that of the fundamentals.
- ✔ **The purchasing power parity puzzle:** Short-term changes in exchange rates don't reflect inflation differentials between countries.

You see that the last two puzzles (the exchange rate disconnect and purchasing power parity puzzles) directly related to exchange rates. The other four imply, among other things, exchange rate risk. Now you examine each puzzle:

The Home Bias in Trade Puzzle

Empirical evidence indicates that, within a country trade is much larger than international trade, which suggests a bias for home goods. This observation implies that international goods markets may be much more segmented than one usually assumes. The existence of national borders may contribute to market segmentation, which, among other things, involves trade barriers.

To explain this bias, one needs to assume empirically plausible trade costs, as well as a lower elasticity of substitution across traded goods. The term *elasticity of substitution* refers to the ease with which domestic goods (nontraded) can be substituted with traded goods. In terms of international trade, border costs imply trade barriers such as tariffs and nontariff barriers (quantitative trade restrictions such as quotas, health and environmental regulations, and customs-related paperwork), transportation costs, and exchange rate risk. Some models suggest that these border costs don't have to be too large to generate the observed bias for home goods. As long as interaction takes place between border costs and the elasticity of substitution between home and foreign goods, a bias for home goods is in play. Additionally, if a bias for home goods does exist, such as having a preference for the "Made in America" label, it works like any other trade cost.

The Home Bias in Equity Puzzle

Most economic models assume that investors take advantage of risk sharing and potential gains in returns provided by international capital markets. But empirical studies show that investors don't optimally diversify internationally, and they favor their home country's equity to the extent of holding almost all their wealth in domestic assets. The question is why domestic investors don't make use of potential gains from foreign investment opportunities. This question is especially puzzling when you consider the rapidly growing international capital markets.

Consider an example that demonstrates why having portfolios consisting of mostly domestic equities is puzzling. Remember the home bias in trade puzzle, which implies a much larger share of country trade in consumption. You know about various trade costs associated with goods trade. But what about international trade in equities? Suppose that every country has equities issued by firms in the traded and nontraded goods sectors. In theory, trading equities between countries should happen without frictions. Now suppose that there's no money in the world, and when you hold equities, you're paid in goods that you consume. Therefore, if you hold an equity (related to firms producing traded or nontraded goods at home or abroad), you're paid in some particular good. In terms of domestic equities, under normal circumstances, the distinction between traded and nontraded goods doesn't matter to you. If you receive your dividends in terms of haircut coupons, you can redeem them in your country. But if you're holding foreign equities, you need to hold the equity associated with the traded good. If you get paid in nontraded goods like haircuts, getting haircuts in a foreign country will be prohibitively expensive (with that airline ticket and all).

Therefore, depending on the share of nontraded goods in home and foreign output, one may expect some representation of foreign equity in domestic portfolios. But the observed domestic equity shares of 80 to 90 percent aren't consistent with optimal portfolio diversification.

Some explanations of this puzzle are based on trade costs, which also include market inefficiencies such as asymmetric information and legal restrictions as a type of trade cost. But these explanations may apply more to developing countries that implement restrictions on capital flows and foreign ownership of domestic assets than to developed countries. Therefore, the question is why there is a bias for home equity even in developed countries. Given the fact that international equity transactions aren't significantly restricted in developed countries, one would not expect a strong home bias in equity holdings of developed countries.

But some studies suggest that potential benefits from investing in foreign equities must be compared to the transaction costs of acquiring these equities. Although transactions costs may be small with fully integrated capital markets, they must be compared with the potential gains from diversification. Another explanation is that the market is inefficient and investors don't recognize the potential gains from including foreign equity in their portfolio. Additionally, some studies suggest that domestic investors are overly optimistic about the returns on domestic equities.

The Feldstein–Horioka Puzzle

In the absence of transaction costs and other frictions, savings and investment shouldn't correlate at the country level for a small country. This prediction implies that, assuming no restrictions between countries, capital should flow from lower-return regions to higher-return regions. This idea makes sense, if you can think of yourself as an investor: You want to invest in a country with the highest return (assuming the same risk and maturity of the instrument).

The overwhelming empirical evidence indicates that savings and investments are highly correlated at the country level. But if capital flows freely between countries, a country's investment shouldn't correlate with its savings. Domestic agents can get funds anywhere in the world and invest in the home country. The most important empirical evidence is obtained in studies that investigate capital flows within the OECD (Organization of Economic Cooperation and Development) countries that consist of mostly developed countries, with minimum restrictions on capital flows. What makes this puzzle even more interesting is that it isn't a short-term phenomenon. The data used in most empirical studies regarding this puzzle involve decade averages.

So why do domestic savings overwhelmingly finance domestic investment? As in the case of other puzzles, among the usual explanations are market imperfections. Costly information about international risk (including exchange rate risk), as well as restrictions in capital flows, may force domestic savings and investment to correlate. As discussed previously, restrictions on capital flows may seem small, but their interaction with information costs may be enough to reject the predictions that savings and investment shouldn't be highly correlated.

The Consumption Correlation Puzzle

In a complete market world in which agents are able to exchange every good with other agents without transaction costs, you may expect that domestic consumption growth doesn't depend too much on country-specific output. Therefore, the theory suggests that consumption should be much more correlated across countries than output. But empirical studies indicate that consumption is much less correlated across countries than output. In other words, there isn't much international risk sharing in terms of consumption. In a way, in the presence of all three previous puzzles (home bias in trade and equity, as well as the Feldstein–Horioka puzzles), it's not surprising that international consumption correlations are low.

Explanations of the consumption correlation puzzles are related to explanations associated with the previous puzzles, which emphasize a variety of market imperfections and, therefore, transaction costs. For example, empirical evidence indicates that financial markets more effectively promote risk sharing *within* a country than *between* countries. Therefore, financial markets are able to smooth consumption among the U.S. states at a much higher degree than among developed countries. In this context, the term *smoothing* refers to counterbalancing the increase or decrease in household consumption by exporting or importing consumption goods, respectively.

The existence of nontraded goods can also break the link between prices and quantities and make it harder for trade to smooth household consumption. Suppose that households consume goods that cannot be traded — for example, services like haircuts. If a positive technology shock increases the supply of services, households cannot smooth their consumption of services by exporting haircuts to other countries.

The Exchange Rate Disconnect Puzzle

This puzzle refers to the weak short-run relationship between the exchange rate and its macroeconomic fundamentals. In other words, underlying fundamentals such as interest rates, inflation rates, and output don't explain the short-term volatility in exchange rates. For example, short-term forecasts of macroeconomic exchange rate models are little better than forecasts of random walk models. A short-term exchange rate determination according to the random walk model implies that tomorrow's exchange rate equals yesterday's exchange rate.

Therefore, you need to put into perspective the models or concepts about exchange rate determination from Chapters 5 through 9 and modify your knowledge. Models of exchange rate determination are good approximations for the long-run relationship between exchange rates and macroeconomic fundamentals. The exchange rate disconnect puzzle implies that macroeconomic fundamentals don't explain short-term variations in exchange rates.

The exchange rate disconnect puzzle and the purchasing power puzzle are considered pricing puzzles. Therefore, explanations of the exchange rate–related puzzles make use of comparing exchange rates to asset prices. As in the case of exchange rates, asset prices such as stock market indices are highly volatile, and the changes in them don't strongly correspond to changes in fundamentals. Similar to exchange rates, random walk models are reasonably consistent with changes in stock prices. In the case of asset prices in general, the assumption is that news affects asset prices. Still, given the relevance of exchange rates as relative prices and their effect on a large number of transactions, it's surprising that disconnect exists between short-term changes in exchange rates and underlying macroeconomic fundamentals.

The exchange rate disconnect puzzle has various manifestations. Predictable excess returns are one of them. According to interest rate parity (IRP), the differences in home and foreign interest rates should be equalized by changes in the exchange rate. But studies find two characteristics of short-run exchange rates that aren't consistent with the IRP:

- ✔ Not only do short-term exchange rates deviate from the IRP, but these deviations are predictable.

- ✔ The variance of these predictable returns is greater than the variance of the expected change in the exchange rate.

Predictable excess returns have two explanations:

- ✔ **Market forecasts are irrational:** This irrationality may arise from the presence of heterogeneous traders in the market. Heterogeneity among traders means that there are different types of traders such as fundamentalists (they keep an eye on macroeconomic conditions that affect exchange rates), chartists (they use charts or graphs about past changes in exchange rates to forecasts future changes), and noise traders (they follow trends in exchange rates and overreact to good or bad news; also called irrational). (Some studies consider all traders who don't make investment decisions based on fundamentals (chartists and noise traders) as noise traders or irrational.) Studies show that irrational traders can affect prices; because they face a higher risk, they can earn higher returns than rational traders.

  Differences may arise in the distribution of perceived and measured economic disturbances (perceived by traders and measured by researchers): In this explanation, market participants are rational. But systematic forecast errors reflect the difference between what traders observe as they experience the situation and how researchers make sense of it ex post (or after the fact). Still, this approach doesn't explain the high variation in excess returns.

- ✔ **Peso problem effect:** A *peso problem* refers to the situation in which market participants' expectations about a future policy change don't materialize within the sample period. In the early 1970s, interest rates on Mexican peso were substantially higher than those in the U.S. This was happening despite the fact that the Mexican peso had been pegged for almost a decade. Nominal interest rates on the Peso were higher than in the United States and reflected higher inflation rates in Mexico along with the probability of a large devaluation of the peso. A couple years passed before, in the late 1970s, the Mexican peso was devalued.

This situation isn't consistent with standard assumptions about forecast errors. Forecast errors should have a mean of zero and shouldn't correlate with current information. But if market participants expect a future discrete change in policy or fundamentals, then rational forecast errors can be correlated with current information and may have a nonzero mean in finite samples.

The Purchasing Power Puzzle

The purchasing power puzzle is an example of the exchange rate disconnect puzzle. As Chapter 9 shows, according to the purchasing power parity (PPP), changes in exchange rates should reflect inflation differentials between countries. However, empirical studies show that short-term deviations from the PPP are quite persistent.

Here I explain the purchasing power puzzle by using the real exchange rate.

The real exchange rate includes the ratio of two countries' price levels and the nominal exchange rate (see Chapter 2). It implies:

$$RER = \left[\left(\frac{\$}{€} \right) \times P_E \right] \div P_{US}$$

Here, RER, P_E, and P_{US} indicate the real exchange rate, the price of the Euro-zone's consumption basket, and the price of the U.S. consumption basket, respectively. In this equation, if you multiply the dollar–euro exchange rate by the price of the European consumption basket (denominated in euro), euros cancel, and you have the price of the European consumption basket in dollars. Therefore, the real exchange rate compares the price of a country's consumption basket to that of another country in a common currency.

You can relate the real exchange rate to the purchasing power puzzle in the following way. The previous equation of the real exchange rate includes the nominal exchange rate, and you know that the short-run changes in the nominal exchange rate don't reflect the changes in macroeconomic fundamentals (in this case, the price levels of two countries). Because the volatility in the nominal exchange rate is much more than the volatility in domestic and foreign price levels, then the volatility in the real exchange rate is high as well.

The question is, what can generate large and persistent international price differentials? Here are some possible answers:

- The *exchange rate pass-through* implies the effect of changes in the exchange rate on import prices in home currency. You may expect that, eventually, the changes in consumer prices will reflect the changes in import prices. But even though the exchange rate pass-through takes place, consumer prices adjust sluggishly to changes in import prices.

- Another popular explanation of persistent international price differentials is based on imperfect competition. As opposed to perfect competition where firms are price takers (they take the market price of their products), in imperfect competition producers have the opportunity to price their products as well as price discriminate in home and foreign markets. Then the argument goes that if most traded goods are produced under imperfect competition, price differentials become persistent. But although the production of some traded goods under the conditions of imperfect competition is reasonable (such as cars), it doesn't apply to other traded goods (such as apparel).

- A variation of the previous argument is used for wholesalers, which doesn't require the firms to be monopolies. Clearly, consumers can't profitably arbitrage price differences in traded goods, but wholesalers should be able to. Apparently, something is preventing wholesalers from engaging in international price arbitrage at the wholesale level. Perhaps wholesalers don't have control over firms' legal rights, such as marketing licenses that enable firms to price discriminate, in other words, to charge different prices in different countries.

Market Imperfection Explanations for Exchange Rate Puzzles

This section focuses on explanations of the famous puzzles that relate to market imperfections. It shows that some of the basic assumptions about markets may not hold in foreign exchange markets.

In most economic models, market behavior has the following characteristics:

- Trading costs and other frictions are small so that they don't affect the market outcome (prices and quantities).
- Whatever the nature of the shock is, market equilibrium prevails.
- Market participants behave rationally.

These assumptions may reasonably explain goods markets, but they seem to not hold completely in financial markets. Because currency markets behave similarly to asset markets, the lack of efficiency in currency markets may partially explain the famous puzzles in international macroeconomics and finance. Even though usually one assumes that competitive markets determine exchange rates in floating exchange rate regimes, foreign exchange markets may be less than efficient.

As in the case of asset markets, the following assumptions of the efficient markets hypothesis may be systematically violated in foreign exchange markets as well:

✔ Trading costs can be quite large. The most important of these costs is the information cost associated with acquiring and analyzing information to assess the risk and return of an asset or a currency.

   • Fragile expectations make assessing risk and uncertainty particularly difficult.

   • Information asymmetry persists. Sharing valuable information may not come with many incentives.

   • Information asymmetry can be a factor for not making use of arbitrage opportunities that are important for market efficiency.

✔ A basic difference exists between commodity and asset markets. To appreciate this difference, consider expectations in any market. A market has a feedback system in terms of expectations. As a market participant, you consider past market behavior to form your expectations and, then your decision determines the current market behavior.

An expectations-based market system can have a positive or negative feedback system. Supply-driven commodity markets have a negative feedback system. When producers expect future prices to be high, they increase production, which results in lower prices of their product. When firms expect future prices to be lower, they decrease production and have to deal with higher prices of their product. In this case, prices quickly converge to their equilibrium value.

Financial markets are demand driven, and there is positive (self-confirming) feedback. When there's an expectation of higher prices of an asset, market participants start buying it, increasing the demand for the asset and, thereby, its price. When market participants expect lower prices, they decrease their demand, and the price of the asset falls. Therefore, positive feedback in asset markets is capable of producing large fluctuations in the actual price of assets.

✔ Herding behavior among asset market participants such as traders, fund managers, and analysts is an important deviation from market efficiency and implies information costs. It means that if you and I are the two traders in the foreign exchange market, I just watch you and sell or buy the currencies that you sell and buy. Why do I mimic your behavior? I must face a prohibitively high information cost, so instead of gathering information to base my trade on, I simply watch you and trade as you do. Information costs generate significant and sometimes persistent deviations from market equilibrium and create path-dependent prices.

Index

• *J* •

• *K* •

Notes

Notes

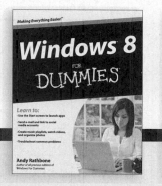

Math & Science

Algebra I For Dummies,
2nd Edition
978-0-470-55964-2

Anatomy and Physiology
For Dummies,
2nd Edition
978-0-470-92326-9

Astronomy For Dummies,
3rd Edition
978-1-118-37697-3

Biology For Dummies,
2nd Edition
978-0-470-59875-7

Chemistry For Dummies,
2nd Edition
978-1-1180-0730-3

Pre-Algebra Essentials
For Dummies
978-0-470-61838-7

Microsoft Office

Excel 2013 For Dummies
978-1-118-51012-4

Office 2013 All-in-One
For Dummies
978-1-118-51636-2

PowerPoint 2013
For Dummies
978-1-118-50253-2

Word 2013 For Dummies
978-1-118-49123-2

Music

Blues Harmonica
For Dummies
978-1-118-25269-7

Guitar For Dummies,
3rd Edition
978-1-118-11554-1

iPod & iTunes
For Dummies,
10th Edition
978-1-118-50864-0

Programming

Android Application
Development For
Dummies, 2nd Edition
978-1-118-38710-8

iOS 6 Application
Development For Dummies
978-1-118-50880-0

Java For Dummies,
5th Edition
978-0-470-37173-2

Religion & Inspiration

The Bible For Dummies
978-0-7645-5296-0

Buddhism For Dummies,
2nd Edition
978-1-118-02379-2

Catholicism For Dummies,
2nd Edition
978-1-118-07778-8

Self-Help & Relationships

Bipolar Disorder
For Dummies,
2nd Edition
978-1-118-33882-7

Meditation For Dummies,
3rd Edition
978-1-118-29144-3

Seniors

Computers For Seniors
For Dummies,
3rd Edition
978-1-118-11553-4

iPad For Seniors
For Dummies,
5th Edition
978-1-118-49708-1

Social Security
For Dummies
978-1-118-20573-0

Smartphones & Tablets

Android Phones
For Dummies
978-1-118-16952-0

Kindle Fire HD
For Dummies
978-1-118-42223-6

NOOK HD For Dummies,
Portable Edition
978-1-118-39498-4

Surface For Dummies
978-1-118-49634-3

Test Prep

ACT For Dummies,
5th Edition
978-1-118-01259-8

ASVAB For Dummies,
3rd Edition
978-0-470-63760-9

GRE For Dummies,
7th Edition
978-0-470-88921-3

Officer Candidate Tests,
For Dummies
978-0-470-59876-4

Physician's Assistant Exam
For Dummies
978-1-118-11556-5

Series 7 Exam
For Dummies
978-0-470-09932-2

Windows 8

Windows 8 For Dummies
978-1-118-13461-0

Windows 8 For Dummies,
Book + DVD Bundle
978-1-118-27167-4

Windows 8 All-in-One
For Dummies
978-1-118-11920-4

Available in print and e-book formats.

Dummies products make life easier!

- DIY
- Consumer Electronics
- Crafts
- Software
- Cookware
- Hobbies
- Videos
- Music
- Games
- and More!

For more information, go to **Dummies.com**® and search the store by category.

FOR
DUMMIES
A Wiley Brand